Prana and Pranayama

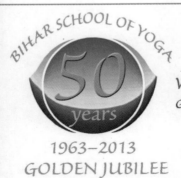

BIHAR SCHOOL OF YOGA

50 years

1963–2013
GOLDEN JUBILEE

WORLD YOGA CONVENTION 2013
GANGA DARSHAN, MUNGER, BIHAR, INDIA
23rd–27th October 2013

Prana and Pranayama

Swami Niranjanananda Saraswati

Johnston Lowry

www.yogaminandbook.org

Yoga Publications Trust, Munger, Bihar, India

Published by Yoga Publications Trust
    First edition 2009
    Reprinted 2010, 2012

ISBN: 978-81-86336-79-3

Publisher and distributor: Yoga Publications Trust, Ganga Darshan, Munger, Bihar, India.

Website: www.biharyoga.net
        www.rikhiapeeth.net

Printed at Thomson Press (India) Limited, New Delhi, 110001

Dedication

In humility we offer this dedication to
Swami Sivananda Saraswati, who initiated
Swami Satyananda Saraswati into the secrets of yoga.

Contents

Introduction

The classical yogic practices of pranayama have been known in India for over 4,000 years. In the *Bhagavad Gita*, a text dated to the Mahabharata period, the reference to pranayama (4:29) indicates that the practices were as commonly known during that period as was *yajna*, fire sacrifice. Many Upanishads written in the pre-Buddhist period also refer to techniques of pranayama (to attain higher states of consciousness). However, it is in the hatha yoga texts such as *Hatha Yoga Pradipika*, *Gheranda Samhita* and *Hatharatnavali*, written between the sixth and fifteenth centuries AD, that we find a detailed description of the practices. It would seem that a need was felt at that time to revive and codify the practices that were until then handed down through the oral tradition. The vedic culture had declined with the advent of Buddhism and many yogic practices were being lost or misapplied by their practitioners. Thus the authors of the texts sought to restore the purity and authenticity of the practices.

A need is felt yet again in the twenty-first century to reinstate the original intent and experience of the practices. The yogic renaissance witnessed in the last few decades has made asana and pranayama into household terms, but the essence and depth of the practices remain unexplored for most practitioners.

It has been the purpose as well as the contribution of Satyananda Yoga to bring the knowledge of the realized rishis to yoga aspirants in a language and method that is applicable in the current age. This is also the gift and blessing of our gurus, Swami Sivananda and Swami Satyananda.

This book provides a complete description of the science of pranayama as presented in the classical texts and as taught in the Satyananda Yoga tradition by the Bihar School of Yoga. Prana and pranayama are investigated as philosophy, physiology and practice. The scriptural analogies of the concept of prana have been rendered comprehensible for the modern reader so that an essential understanding of the basis of the practices is acquired. In addition, the scientific framework of the concepts is explained, and the practices are presented in a stage-by-stage, systematic method so that the yogic counsel of gradual perfection may be understood and practised.

The book is divided into three parts. *Part 1* explains the theory of prana, and related yogic concepts such as koshas, chakras, nadis and mantra. *Part 2* describes respiratory physiology as relevant in understanding yogic and pranic physiology, the process of pranayama and the research undertaken by science on pranayama and related practices. *Part 3* provides the guidelines for practising pranayama, and the preparatory and classical practices of pranayama. There are also four appendices describing yogic practices that complement pranayama, including neti and agnisar kriya, asanas, mudras and bandhas. The pranayama sutras from the *Hatha Yoga Pradipika* are also provided as an adjunct.

Prana

The Upanishads tell the following story. Once all the deities that reside in the body – air, fire, water, earth, ether, speech and mind – had an argument. Each claimed that it was superior to all others, declaring, "I sustain this perishable body." Prana was listening to this debate, and ultimately said to them, "Do not delude yourself. It is I, having divided myself into five parts, who supports and sustains this body." The deities did not believe him. Indignantly, Prana began to withdraw from the body. Instantly, all the other deities found themselves withdrawing too. When Prana again settled in the body, the deities found that they had assumed their respective places. Convinced of Prana's superiority, all now paid obeisance to Prana.

Prana is the vital force that sustains not only the body, but also creation at every level. The seers of India have always known what modern science has been trying to fathom: the existence of a primeval force, its nature, potential, and how to harness it. Every yogic science – mantra, yajna, austerities, different forms of concentration and meditation – is aimed at awakening and enhancing this vital force within the unit of the individual or the wider universe.

The Sanskrit word *prana* is a combination of two syllables, *pra* and *na,* and denotes constancy, a force in constant motion. Prana exists in sentient beings as the energy that drives every action, voluntary and involuntary, every thought, every level of the mind and body. Scientific research describes prana as a complex multidimensional energy: a combination of electrical, magnetic, electromagnetic, photonic, ocular, thermal and mental energies.

Prana also exists in the insentient world, causing motion, growth and decay at this level. Prana is, indeed, the basis of manifested creation. It is the force that emerged out of the 'original willing' of the primal consciousness to bring about creation. The *Chhandogya Upanishad* (1:11:5) says:

सर्वाणि ह वा इमानि भूतानि ।
प्राणमेवाभिसंविशंति प्राणमभ्युज्जिहते ॥

In prana all moveable and immoveable beings merge (during dissolution) and rise out of prana (during creation).

In the individual being, prana pervades the entire being, projecting itself in what the yogis called pranamaya kosha – a level of existence subtler than the physical. The existence of this pranic field has been proven by modern science too. In particular, the highly sensitive system of Kirlian photography noted the existence of a halo around people as well as objects. It also found that the halo changed according to the state of the being. This pranic field is sometimes called psi plasma due to the fact that it can be likened to the plasma (charged gases) described in plasma physics; it has been described as a vapour of charged particles which can be affected internally by the mind and externally by electric, magnetic or electromagnetic fields.

In the pranic body, prana flows through *nadis*, energy channels, and is stored in *chakras*, energy vortices. According to some researchers, the electromagnetic energy in prana gives rise to radiation in which the waves of electric energy and magnetic energy are at ninety degrees to each other, resulting in what looks like a spiral. Indeed, the spiral radiation structure around chakras has been seen, described and drawn by sages and savants from all parts of the world at different times.

Prana is inherent to a being. We are born with a certain quantum of prana, and we maintain it, increase or decrease it through the air we breathe, the food we eat, the thoughts we think, the actions we perform and the kind of life we lead. When we die, the accumulated prana leaves the body.

Pranayama

The science of pranayama was developed by highly evolved yogis through an intuitive and experiential understanding of prana and its influence on the human mechanism at various levels. The agency of the breath was used to access the pranic field, to attain balance in the body and control of the mind. The practices would render the body-mind instrument capable of experiencing higher states of consciousness so that the ultimate union with the transcendental reality could be experienced.

The breath being the medium of pranayama, the system is based on the three stages of respiration: inhalation (*pooraka*),

4

retention (*kumbhaka*) and exhalation (*rechaka*). By permuting and directing these three stages, the different practices of pranayama are obtained. Technically speaking, pranayama is actually only retention. Maharshi Patanjali's *Yoga Sutras* state (2:49):

तस्मिन्सति श्वासप्रश्वासयोर्गतिविच्छेद: प्राणायाम: ॥

Pranayama is the pause in the movement of inhalation and exhalation when that is secured.

Inhalation and exhalation are methods of inducing retention. Retention is the key because it allows a longer period for the assimilation of prana, just as it allows more time for the exchange of oxygen and carbon dioxide in the cells. As the breath is also intimately connected with various functions and organs of the body as well as the mind, by controlling the breath we also influence all these dimensions.

At the pranic level, in their initial stages the practices of pranayama clear up the *nadis*, energy pathways in the body. The scriptures say there are over 72,000 nadis or pathways of prana in the pranic body and six main chakras. However, in the average individual, many of these pathways are blocked and the chakras release energy only partially. In other words, we do not utilize our full potential in terms of energy, mind and consciousness. The negative conditions we experience, whether physical or mental, are the cause as well as the consequence of the blockages. The state of our nadis and chakras are defined by our *samskaras*, conditionings carried in seed form, as well as *purushartha*, self-effort and *anugraha*, grace. With the practice of pranayama, these pathways of energy are gradually freed so that prana moves through them smoothly.

At higher levels of practice, the direction of the pranic flows is influenced and a greater quantum of energy is released from the chakras. As these processes are activated, many new experiences unfold. Expert guidance is essential to steer the practitioner through these stages.

Remember that pranayama is not a stand-alone yogic practice. In the system of ashtanga yoga, it is preceded by sustained practice of yamas and niyamas, shatkarmas and asanas, and is followed by pratyahara, dharana, dhyana and samadhi. A balanced, sequential movement from gross to subtle, from annamaya kosha to anandamaya kosha, is the aim. In the *Hatha Yoga Pradipika* (1:67) it has been said:

पीठानि कुंभकाश्चित्रा दिव्यानि करणानि च।
सर्वाण्यपि हठाभ्यासे राजयोगफलावधि: ॥

Asanas, various types of kumbhaka (pranayama) and the other various means of illumination should all be practised in the hatha yoga system until success in raja yoga is attained.

In this context, the aim of pranayama is to perfect pratyahara, which in the traditional texts has been described as not just sense withdrawal, but the state where we perceive every sensory input as a manifestation of the Supreme, and have expanded the pranic capacity to the extent that we can retain the breath for three hours. The *Shiva Samhita* (3:57) states:

याममात्रं यदा धर्तुं समर्थ: स्यात्तदाद्भुत: ।
प्रत्याहारस्तदैव स्यान्नांतरा भवति ध्रुवम् ॥

When one attains the power of holding the breath for three hours, then certainly the wonderful state of pratyahara is reached without fail.

The practice of yoga, in fact, begins when we come to the pranayama series. With the practice of asanas, we arrive at the state where we are able to work with the energies controlling the body. With pranayama, through the breath, we develop an awareness of the subtle force within the body, and directing the mind to become aware of the subtle activities is the beginning of yoga.

Philosophy of Prana and Pranayama

1

What is Prana?

What makes any motion possible: the blink of an eye, the budding of a flower, the splitting of atoms or the fall of a meteor? Thousands of years ago, the yogis living in the shadow of the Himalayas fathomed the inherent quality of motion in creation and they called it prana. One may roughly translate the word *prana* as 'energy' or 'vital force', but neither definition offers a precise equivalent of the Sanskrit term that emerged from higher states of contemplation. The word prana assumes the quality of 'livingness'. From the yogic point of view, the entire cosmos is alive, throbbing with prana.

Prana is ever present in every aspect of creation. The prana within every created object gives existence and material form, whether it is a planet, an asteroid, a blade of grass or a tree. If there were no prana, there would be no existence. If prana were withdrawn from the universe, there would be total disintegration. All beings, whether living or non-living, exist due to prana. Every manifestation in creation forms part of a never-ending matrix of energy particles, arranged in different densities, combinations and variations. The universal principle of prana may be in a static or dynamic state, but it is behind all existence on every plane of being from the highest to the lowest.

Prana is the simplest as well as the most profound concept propounded by the seers. A stone worshipped sincerely may have a finer quality of prana than the force of a leopard in full flight. The tangible strength that enables the movement of one's hand is prana and the intangible force invoked through a complex fire ritual is also prana. The wind blows and rivers flow because of prana. Aircrafts, trains and cars move because of prana; laser beams and radio waves travel because of prana. Every object in creation is floating in the vast, all-encompassing sea of prana, and receiving everything they need to exist from it. It is said in the *Kathopanishad* (2:3:2):

यदिदं किं च जगत्सर्वं प्राण एजति निःसृतम् ।

This whole world – whatever there is – vibrates having originated from prana.

This cosmic prana, also called *mahaprana*, came into being at the time of creation. Thus, in order to fully understand prana, one must go back to the beginning of creation.

Universal prana

At the very beginning, there was nothing, not even creation. What existed was an all-pervasive, unmanifest consciousness, known in the scriptures as *Para Brahman*. It contained within it all the qualities and components necessary for creation. The whole universe lay infinitely contracted in it as mere potency; prana remained completely absorbed in it as if in a union of deep embrace. It was a state of perfect equilibrium and harmony.

In this utter stillness, there is a movement. The tantric and vedic literatures state that a desire arose in that absolute principle: *Ekoham bahusyam* – "I am one, let me become many." The desire is the first creative impulse, which results in 'willing'. The willing of the unmanifest consciousness causes the first *spandan*, vibration, and energy issues forth. It is the first movement: the first moment of becoming from being, the first manifestation of prana.

This primal energy, called mahaprana, is variously known as mahashakti, mahamaya, the cosmic creatrix or the Cosmic Mother. Prana was never separate from consciousness; it existed eternally as potential in consciousness, but now it assumed itself. Thus energy and consciousness began to interact with each other. They indulged in cosmic play, *lila*, which caused *srishti*, creation. The awakening of mahaprana was like a self-projection of the 'I-ness' of the infinite consciousness – the unchanging consciousness could experience itself through the movement of prana. In the course of time, modifications took place in the states of consciousness and energy, and with each modification a different level of creation came into being. Different levels of existence manifested: beings and matter, elements and energies, light and dark, positive and negative, animate and inanimate, male and female. Together, consciousness and energy expanded the universe, and at the end of every age dissolved it, gathering the universe back into themselves.

The many subtleties of prana and *chitta* (consciousness) are the ladders of all spiritual practices, the ultimate rung being involution to the state where all that exists is pure consciousness. This is the process of going back to the 'source'.

Play of prana and chitta

चले वाते चलं चित्तं निश्चले निश्चलं भवेत् ।
योगी स्थाणुत्वमाप्नोति ततो वायुं निरोधयेत् ॥

When prana moves, chitta (consciousness) moves.
When prana is without movement, chitta is without movement.

Hatha Yoga Pradipika (2:2)

Both prana and consciousness must be present for life to exist. The conscious experience is chitta; that which takes one closer to the conscious experience is prana, and that which motivates prana is *vasana*, inherent desire. So, prana and vasana are the two supports of consciousness. A living being is called a *prani*, one who has prana and thus consciousness. It is not that consciousness is the cause of existence and prana the result; nor is prana the cause or consciousness the result. They are two aspects of existence which determine the nature of everything.

Consciousness is being, awareness, knowledge; prana is becoming, manifestation through motion. Consciousness is a dormant experience whereas prana is the active principle of manifest energy. They are the two eternal principles that are the basis of the macrocosmos and the microcosmos. Everything is a combination of prana and chitta. The entire universe, creation and existence are a play of consciousness and energy. The life force and mental force permeate every atom and cell of the universe, though remaining at different degrees of separation.

Individual prana

In the *Shiva Swarodaya*, Devi asks Shiva: "In this universe who is the greatest friend of man?" Shiva replies (v. 219):

प्राण एव परं मित्रं प्राण एव पर: सखा।
प्राणतुल्य: परो बन्धुर्नास्ति नास्ति वरानने ॥

Prana is the greatest friend, prana is the greatest companion.
O fair one, there is no closer friend in this universe than prana.

All beings are composites of prana, which gives them life and existence. The quantum of prana of each individual is indicated by the power of the personality, which reflects one's natural capacity to wield prana. Some persons are more successful, commanding and fascinating than others due to the level of their prana. The *Prashnopanishad* explains that prana springs from the atman and is as inseparable from the self as the shadow from one who casts it.

Often the word prana is translated as breath. However, prana is not the oxygen or the air that one breathes. Yogis have proved that one can stop breathing for long periods of time and yet continue to live. An experiment was conducted at the Menninger Foundation, USA, on Swami Nadabrahmananda

12

Saraswati, an initiate disciple of Swami Sivananda Saraswati of Rishikesh. Swami Nadabrahmananda had perfected *Nada Brahma*, attunement with the primordial sound vibration, and the experiment intended to verify his claim that he could remain comfortably without breathing for extended periods. He was placed in an airtight glass chamber. A lit candle and a live monkey were placed in similar chambers. Electrodes were connected to his heart, brain and different parts of the body, and he was asked to play the tabla while instruments monitored his parameters. His nose and ears were blocked and his whole body was smeared with wax, so that air would not pass through the pores.

After three minutes the candle went out, and after fifteen minutes the monkey fell unconscious, but Swami Nadabrahmananda continued to play the tabla for more than forty minutes. During this period he was not breathing and when a coin was placed on top of his shaved head, it bobbed up and down. When a microphone was placed against any part of his body, a loud, constant sound like that of a waterfall was heard. He explained that this sound was the movement of prana, adding that one continues to live as long as the pranas are active, even if one stops breathing. The *Hatha Yoga Pradipika* (2:3) echoes his statement:

यावद्वायुः स्थितो देहे तावज्जीवनमुच्यते ।
मरणं तस्य निष्क्रांतिस्ततो वायुं निरोधयेत् ॥

As long as the vayu (prana) remains in the body, there is life.
Death occurs when the vayu leaves the body, therefore, retain the vayu.

Receiving prana

Prana is the dynamic principle within everything. Everyone is born with a certain quantum of prana, but the quantity and quality change continuously, as one goes through life. Positive thoughts, higher feelings and yogic practices generate higher levels of prana. When the sexual energy is sublimated or transformed, substantial prana is conserved within the system and converted into *ojas*, a subtler form of energy. This energy accumulates in the brain and is utilized for creative and spiritual development. A yogi stores an abundance of prana within him, just as batteries store electricity. The megawatts of his prana radiate strength, health and vitality to all around him. He is a powerhouse of energy, providing prana to everyone who comes in contact with him. Swami Sivananda says, "Just as water flows from one vessel to another, prana flows like a steady current from a developed yogi towards weak persons."

At the material level one also receives prana from the environment, food, water, sun and air. All the elements are comprised of prana. So, the quantum of prana within each individual is influenced by the quality of the elements to which one is exposed and which one ingests in the course of everyday life.

Pranic value of food: The *Bhagavad Gita* refers to the quality of prana in different foods by categorizing them as sattwic, rajasic and tamasic (17:8–10). In recent times, a method was developed by André Simonéton in France for establishing the pranic value of food. He used a simple pendulum on a piece of string, similar to that used by water diviners for dowsing, for this purpose. The subtle radiations emitted by organic matter affect the motion of a pendulum, causing it to swing and spin. By measuring the distance of a pendulum's arc, and the speed of its spin, Simonéton was able to measure specific wavelengths, which indicate the intrinsic vitality and relative freshness of different foods. He published his research in *Radiation des Aliments, Ondes Humaines, et Santé*.

On the basis of his findings, Simonéton divided food into four general classes. On a scale of zero to 10,000 angstroms, he found the basic human wavelength to be about 6.5 thousand. Foods that have wavelengths between this and 10,000 angstroms, he regarded as those of the highest quality. In this first class are fruits, fresh vegetables, whole grains, olive oil, ocean fish and shellfish. In the next class, with radiations 6.5 thousand to 3,000 angstroms are eggs, peanut oil, wine, boiled vegetables, cane sugar and cooked fish. The third category, with very weak radiations below 3,000 angstroms, is comprised of cooked meats, sausages, coffee, tea, chocolate, jams, processed cheeses and white bread. The fourth category exhibits practically no life force and includes margarine, conserves, alcoholic spirits, refined white sugar and bleached flour.

Simonéton also found that food with a vital radiance of 8,000 to 10,000 angstroms caused the pendulum to rotate at the amazing speed of 4–500 revolutions per minute over a radius of 80 millimetres. Those between 6,000 and 8,000 angstroms spin at 3–400 revolutions per minute over a radius of 60 millimetres. However, meats, pasteurized milk and overcooked vegetables, which have a value of less than 2,000, are too low in energy to cause the pendulum to revolve at all. This substantiates the recurrent yogic advice to maintain purity of diet, especially while practising pranayama.

Pranic value of air: Pure air is essential for life and health, not only to satisfy the requirement of oxygen, but also the need for prana. The quality of air one breathes affects one's energy level directly. The exhilaration and vitality experienced near a waterfall or high in the mountains is because the quantum of prana in the air is significantly higher in these places. On the other hand, when one is exposed to air pollution or recycled air, the energy level quickly begins to decline. Science has explained this phenomenon in terms of ions, charged particles in the air that are formed when enough energy acts on a gaseous molecule to eject an electron. Ions may be negative or positive. When the displaced electron attaches itself to an adjacent molecule, it becomes a negative ion. The original molecule then becomes a positive ion.

These positive and negative ions are the components of the air one breathes. When one inhales negative ions, they

15

increase the level of prana in the body. The opposite effect is experienced on inhalation of positive ions. Inside a closed room in a modern city there may be less than 50 negative ions per square foot and in the mountains there are about 5,000. It is now an established scientific fact that depletion of negative ions leads to discomfort, enervation, lassitude and some degree of mental and physical inefficiency. Negative ions are therapeutic partly because they kill germs. In human beings, they act on the capacity to absorb oxygen, accelerating the blood's delivery of oxygen to cells and tissues. Negative ions are not prana, but when one inhales them the level of prana in the body increases. In this context it is interesting that negative ions work only so long as they are being inhaled. It has also been observed that the ability to assimilate negative ions goes up during yogic practices such as pranayama.

Working with prana

Prana is not received solely from external sources; it is also self-generated and its quality can be refined and directed. One can work with one's own prana to enhance vitality, will and strength, cure diseases, boost capability and efficiency, and evolve to a higher consciousness. In fact, one must work with *prana shakti*, force of prana, in order to perfect any experience in life. This is the aim of pranayama and prana vidya, which are tangible methods to enhance and guide prana.

The breath is the external manifestation of prana. The yogis state that prana is sustained and the duration of life is prolonged by deliberately decreasing the distance of the exhaled air. Based on this fact, they devised a technique to measure the prana expended during different actions. They stated that the pranic outflow can be gauged by observing the length of the exhalation during different actions. The longer the air current, the more prana is utilized. The average length of exhaled air is twelve digits (nine inches). While singing the length becomes sixteen digits (one foot), while eating twenty digits (fifteen inches), while sleeping thirty digits (twenty-two inches), while copulating thirty-six digits (twenty-seven inches), and while performing physical exercise, it is much longer.

Maximum prana is utilized by the brain. If the brain is not supplied with sufficient prana, the mind becomes restless and disturbed, and constantly dives into negative thoughts. This is evident from the fact that when one is hungry or ill, one tends to become irritable. The quantum of prana in the body has gone down and the brain circuits are protesting the lack.

Although the breath is gross and prana is subtle, the two are intrinsically connected. One can influence the level of prana shakti in the body with the help of the breath. When prana is influenced through modification of the breath, all the functions of the body, brain, mind and consciousness are affected. The practices of pranayama raise the levels of prana by working with the breath and lead to *prana vidya*, inner knowledge or experience of prana. A significant outcome of pranic awareness is that one is able to gain control over the mind.

When prana moves, the mind thinks and the senses perceive their respective objects. By developing sensitivity to prana, one becomes more aware of the subtle forces of the mind, which arise in the form of thoughts, feelings, emotions, responses, impressions, symbols and knowledge. Prana is grosser than the mind and hence easier to control. Thus, when prana is caught the flighty mind is caught too. The *Hatha Yoga Pradipika* (2:42) states:

मारुते मध्यसंचारे मन:स्थैर्यं प्रजायते।
यो मन:सुस्थिरीभाव: सैवावस्था मनोन्मनी॥

The movement of the breath in the middle passage makes the mind still.
This steadiness of mind is the state of manonmani (devoid of thought).

As one works with prana and its quantum and quality improve, the dormant areas of the brain awaken. Normally only one-tenth of the human brain is active and the other nine parts remain inactive. This is because a high level of energy is required for the whole brain to function simultaneously. The yogic practices are able to supply such a quantum of energy and awaken the genius in an average individual. However, just a few rounds of pranayama performed hurriedly will not achieve this. Sustained practice with deep concentration, acute awareness and unshakeable faith are the requisites of a yogi.

Experience of cosmic prana

The individual prana within each being is a part of the cosmic sea of mahaprana, but until this truth is realized experientially, one sees oneself as separate from the rest of the universe. Pranayama practices activate the individual prana and raise it to a higher frequency. They generate a certain amount of heat or creative force throughout the body. This influences the existing quantum of prana, which makes its way up to ajna chakra, the psychic centre in the midbrain, and can then be directed to different areas of the body. This process is the basis of prana vidya.

When prana sadhana assumes an even higher level, the amount of heat generated within the system becomes more intense. This leads ajna chakra to monitor a message back to mooladhara chakra, the psychic centre located at the perineum. Mooladhara is the abode of kundalini, where the cosmic prana lies dormant. The entire experience from creation to dissolution is embedded within the folds of kundalini, hence it is also known as *atma shakti* or soul force. The message from ajna stirs this force and an awakening of the great prana takes place. When the full potential of this energy is released, it travels up through the sushumna nadi, bringing about a complete metamorphosis of the individual. Cosmic prana and kundalini are synonymous terms. In awakening the kundalini, one unites with the cosmic prana.

At the time of the awakening, the two forces of prana and chitta assume perfect balance within the individual and become one. The mind undergoes a state of fission and energy issues forth. There is an explosion of *satya*, a moment of Truth, when one sees everything as luminous. One experiences oneself in every object of the universe, every person, leaf and rock. The realization of cosmic prana is attained and the experience of separation dissolves. People who have experienced this union are called saints or liberated beings, as they have transcended duality by taming the infinite, universal energy within the microcosmic unit. The ultimate yoga is experienced at this level, where one discovers the abiding consciousness, *sat-chit-ananda*, truth, expansiveness and beatitude.

2

Pancha Kosha: Vital Sheaths

According to yoga, a human being is capable of experiencing five dimensions of existence, which are called *pancha kosha* or five sheaths. These are the five spheres in which a human being lives at any given moment and they range from gross to subtle. The pancha kosha are: i) annamaya kosha, ii) pranamaya kosha, iii) manomaya kosha, iv) vijnanamaya kosha and v) anandamaya kosha.

The first sheath or level of experience is the physical body, or *annamaya kosha*. The word *anna* means 'food' and *maya* 'comprised of'. This is the gross level of existence and is referred to as the food sheath due to its dependence on food, water and air. This sheath is also dependent on prana. While it is possible to live without food for up to six weeks, water for six days, and air for six minutes, life ceases immediately the moment prana is withdrawn from it.

The second sheath is *pranamaya kosha*, the energy field of an individual. The level of experience here is more subtle than the physical body, which it pervades and supports. This sheath is supported in turn by the subtler koshas. Together, the physical and pranic bodies constitute the basic human structure, which is referred to as *atmapuri*, city of the soul. They form the vessel for the experience of the higher bodies.

The pranamaya kosha is the basis for the practices of pranayama and prana vidya. It is also described as the pranic, astral and etheric counterpart of the physical body. It has almost the same shape and dimensions as its flesh and blood vehicle, although it is capable of expansion and contraction. It has been said in the *Taittiriya Upanishad* (Brahmandavalli:2):

तस्माा एतस्मादन्नरसमयात् । अन्योऽन्तर आत्मा प्राणमय: ।
तेनैष पूर्ण: । स वा एष पुरुषविध एव ।
तस्य पुरुषविधताम् । अन्वयं पुरुषविध: ॥

Verily, besides this physical body, which is made of the essence of the food, there is another, inner self comprised of vital energy by which this physical self is filled. Just as the fleshly body is in the form of a person, accordingly this vital self is in the shape of a person.

Clairvoyants see the pranic body as a coloured, luminous cloud or aura around the body, radiating from within the physical body, like the sun flaring from behind the eclipsing moon. Researchers working with a Kirlian high voltage apparatus have obtained similar effects on film. The pranic body is subtler than the physical body and takes longer to disintegrate. This is why the energy field of an amputated limb can be felt for quite some time. As demonstrated in experiments with Kirlian photography, this matrix of energy also allows a damaged part to assume its original shape when healed.

The third sheath is *manomaya kosha*, the mental dimension. The level of experience is the conscious mind, which holds the two grosser koshas, annamaya and pranamaya, together as an integrated whole. It is the bridge between the outer and inner worlds, conveying the experiences and sensations of the external world to the intuitive body, and the influences of the causal and intuitive bodies to the gross body.

The fourth sheath is *vijnanamaya kosha*, the psychic level of experience, which relates to the subconscious and unconscious mind. This sphere pervades manomaya kosha, but is subtler than it. Vijnanamaya kosha is the link between the individual and universal mind. Inner knowledge comes to the conscious mind from this level. When this sheath is awakened, one begins to experience life at an intuitive level, to see the underlying reality behind outer appearances. This leads to wisdom.

The fifth sheath is *anandamaya kosha*, the level of bliss and beatitude. This is the causal or transcendental body, the abode of the most subtle prana.

The Pancha Koshas

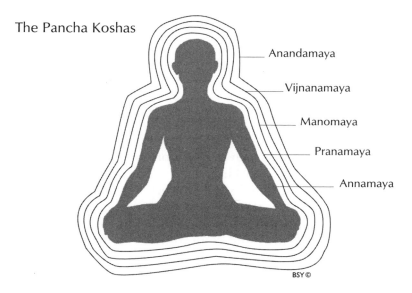

Anandamaya

Vijnanamaya

Manomaya

Pranamaya

Annamaya

BSY©

Prana and the koshas

All the five sheaths are pervaded by prana, which nourishes and sustains them and maintains their appropriate relationship. The movement from one kosha to another is also achieved with the help of prana. How prana operates in between the koshas can be understood by the example of a gearshift in a car. One moves in between the gears through the neutral. The car is also stopped and reversed by first putting it into neutral. Neutral is not a gear; the gears are first, second, third, fourth and reverse. However, without the neutral space in between, one cannot shift from one gear to another. The same principle applies to the koshas.

The pranamaya kosha acts as the neutral space, allowing one to move from annamaya to manomaya, manomaya to vijnanamaya, vijnanamaya to anandamaya, and so on. One must use the faculty of prana shakti in order to move from any one state to another. Therefore, the dimension of energy is like the neutral space in the gear box. With the activation of prana, one gains access to the physical, mental, psychic and spiritual dimensions.

Ascending through the koshas

The aim of a yoga aspirant is to attain higher levels of consciousness by piercing through kosha after kosha. All yogic practices facilitate this aim. The shatkarmas, for example, directly influence annamaya kosha and allow the consciousness to penetrate the next level, pranamaya kosha, by freeing the flow of prana. The asanas have a similar influence; they clear the blockages in the annamaya kosha and as a consequence, influence the pranamaya kosha. As one advances in the practice of asanas, their range of influence becomes subtler and the pranamaya kosha is more directly influenced. Pranayama practices influence pranamaya kosha and indirectly affect manomaya kosha.

Purification of the first three sheaths opens the door to the fourth sheath, vijnanamaya kosha, the sheath of intuition. How and when anandamaya kosha is penetrated, however, remains a mystery. In the transcendental realm the sequential logic of practices and their effects does not apply. Nevertheless, the five sheaths are interlinked and what happens in one affects the others. The activation of pranic force leads to the development of healing abilities, so that the energy can be used to repair the wounds of life. Purification of manomaya kosha results in clarity of thought and balanced expression of emotions and ego. There is a better understanding of different conditions and situations, and greater creativity in the realms of *buddhi*, intellect, and *kriya*, action.

When annamaya and pranamaya are cleansed, there is no longer any barrier between them and manomaya. Mind, body and energy can work in unison, and that tears the veil to vijnanamaya kosha. When the psychic sheath is accessed, concentration becomes refined and the deeper mind comes to the surface. The psychic experiences and extrasensory perceptions manifest and deep-rooted samskaras are purged. As vijnanamaya kosha is cleared, creativity becomes inspired and clarity comes intuitively and effortlessly. At this stage the mind is actually and truly being emptied and prepared to experience anandamaya kosha.

The process of gradual ascent through the koshas may be reversed for the rare yogi who is endowed with grace. In this case the experience of anandamaya kosha brings about purification at all the other levels.

Kosha consciousness

The yogic practices that one selects should be based on the major kosha in which the consciousness rests. The different levels of consciousness represented by the koshas relate to: i) body, ii) life, iii) mind, iv) psyche and v) Self. Each practitioner belongs to one realm predominantly among these five levels of consciousness based on his state of evolution. If the consciousness is mainly in annamaya kosha, one will identify strongly with the body, as many epicureans and hedonists do. If the consciousness is in pranamaya kosha, one will identify with power and vitality, as athletes do. If the consciousness is in manomaya kosha, one will identify with the analytical mind.

When the consciousness has evolved to the level of vijnanamaya kosha, where the tamasic and rajasic tendencies are reduced, there is clarity of cognition based on intuitive intelligence. Here all experiences are seen in the light of the psyche and assume a deeper significance than is apparent. In this dimension one begins to experience the subtle, expressive nature of a higher consciousness. One who identifies with anandamaya kosha is a yogi. He has evolved to the spiritual realm, where all experiences are spiritual experiences.

24

One's experiences in life indicate the realm of consciousness to which one has evolved. However, blockages in other koshas still exist despite the focus of consciousness in a particular kosha. For this reason, an integral path of yoga is advised. The time spent on each limb of yoga will vary from individual to individual, depending on the kind of blockages and the level of evolution one has attained. Expert guidance is essential to ascertain the correct practices for each kosha, which will in turn influence the other koshas.

Perception of prana in different koshas

The aim of the practitioner who focuses on pranayama and prana vidya is to work with the pranamaya kosha until the activation and perception of prana becomes subtle enough to penetrate the other koshas. The techniques of prana vidya train one to perceive and experience prana directly at different levels of subtlety. After the awakening of prana, its flow, form, colour and quality are experienced at all levels.

At the level of annamaya kosha, prana is experienced in the form of nervous energy. The awareness of prana shakti in the other sheaths develops through *pratyahara* or sensory withdrawal, by transcending the gross body and external environment. The perception of prana in manomaya kosha can be compared to a house at night with the lights switched on. The quality and luminosity of that light depends on the purity of the mind. Some people experience manomaya kosha as a sheath of light, having a shape and form, others as light emanating cyclically from a central source.

A systematic and sustained period of practice at the level of manomaya opens the door to vijnanamaya kosha. The inner visions, smells, sounds and sights perceived in deeper states of meditation are the manifestations of prana in vijnanamaya kosha. The first glimpse of psychic experience, however, does not indicate that the practices have borne fruit or can be dispensed with. As the koshas begin to function more coherently, a slight nudge here may cause a little experience there. So, one must persevere until complete integration is achieved. In fact, once vijnanamaya kosha is unlocked, the sadhana requires maximum effort and attention on the part of the aspirant, as it is possible to wander endlessly in its realms, so vast is its scope and so fascinating and absorbing its stuff.

As vijnanamaya kosha becomes progressively cleared through the sustained practices, one may get glimpses of anandamaya kosha – moments when everything appears luminous. One may be suffused with visions of a luminous Shivalingam or such like. However, this too is a relative experience, for one truly abides in ananda only when the entire mind-stuff has been purged. The aim of the practices at this level is to clean the slate completely. Swami Satyananda once said: "A yoga practitioner may have a developed vijnanamaya kosha, but one who has achieved the result of yoga rests in anandamaya kosha."

The enlightened yogi is, in fact, able to experience a sixth kosha – the *atmamaya kosha*. This is the state where complete union with the higher Self is lived and one begins to perceive the entire world as an emanation of beauty, contentment, joy and truth. One who abides in atmamaya kosha is recognized as a *siddha*, a perfected being.

3

Chakras:
Energy Vortices

The pranic body is fuelled by the *chakras*, or psychic centres, which are subtle, high-powered vortices of energy in the body. They receive and store the cosmic prana, and act as transformers to step down the level of energy, so that it can be used by the different organs and parts of the body. They also act as switches for illumining the higher faculties and dimensions of consciousness. The chakras have been discovered by yogis, rishis and sages of various traditions in India and throughout the world. They have been seen, not by physical dissection of the body, but by psychic introspection. From the knowledge of these centres, the great science of kundalini yoga has developed, which is concerned with awakening the chakras.

The six main chakras located along the spinal column are: mooladhara, swadhisthana, manipura, anahata, vishuddhi and ajna. Although these centres are situated in the subtle body, they correspond to the nerve plexuses in the gross body. Beyond the six are two other centres of awakening: bindu and sahasrara, whose perception is acquired only at significantly evolved states of consciousness.

Each chakra vibrates at a particular rate and velocity. The chakras at the lowest point of the energy circuit operate at a lower frequency. They are grosser and create grosser states of awareness. Chakras at the top of the circuit operate at a higher frequency and are responsible for higher intelligence and subtler states of awareness. The different systems of yoga, especially hatha and kriya yoga, systematically purify, rebalance and awaken the chakras individually and also as a whole. When the chakras are properly prepared by such practices, the pranic level is higher and more stable, and there is little difficulty in awakening and experiencing the transmission of prana.

Mooladhara chakra

Mooladhara is the root chakra and the seat of primal energy, kundalini shakti. In philosophical terms the concept of mooladhara is understood as *moola prakriti*, the transcendental basis of physical nature. All the objects and forms in this universe must have some basis from which they evolve and to which they return after dissolution. This basis is called moola prakriti, the original source of all evolution. Mooladhara, as moola prakriti, is therefore responsible for everything that manifests in the world of name and form.

In pranic science, mooladhara is the generating station for prana. The awakening of prana starts from mooladhara and ascends the spinal cord via the pingala nadi. Pingala is merely the channel; the energy comes from mooladhara. This centre is also the direct switch for awakening ajna chakra. Without the awakening of prana in mooladhara, there can be no corresponding awakening in ajna. Hence, the relationship between mooladhara and ajna is very important. Mooladhara is the generator and ajna is the distributor.

The location of mooladhara in men is at the perineum, midway between the genital organ and the anus, and about two centimetres inside. In women, it is located at the posterior side of the cervix, midway between the vagina and the uterus. Mooladhara is also the location of *brahma granthi*, the knot of Brahma. As long as this knot remains intact, the energy located in this area is blocked. Prana shakti awakens the moment this knot is undone. Infinite energy and spiritual experience emanate from mooladhara.

Mooladhara is associated with annamaya kosha and the earth element. In psychological terms, mooladhara is associated with the unconscious mind where the most primitive and deep-rooted instincts and fears lie. It is therefore the gateway to hell as well as to heaven; to the lower as well as the higher life.

Mooladhara chakra may be seen in a state of meditation as a deep red lotus flower with four petals. The red petals are seen in meditation because of electrical discharges, which emit light particles in this region. The pattern of the four-petalled lotus is formed due to the relative proximity of the discharges. Thus the chakras are also known as lotuses. Each chakra has a different number of petals, which indicate the level of pranic intensity in that particular region. The bija mantra, or master key, to mooladhara is *Lam*.

Location of the Chakras

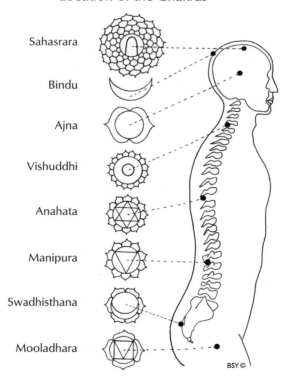

Sahasrara

Bindu

Ajna

Vishuddhi

Anahata

Manipura

Swadhisthana

Mooladhara

BSY©

Swadhisthana chakra

Swadhisthana means 'one's own abode'. It is located at the coccyx, very near to mooladhara, and is also responsible for the awakening of prana shakti. This centre is the storehouse of all the latent samskaras and impressions, which are considered to be the substrata of individual existence. Therefore, it forms a karmic block, making it difficult for the awakened prana to pass through this area.

In psychological terms, swadhisthana is associated with the subconscious mind and is responsible for drowsiness and sleep. It is also related with the reproductive organs and the sense of taste. The desire for pleasure, especially in the form of food and sex, increases when this centre is activated. These desires can become an obstacle to the awakening of prana at this level. In order to pass through this centre one needs to develop willpower.

In relation to the three *gunas*, or qualities of nature, mooladhara and swadhisthana are predominantly influenced by *tamas* or lethargy, dullness and ignorance. Swadhisthana is associated with pranamaya kosha and the water element. It is represented by a lotus flower with six vermilion petals. The bija mantra for this centre is *Vam*.

Manipura chakra

Manipura literally means 'the city of jewels'. Located behind the navel in the spine, its development is very important for success in the pranic science, as it is the storehouse of prana. This centre is associated with heat, vitality, dynamism, generation and preservation. Manipura is often compared with the dazzling orb of the sun, without which there would be no life. As the sun radiates light and energy, so manipura radiates and distributes pranic energy throughout the body, regulating and fuelling life's processes.

Manipura is predominantly influenced by *rajas* – activity, dynamism, strength and will. This centre is associated with pranamaya kosha and its element is fire. It is represented by a bright yellow lotus with ten petals. Its bija mantra is *Ram*.

Anahata chakra

Anahata means 'unstruck' or 'unbeaten'. It is the seat of *anahad nada*, the cosmic sound, which is experienced only in the highest state of meditation. This sound is unstruck, because it is not caused by any external form of friction nor can it be heard by the ears, mind or psyche. It is transcendental sound, which can only be perceived by the pure consciousness.

Anahata is the heart centre and is responsible for the awakening of refined emotions. The person with a developed anahata is generally very sensitive to the feelings of others. This centre relates to the sense of touch and its awakening bestows the power to heal others either by touch or by radiating energy. Many people who perform miraculous healing do so through the agency of anahata.

The heart centre is the seat of divine love. It is here that emotion is channelled into devotion. *Vishnu granthi*, the second psychic knot, representing the bondage of emotional attachment, is located here. When this knot is opened, one becomes free of all selfish, egoistic and emotional attachment, and attains mental and emotional control, equilibrium and peace.

Anahata is associated with manomaya kosha, the mind and emotions. At this level one becomes free of fate and takes control of one's destiny. Hence, the symbol of *kalpataru*, the wish-fulfilling tree, is also found at this centre. When this tree starts to fructify, whatever one thinks or wishes for comes true. Anahata is located behind the heart in the spine. Its element is air and it is represented by a blue lotus with twelve petals. The bija mantra is *Yam*.

Vishuddhi chakra

Vishuddhi is the purification centre and is known as the fountain of youth. According to tantric philosophy, *amrita* or the nectar of life falls down from *bindu* into this chakra, generating vitality, health and longevity. In the yogic texts it is stated that with the awakening of this centre all diseased

31

states can be reversed, and even an old person can become young once again.

When vishuddhi is activated cool, sweet drops of nectar drip down into the throat, causing a feeling of blissful intoxication. The ability to neutralize poison, both internally and externally, is also associated with vishuddhi. At this level all the poisonous and negative experiences of life can be absorbed and transformed into a state of bliss.

Vishuddhi is associated with vijnanamaya kosha and initiates higher mental development. It is the centre for receiving sound vibrations and acts like a transistor radio, allowing one to tune into the thoughts of others, whether close by or far away. When vishuddhi is purified, the sense of hearing becomes very sharp, not only through the ears, but through the mind.

Vishuddhi is located behind the throat pit in the spine and is associated with the thyroid gland. The element is ether or *akasha*. By meditating on vishuddhi, the mind becomes free of thought, pure and empty, like space. Vishuddhi is seen as a violet lotus with sixteen petals. Its bija mantra is *Ham*.

Ajna chakra

Ajna literally means 'command' and is the monitoring centre, also known as the guru chakra. It is the point of confluence where the three main *nadis*, energy channels: ida, pingala and sushumna, merge into one stream of consciousness and flow up to sahasrara. During deep meditation, when all the senses have been withdrawn and one enters into the dimension of *shoonya*, or void, guru or the higher consciousness guides the aspirant from ajna to sahasrara by issuing commands through this centre.

Ajna is the centre of mind and represents a higher level of awareness. It is also known as the eye of Shiva, the third eye or the eye of intuition, which gazes inward rather than outward. It is often called *divya chakshu*, the divine eye, or *jnana chakshu*, the eye of wisdom, because the spiritual aspirant receives revelation and insight into the underlying nature of existence

32

through this centre. Ajna is the doorway through which one enters the psychic or astral dimension. When this centre is developed one acquires psychic powers. Direct mind-to-mind communication takes place at this level.

At ajna lies the *rudra granthi*, the knot of Shiva. This knot is symbolic of attachment to the psychic personality and to the siddhis which accompany the awakening of ajna chakra. It effectively blocks one's spiritual evolution until attachment to psychic phenomena is overcome and the knot is freed. The trigger point for ajna is located at the eyebrow centre. It is known as bhrumadhya and is an important focal point for the practice of meditation, concentration and visualization.

The development of ajna is very important for success in pranic science. Prana can never be experienced in the form of light unless ajna is developed to some extent. The vision of light is usually seen first at ajna or bhrumadhya, or in *chidakasha*, the space of consciousness, which is directly associated with ajna. In the practice of prana vidya, ajna acts as the control centre for the distribution of prana. If the vision of light at ajna is well developed, one will have no difficulty in visualizing the raising of prana and its movement throughout the body. Otherwise, the imagination must be used until the actual experience develops.

Ajna is associated with vijnanamaya kosha. It is located at the top of the spinal cord in the mid-brain and corresponds to the pineal gland. The *tattwa* or element is mind. This is the point where the mind changes from gross to subtle, from outward to inward. Ajna is represented by a silver lotus with two petals. The bija mantra is *Om*.

Bindu

Bindu means 'point'. It is the point of creation where oneness first divides into multiplicity, the ultimate point from which all things manifest and into which all things return. Within bindu is contained the evolutionary potential for the myriad objects of the universe, the blueprint for creation. Bindu is the gateway to shoonya. It is located at the top back of the head, at the point where Hindu brahmins keep a tuft of hair called *shikha*.

Bindu is represented by a crescent moon and a drop of white nectar. The tantric texts describe a small depression or pit within the higher centres of the brain which contains a minute secretion of fluid. In the centre of that tiny secretion is a small point of elevation, like an island in the middle of a lake. In the psycho-physiological framework, this tiny point is considered to be bindu.

The moon at bindu produces *amrita*, the life-giving nectar, and the sun at manipura consumes it. This means that during the course of life, the drop of nectar produced at bindu falls down to manipura, where it is consumed by the fire element. Due to this process one suffers from the three ailments of *vyadhi*, disease; *jara*, old age; and *mrityu*, death. Yoga and tantra employ techniques by which one is able to reverse this process, so that the amrita is retained at vishuddhi, or sent back up from manipura to vishuddhi, and then to bindu. In this way perfected yogis have experienced immortality.

The first manifestation of creation was *nada* or sound, and bindu is also the point where the original nada emanates. Bindu is associated with anandamaya kosha. When bindu is awakened, the transcendental sound of *Om* is heard. Bindu is very important in prana vidya and in many higher yogas.

Sahasrara

Sahasrara is the seat of supreme consciousness, located at the crown of the head. Actually it is not a psychic centre at all, because it is beyond the realm of the psyche. Sahasrara is the totality, the absolute, the highest point of human evolution, which results from the merging of cosmic consciousness with cosmic prana. The experience of cosmic prana is the aim of the science of prana. Once mahaprana is experienced, one no longer needs to practise techniques. Transmission of energy will take place spontaneously with a thought, gesture, word or look.

Sahasrara is the master key that controls the awakening of all the chakras from mooladhara to ajna. The chakras are only switches; their potential power lies in sahasrara. When the kundalini shakti reaches sahasrara, self-realization or *samadhi* dawns. At this point, individual consciousness dies and universal consciousness is born. Sahasrara is infinite in dimension, like a huge radiant dome. It is visualized as a thousand-petalled lotus, unfolding from the crown of the head in all directions into eternity. Sahasrara is associated with anandamaya kosha.

4

Nadis:
Channels of Prana

Imagine the rush of energy that you experience during a moment of exhilaration. Now feel the channels through which the energy travels during such experiences. At first this may seem incomprehensible, but these flows may be traced when the concentration becomes deeper. Modern science explains this process in terms of nerve impulses, but the ancient seers perceived it as energy and consciousness flowing through interconnected channels in the body called nadis, which form an energy network. The word *nadi* means 'flow'. In this sense, nadis are subtle flows of energy, just as electricity, radio waves and laser beams are subtle flows. Nadis relate to the energy body and should not be confused with nerves, which relate to the physical body.

Nadis are pathways of pranic, mental and spiritual currents, which form a matrix throughout the physical body. They provide energy to every cell, organ and part through their vast network, carrying prana back and forth in every direction. Nadis are not physical, measurable or dissectible structures within the body, but channels of energy which underlie and sustain life and consciousness. In higher states of consciousness the nadis can actually be seen as flows of energy, as described by the yogis. They can be perceived at the psychic level as distinct channels of light, colour and sound. At the same time, the nadis underlie and are mirrored in all bodily functions and processes.

Scientific research has been carried out to verify the existence of the nadis. Dr Hiroshi Motoyama pioneered this research and found stable voltages of electromagnetic currents flowing within close proximity to the nervous system, which he cited as evidence for the existence of nadis. The network of nadis is so subtle and vast that even the yogic texts differ in calculation of their exact number. References in the *Goraksha Samhita* and *Hatha Yoga Pradipika* place the number at 72,000; the *Prapanchasara Tantra* gives the number of 300,000; while the *Shiva Samhita* states that 350,000 nadis emerge from the navel centre.

Major nadis

Out of the thousands of nadis, which include all the major and minor flows, seventy-two are considered important. Out of these seventy-two, ten are considered to be major. Among the ten major pranic flows, three are most significant: ida, pingala and sushumna. These three major nadis are situated in the spinal column and pass through every chakra. *Ida nadi* is the mental channel, *pingala nadi* the vital channel and *sushumna nadi* the spiritual channel. Ida, pingala and sushumna are the three main channels for the distribution of energy throughout the entire pranic network. Maximum pranic charges flow through them and they impact the entire network instantly; they are the high voltage wires that conduct the energy from the substations or chakras situated along the spinal column to all the other nadis.

After ida, pingala and sushumna, the seven lesser major nadis include: gandhari, hastijihva, yashaswini, pusha, alambusha, kuhu and shankhini. Some texts mention 19 major nadis and include: jihva, koorma, payaswini, saraswati, saumya, shura, varuni, vilambha and vishwodari. For all practical purposes, however, one need only concentrate on ida, pingala and sushumna, as these three govern the whole system of the nadis and all the body processes. In pranayama and prana vidya the practitioner works chiefly with these three channels. These three paths are also known as ganga (ida), yamuna (pingala) and saraswati (sushumna) after the three most important rivers in India, the last being an underground flow. The junction where these three rivers join is called Prayag, located outside of Allahabad in north India. In the pranic body, they converge at ajna chakra. Pingala is also known as the *surya*, or solar nadi, and ida as the *chandra*, or lunar nadi. Ida and pingala indicate time, while sushumna is the devourer of time, since it leads to timelessness or eternity.

Location of the nadis

The system of kundalini yoga describes mooladhara chakra as the main plexus of the pranic body from which the nadis emanate. Ida, pingala and sushumna originate here and then ida and pingala flow alternately, coiling around the spinal passage from left to right, while sushumna flows straight up through the middle. Ida emerges from the left of mooladhara, pingala from the right, and sushumna flows straight up through the centre.

Ajna

Ida

Pingala

BSY©

Mooladhara

From mooladhara chakra, pingala curves to the right and crosses swadhisthana, goes to the left to manipura, then to the right to anahata, to the left to vishuddhi, to the right to ajna at the top of the spine and then straight to sahasrara. Ida follows a similar path, but on the opposite side. As pingala crosses to the right, ida crosses to the left and so on (see diagram). As ida and pingala cross over at each chakra, their energy currents branch off via the network of nadis to all the respective organs and parts of the body. In this way the matrix of nadis carries these two opposite forces to every cell, organ and part of the body.

38

Ida governs the left side of the body and pingala the right. This can be explained with the analogy of a magnet. If a magnet is cut in half, either end of the magnet assumes opposite polarity. Similarly, the body is polarized, so that pingala governs the right side and ida the left. The central axis of ida and pingala is sushumna. This nadi is the mystical path of yoga that flows in between ida and pingala. Sushumna rises straight up through the centre of the spine, meeting ida and pingala at the points where they cross the chakras, and uniting with them at ajna chakra.

Sushumna is the pathway through which the kundalini rises, and thus forms the basis for the progressive awakening of higher knowledge. However, this pathway remains dormant in most people until a higher state of evolution is reached. The inner structure of sushumna comprises three subtler nadis, which become active when sushumna is awakened. Inside sushumna is vajra nadi, within which lies chitra or chitrini nadi, and at the centre is brahma nadi, the subtlest flow. Brahma nadi is so called because the higher centres of consciousness are directly activated via this channel. When the kundalini shakti passes through this channel, transcendental experiences take place.

The locations of some the other major nadis are as follows:
1. *Gandhari* flows from the corner of the left eye to the left big toe. It is situated on the side of ida and supports it. Gandhari can be stimulated by baddha padmasana.
2. *Hastijihva* flows from the right eye to the left big toe and carries energy to and from the lower part of the body. Hastijihva and gandhari support ida and together form the left channel.
3. *Yashaswini* flows from the right big toe to the left ear and supports pingala.
4. *Pusha* flows from the left big toe to the right ear. Pusha and yashaswini support pingala and together form the right channel.
5. *Alambusha* begins in the anus and terminates in the mouth.
6. *Kuhu* begins in the throat and terminates in the genitals.

Seminal essence is transformed to soma by this nadi. Kuhu is awakened by the practice of vajroli.

7. *Shankhini* begins at the throat and terminates in the anus. It flows on the left side of sushumna between saraswati and gandhari. Shankhini is activated by the practice of basti (yogic enema).

8. *Saraswati* is the nadi situated on the tongue. Those who possess gifted speech have an awakened saraswati.

9. *Payaswini* flows on the right side between pusha and saraswati, and is complementary to pingala. Its termination point is the right ear. The sect of ascetics called Kanphata Yogis awaken this nadi by wearing large earrings.

10. *Varuni* purifies toxins in the lower pelvic area along with kuhu. It terminates at the anus and is activated by basti and other kriyas.

11. *Vishwodari* resides in the area of the navel and flows between kuhu and hastijihva. It is related to the adrenal gland and the pancreas, and is activated by nauli kriya and uddiyana bandha. It improves the flow of prana throughout the body, and helps in the rising of prana along sushumna.

Polarity principle of ida-pingala

The entire universe is comprised of two forces, consciousness and energy, which are interdependent and opposite, yet complementary. The universe hangs as a kind of web of interacting energies, suspended and functioning within the framework of tensions developed by this fundamental polarity. Wherever one looks, within nature, within the body and within the mind, this polarity can be seen as light and dark, positive and negative, male and female, and so on. At every level, these two great principles or forces are at work, creating and motivating the universe.

When this cosmic polarity of prana and consciousness manifests in the microcosmic unit of the human body, it takes the form of chitta shakti and prana shakti, which correspond to ida nadi and pingala nadi. These two mental and physical channels within the body apply to all levels of being from gross to subtle, forming the basis for every perception, activity and experience. They represent the two distinct forces within the human environment – the ebb and flow of human existence.

Pingala represents the positive polarity and is the solar force. Physical vitality, dynamic activity and tension are qualities of pingala energy. It is hot in nature and corresponds to the sympathetic nervous system. Ida represents the negative polarity and is the lunar force. It is cold in nature and corresponds to the parasympathetic nervous system. Relaxation, passivity and sedentary activity are qualities of ida. The two mantras comprising the word 'hatha' correspond to the ida and pingala nadis. *Ham* relates to pingala nadi and *tham* or *ksham* to ida nadi. This symbology is also seen on the two petals of ajna chakra.

Pingala, the extroverting force, generally predominates during the daylight hours, especially in periods of physical and mental exertion, and activities requiring external interaction and attention. Ida also flows at such times, but it is subordinate to the pingala flow. In order to maintain a balance, ida generally predominates at night, counteracting the predominant flow of pingala during the day. Ida, the introverting force, is active while relaxing, reading, thinking, viewing television or sleeping.

Link with flow of nostrils: Ida and pingala dominance is directly related to the flow of breath in the nostrils. If one checks the flow of breath at any moment, one will usually find that one nostril is more open than the other. When the flow of breath is stronger in the left nostril, it indicates that ida is dominant; when the flow is stronger in the right nostril it indicates that pingala is dominant. When one is sleepy or drowsy, one will notice that the left nostril is flowing. When one is physically active, the right nostril begins to flow predominantly. Observing this phenomenon, the yogis devised breathing techniques to regulate the flows of ida and

41

pingala (and consequently sushumna) in order to intensify the experience of the pranic body.

Link with right and left brain: The specific functions of the brain also correlate with the activities of ida and pingala. The cerebrum is symmetrical, consisting of right and left hemispheres. The right hemisphere governs the left side of the body and the left hemisphere governs the right side of the body. Ida is connected to the right hemisphere and pingala to the left. The right hemisphere processes information in a diffuse and holistic manner. It controls orientation in space and is particularly sensitive to the vibrational realm of existence and those experiences which are intangible to the external senses. Thus it stimulates creative, artistic and musical abilities and is responsible for mental, psychic and extrasensory perception. Conversely, the left hemisphere which relates to pingala processes information in a sequential, linear and logical manner, and is responsible for rational, analytical and mathematical ability. In this way the nadis and brain hemispheres determine and motivate one's responses in day-to-day life.

Link with koshas: The ida force is the subtle energy that controls the manomaya and vijnanamaya koshas, whereas pingala controls the annamaya and anandamaya koshas. In pranamaya kosha, the ida and pingala forces reach out in both directions. The thoughts and mental experiences that remain confined to manomaya kosha, or the mental dimension, are known as ida activity until they become physical. Desires, thoughts, emotions and feelings are given form and direction by the force of ida. Vijnanamaya kosha, the body of psychic and intuitive knowledge that one gains through sadhana, is also an aspect of ida, the mental force. Extrasensory powers, such as clairaudience and clairvoyance or telepathy, are developed within the range of ida. The range of pingala, the vital force, is experienced as physical vitality in annamaya kosha. In anandamaya kosha, the awareness which remains even in the deepest state of meditation, after the dissolution of all the samskaras and karmas, is the result of an awakened pingala. The awareness in samadhi is pingala energy; this is the subtlest aspect of prana.

Sushumna: the neutral channel

When the two forces of ida and pingala are balanced, the third channel of sushumna becomes active. It is a fact that when two opposing forces are equal and balanced, a third force arises. By striking a match against a corrosive surface, fire is created. By bringing positive and negative currents together, machinery can be operated. Similarly, when the body and mind are united, a third force arises. This force is called sushumna, the spiritual energy. The working of these three forces can also be understood through the analogy of an electromagnetic circuit with the north pole being ajna and the south pole mooladhara. Ida is the negative charge, pingala the positive charge, and sushumna the neutral.

At each node of ida and pingala there is a concentration of energy, which forms pulsating patterns in the horizontal plane. These nodes are the chakras, force fields that expand and contract, depending on physical and mental activities. When there is an intensity of energy between ida and pingala, the chakras manifest in the form of light and sound. This manifestation occurs to a minor extent in normal breathing, but much more during pranayama practices such as nadi shodhana, and meditation. While ida and pingala conduct mental and physical energy, sushumna conducts a higher form of cosmic energy. The pranic and mental energies are finite, whereas the energy of sushumna is infinite.

When sushumna is active, the breath flows through both nostrils simultaneously. Normally this happens only for a few minutes when the breath dominance changes over from one nostril to the other, which usually takes place every ninety minutes. Sushumna flows after practising pranayama, prayer and meditation, and also when one is about to commit a criminal act. When sushumna flows, the whole brain operates, but only half of the brain is active during the flow of ida or pingala. At the time of sushumna, both *karmendriyas*

43

and *jnanendriyas*, physical organs and mental organs, function simultaneously and one becomes very powerful. Feelings of equanimity and steadiness arise, because sushumna is the conductor of mahaprana, the kundalini energy. Meditative states dawn spontaneously, even in the middle of a traffic jam. The flow of sushumna is considered to be the most favourable for any type of sadhana.

Sushumna represents the integration and harmony of opposites at all levels. It indicates the balance and fusion of the opposite principles of ida and pingala. The following chart shows the experience of these three forces at various levels:

Ida	Pingala	Sushumna
chitta	prana	kundalini
mental	vital	supramental
negative	positive	neutral
feminine	masculine	androgynous
yin	yang	tao
moon	sun	light
cold	hot	temperate
imagination	logic	wisdom
desire	action	knowledge
internal	external	centred
night	day	dusk/dawn
passive	dynamic	balanced
subjectivity	objectivity	awareness
parasympathetic	sympathetic	cerebrospinal
blue	red	yellow
Ganga	Yamuna	Saraswati
Brahma	Vishnu	Rudra
subconscious	conscious	unconscious
sattwa	rajas	tamas
A	U	M

Purpose of yoga

There are planes of existence and areas of consciousness that remain in absolute darkness for the average individual. These planes are much more beautiful and creative than those one lives in now. By penetrating and illumining them, one is able to experience different states of consciousness,

44

just as one experiences the state of dream or sleep. When the pranic energy is awakened, it circulates to these dark areas of consciousness. Then the inner city is illumined and the soul is reborn into a new dimension of existence, a new area of experience.

This process, however, takes place gradually. First, the body is rendered subtle and pure through yogic practices, and transformed into a yogic body. The very physical molecules in the body are altered, and the pranic and mental forces undergo a metamorphosis. This is achieved through the purification of the nadis, which enables the pranas to awaken. The awakened pranas then gradually illumine the whole consciousness.

Purifying the pranic body: All yogic practices purify the pranas, but pranayama is considered the principal among these. In the *Yoga Sutras* (2:52) Maharshi Patanjali states, "Thence the covering of the light is destroyed", with reference to the effects of pranayama. This covering is the residue of tamas and rajas, and through pranayama the sattwic nature of the chitta shines forth. Tamas and rajas exist in the form of blockages in the nadis. These blockages may be caused by disease, tension, accumulation of impurities, negative thoughts or samskaras, mental patterns lodged in the subconscious and unconscious. Just as the nadis are not physical but pranic entities, the blockages too are pranic and may be experienced, but not quantified.

The thoughts and *vrittis*, mental formations and modifications, exist in the mind and consciousness as energy waves. Therefore, they influence the energy patterns in the nadis directly and inherently. Depending on the nature of a thought or vritti, the respective nadis as well as the chakras, elements and doshas are affected, creating a spiralling effect throughout the energy network. If the thoughts are left unchecked, the energy system will be depleted over time. In this way the negative thought patterns and vrittis are reinforced and the mind is weakened. For this reason it is difficult to free oneself of obsessions and samskaras.

Indulging in an experience of arrogance, for example, will create a block in the manipura/anahata region and the network of nadis there. Every further wave of arrogance will fortify the block. A tendency to hold back will create a block in the anahata/vishuddhi region. These blockages in the nadis often manifest as disease in the annamaya kosha. On the other hand, even if a disease has been caused by purely physical circumstances, it will be transmitted to the pranic and psychic realm as well. The nadis in that region will become weak and the network of flows will tend to bypass that region, just as a river tends to bypass a rock. This region will be depleted of energy and will become weaker and weaker.

During pranayama, especially nadi shodhana, as one takes slow, deep breaths, the prana is forced to flow through the blocked areas, indeed, through the entire system of nadis. By this process, the energy circuits are restored and the weak areas gradually regain strength. Just as an emotion of arrogance creates a blockage in the manipura/anahata area, increasing the pranic flow through the nadis of this region clears up the blockage. Thus the *Shiva Samhita* states (3:49), "Through the regulation of breath the wise practitioner surely destroys all of his karmas, whether acquired in this life or in the past." *Manusmriti* also tells us, "Let the defects be burnt up by pranayama."

Even if one were unaware of one's specific blocks, the very nature of pranayama, when practised correctly, is such that the entire energy circuitry is influenced and cleared over a period of time. Purification is achieved at the pranic level and simultaneously at the physical and mental levels as well. This brings about many positive transformations. As the *Hatha Yoga Pradipika* (2:20) says, "With the nadis purified, the inner sound or nada awakens and one is free from disease." At this point, one is ready to commence higher sadhanas.

Awakening of prana: Human evolution depends on the awakening of prana shakti, as much as it depends on optimum health of the body. The awakening of prana

46

takes place when the nadis flow regularly, rhythmically and continuously, and no blockages or physiological discomfort is encountered in the breathing process. This stage is known as *pranotthana*, awakening of the pranas, more specifically of ida and pingala. When the awakening of ida and pingala occurs, sushumna awakens. The awakening of this third force is considered the most important event in pranayama, kriya yoga and kundalini yoga. Pranayama actually begins with the awakening of sushumna, because then the pranic field expands. Until this awakening occurs, the purification of ida and pingala continues throughout the practices.

After the pranas have awakened, the practitioner is ready to undertake the practice of prana vidya. The practitioner must be able to direct prana as necessary, not only within his own body but also the omnipresent, manifest power from which all energies originate. The adept yogi can withdraw prana from any area of the body, so that it becomes impervious to heat, cold or any other sensations. He can also send prana to any area and make it oversensitive. He can send prana to the eyes and see distant objects, to the nose and experience divine aromas, or to the tongue and experience super-sensuous taste. One can learn to use the cosmic energy, which is freely available to all, to create further changes in the patterns of the body, mind and consciousness. Such an awakening of pranic energy indicates the evolution of pranamaya kosha, whereby one is able to go deep into and become established in the higher meditative states.

5

Pancha Prana:
Pranic Force Fields

There are five primary forces, known as *pancha prana*, which operate in the physical body at all times. Prana shakti, the one sustaining force, assumes these five fields to enable the body to accomplish its various functions. Thus prana is experienced differently in different parts of the body simultaneously. These five forces also act on subtler levels, influencing and in turn being influenced by the mind and consciousness. The seers identified these five pranas as: prana, apana, samana, udana and vyana. The five pranas are also known as prana vayus. The term vayu is derived from the root *va*, meaning 'motion' or 'that which flows'. So the prana vayus represent the inherent quality of motion which energizes every action from secretion of the digestive juices to the movement of the hand. They flow through all the elements, organs and the mind.

The five pranas are responsible for creation and existence at the individual level. In human beings they are created during the first four months of development in the womb. During the first and second month, the foetus lives on the prana of the mother. By the third month the foetus has its own battery installed. By the fourth month, the five physical pranas become active with the formation of the body, and the soul enters the new body as a result of this pranic activity.

The five pranas maintain the balance between the physical and mental levels. Their physical locations are relevant in

48

regard to the functions of the body; however, they function more homogeneously in the subtler levels of mind and consciousness, where their distinction is qualitative rather than physical. In this context, the yogic texts often differ in their description of the five pranas and their locations. This should not confuse the practitioner. One should remember that the energy body is comprehended in the realm of experience, where the boundaries are neither black nor white. The key is to continue honing one's own experience.

Sthoola prana

Physical level: Prana is the first of the pancha pranas. This prana is also known as *sthoola* (gross) prana to differentiate it from the all-pervasive vital force. Sthoola prana refers to the energy currents located in the thoracic region between the diaphragm and the base of the neck. It is the centre of circulation of life energy. This force maintains the heart and lungs, and all the activities in the chest region such as breathing, swallowing and circulation of blood. When the rate of breath or heartbeat increases due to strenuous work, etc. the level of sthoola prana also increases. This force is so essential that if its activity is obstructed or ceases for any reason, death may occur.

Sthoola prana is experienced in the form of light particles moving upwards in the chest region. Among the fivefold pranas, it occupies the pivotal position and controls the other four. Pranayama in particular raises the level of this prana and prevents congestion of blood in the arteries around the heart. When sthoola prana is strong, the heart does not become weak; one does not suffer from high or low blood pressure, and thus lives longer.

Subtle level: At the level of mind, prana is responsible for the intake of impressions and ideas. Prana energizes all the koshas and is active all the time. It pervades the region from anahata up to vishuddhi chakra. When the force of prana is strong and flowing uninterruptedly, purer qualities of the heart, such as strength, courage and greatness are expressed.

This prana is the energy by which one-pointedness of mind and intuitive knowledge can be experienced. It holds the intelligent energy of the soul, which abides in the heart. By enhancing this prana, the yogis reach the soul. In the *Brihadaranyaka Upanishad* (3:7:16), it is said:

य: प्राणे तिष्ठन् प्राणादन्तरो यं प्राणो न वेद यस्य प्राण: शरीरं ।
य: प्राणमन्तरो यमत्येष त आत्मान्तर्याम्यमृत: ॥

The intelligent soul is placed in prana, inside the prana, it pervades the prana, yet the non-intelligent are unaware of it. Prana itself has become the body of the chief master, who controls it from the inside. Thus the soul is immutable, indestructible and immortal.

Prana is the guide and medium for realization of the soul. When meditating on the heart centre, the identification with prana is most intense; one feels as if one has become prana.

Indications of imbalance: When the pathways of prana are not clear, the heart and lungs malfunction and there is poor intake of oxygen. At the mental level, one is not able to bring in positive impressions. It is difficult to concentrate or access intuitive knowledge.

Apana

Physical level: Apana is the second prana, which operates in the pelvic region between the navel and the perineum. It sustains the functions of the kidneys, bladder, bowels, excretory and reproductive organs. It is responsible for the expulsion of gas, wind, faeces, urine, semen and ova. It nourishes the foetus and expels it from the uterus at the time of birth. Apana is experienced in the form of light particles moving downwards from the navel to the perineum. Due to the presence of the earth and water elements in this region, apana is felt as a heavy force.

Subtle level: Apana brings energy down through the koshas. Swadhisthana and mooladhara chakras are within the range of apana. By realizing apana, these chakras are

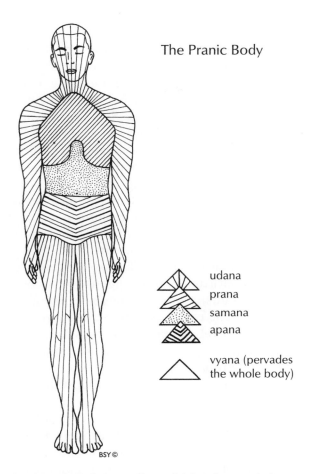

The Pranic Body

udana
prana
samana
apana

vyana (pervades
the whole body)

BSY©

also realized. The kundalini force lies within the periphery
of apana, and it assists in the awakening of kundalini,
while prana helps in its upward ascent. Thus mahaprana
is experienced in the region of apana. Control of apana
is also control of the sexual instinct and the instilling of
brahmacharya. At the mental level, apana removes negative
thoughts and emotions.

Indications of imbalance: When apana is imbalanced,
there is poor elimination, a feeling of being pulled down by
gravity, depression and negativity.

Samana

Physical level: Samana is the third prana. It operates between the navel and the diaphragm. The word samana is derived from the root *saman*, meaning 'equal' or 'balanced'. Thus it acts as a balancer or equalizer for the two opposite forces of prana and apana. Samana activates and maintains the digestive organs and their secretions, and is responsible for metabolism. It is associated with the digestive fire, *jatharagni*. Samana is experienced as a sideways movement of light, like the swinging of a fast pendulum, from right to left and left to right. It is responsible for the manipura experience of vitality and dynamism.

There are six major organs of digestion: liver, stomach, duodenum, spleen, and the small and large intestines, all fall within the field of samana. The body receives its life support and healthy nourishment by the agency of samana. The distinctive feature of samana is that although it is a single force, it is capable of different activities in all these different organs.

Subtle level: Samana maintains the cohesion and balance between the koshas. It is subtle in comparison to apana and gross in comparison to prana. Just as it helps digest food, samana is also responsible for digesting the mind-stuff.

Indications of imbalance: Samana, the equalizer, is disturbed whenever one's mental peace and harmony are disturbed. Whenever there is turbulence in the body and the senses, samana becomes agitated and causes disorders. Poor assimilation of food is a result of samana imbalance, causing build-up of toxins as well as psychological blockage.

Udana

Physical level: Udana is the fourth manifestation, which operates in the extremities: the arms, legs, neck and head. This prana is responsible for all the sensory organs, *jnanendriyas*, and the organs of action, *karmendriyas*. It coordinates and controls the movements of the legs, arms and neck and directs the activities of the brain and sensory organs that are situated in the head region. These include: eyes, vision; ears, hearing; tongue, taste; nose, smell; skin, tactile sensation. The organs of action controlled by udana are three: hands, feet and speech. The other two, the excretory and reproductive organs, are under the control of apana.

Udana also assists prana in inhalation and exhalation, intake of food and drink, as well as vomiting, spitting and swallowing saliva. All the functions of the throat and mouth are sustained by udana and its influence begins from the region of vishuddhi chakra. It also maintains the pranic link between the heart and the brain. In addition, udana aids the minor pranas (see below) in carrying out their activities due to its close proximity to them. All the five minor pranas function due to the energy derived from udana.

Udana sustains the sense organs and their activities. The enjoyment of senses keeps udana active, because it functions according to their needs. The force of udana keeps the body upright; it is responsible for anti-gravitational activities of the body (particularly by the hands and the feet).

Subtle level: Udana allows one to perform positive mental work. It is responsible for sweet, melodious and impressive speech. It allows for the exchange of prana between the head and heart, thereby establishing contact between the subtle and causal bodies. It maintains the relationship between the gross, subtle and causal bodies. Udana is experienced as spiralling flows of light down the arms and legs and up through the head.

Udana pervades ajna, bindu and sahasrara chakras. It brings energy up the koshas from the gross to the subtle. When the yogi fixes his attention on udana, he becomes free from hunger, thirst, sleep and drowsiness. The activity of udana becomes extremely slow and subtle during meditation and samadhi.

Indications of imbalance: An irregular udana causes breathing troubles, inefficiency in physical and mental work, inability to think clearly or express oneself, uncoordinated speech, weakened will and lack of cheer.

Vyana

Physical level: Vyana, the fifth prana, pervades the whole body and acts as reserve energy. It helps all the other pranas when they require an extra boost. When one overexerts and feels extremely tired, a rush of energy comes, which enables one to continue. This 'second wind' is the vyana experience. Vyana also regulates and coordinates all the muscular movements, aids in sending impulses to different parts of the body, and causes the flow of perspiration and gooseflesh. Vyana causes all the pranas, major and minor, to function by being their accessory.

Subtle level: Vyana brings about circulation through all the five koshas and is responsible for their differentiation. It pervades the spatial element in the body, and is the vehicle of consciousness through the body. In the condition of excitement, due to its swift motion, it makes the mind excited and deluded. The motion of consciousness becomes intense at such times.

Indications of imbalance: When vyana, the expansive energy, is imbalanced, there is lack of coordination, tremors, inability to reach out to people, and the mind is erratic.

Density and colour of pranas

The five pranas have varying densities of ionic fields. Udana is the least dense, then follow prana, samana and apana. Vyana, which flows throughout the whole body, has a density which is the average of all the others. The ionic fields of the pranas may be visualized as swirling clouds of differing colours and hues, capable of expanding and contracting. The colours are created due to the emission of photons, when electrons change their energy levels from higher to lower frequencies. The *Amritanada Upanishad* describes the colours of the different pranas thus (v. 34–37):

रक्तवर्णो मणिप्रख्य: प्राणवायु प्रकीर्तित: ।
अपानस्तस्य मध्ये तु इंद्रकोपसमप्रभ: ।

54

समानस्तु द्व्योर्मध्ये गोक्षीरधवलप्रभः ।
आपाण्डर उदानश्च व्यानो ह्यर्चिसमप्रभः ॥

Prana is said to be blood-red, the colour of ruby or coral;
apana is the colour of *indra-gopa* (an insect which is white
or red in colour); samana is in-between the colour of pure
milk and crystal (oily and shining), udana is *apandara* (pale
white), and vyana is the colour of *archis* (a ray of light).

Union of prana and apana

Of the five pranas, the two most influential are prana and
apana. The *Shiva Samhita* (3:6) states:

अत्रापि वायवः पंच मुख्याः स्युर्दशतः पुनः ।
तत्रापि श्रेष्ठकर्त्तारौ प्रानापानौ मयोदितौ ॥

Out of the ten (major and minor pranas), the first five are
the leading ones; even among these, prana and apana are
the highest agents.

Prana and apana are the two opposite forces in the
physical body; prana moves upward from the navel and apana
downward. Under the influence of apana, the consciousness
is drawn down to mooladhara, which is associated with the
earth element, the grossest level of manifestation. There it
generates desires and interacts with the world. Under the
influence of prana, the consciousness is drawn upward towards
sahasrara, which is associated with ether, the subtlest element,
and with the unmanifest dimension, where it experiences its
higher nature.

In the practice of yoga the direction or movement of prana
and apana are changed. The upward flow of prana is directed
downward and the downward flow of apana is directed
upwards. In this way they both move towards one another and
meet at samana. At this meeting point the energy of *yogagni*,
fire of yoga, arises. When these two aspects of life, the inner
and the outer, the mundane and the spiritual are brought
together and united, the kundalini awakens.

In the fourth chapter of the *Bhagavad Gita*, Sri Krishna instructs Arjuna on raja yoga and hatha yoga. His basic advice is: unite prana with apana or unite apana with prana (4:29):

अपाने जुह्वति प्राणं प्राणेऽपानं तथाऽपरे ।
प्राणापानगती रुद्ध्वा प्राणायामपरायणाः ॥

Apana is absorbed in prana (by some), and prana in apana by others. By restraining the courses of prana and apana, (the yogi is) wholly occupied in pranayama.

The union of prana and apana, or apana and prana, or the suspension of both, can be attained through the practices of yoga. There are many practices for bringing about this union. When siddhasana is practised and the inspired breath is taken to the region of samana, prana and apana unite at this centre. The practices of kriya yoga bring about the same effect. When the three bandhas are performed, jalandhara bandha stops prana from ascending, moola bandha stops apana from descending, and uddiyana bandha creates a suction process, which affects the behaviour of both prana and apana. A shatkarma like nauli kriya also creates union between prana and apana. When pranayama is practised with inhalation, exhalation and retention, the union of prana and apana takes place at ajna chakra.

The union of prana and apana is one of the most important aims of yoga. Until the practitioner is able to channel these two forces, he continues to be under the influence of duality and the mind remains dissipated. The *Yoga Chudamani Upanishad* says (v. 27):

आक्षिप्तो भुजदण्डेन तथा यथोच्चलति कन्दुकः ।
प्राणापानसमाक्षिप्तस्तथा जीवो न तिष्ठति ॥

Just as a ball goes up and down when thrown by the hand, similarly, the individual soul is thrown up (and down) by the movement of prana and apana (and therefore) does not remain still.

Five minor pranas

Along with the five major pranas, there are five minor or *upa* pranas, actually called *pancha vayus*. These are: naga, koorma, krikara, devadatta and dhananjaya. The pancha vayus are grosser and more limited manifestations of energy compared to the pancha pranas. The *Gheranda Samhita* qualifies the difference between the two by calling them 'inner vayus' and 'outer vayus'. It must however be mentioned that most scriptural authorities use 'vayu' as a generic term to refer to all the pranas. The *Hatha Yoga Pradipika* uses the term 'vayu' and 'prana' interchangeably throughout its slokas; the *Gheranda Samhita* refers to the 'ten vayus' and so on. Works such as the *Yoga Chudamani Upanishad* even refer to the pancha pranas as pancha vayus. However, in works such as the *Shiva Swarodaya* and the *Dhyana Bindu Upanishad*, we find a categorical distinction in the usage of the terms 'pancha prana' and 'pancha vayu'. This distinction is preferable as the experience of prana at the level of the pancha pranas and the pancha vayus is qualitatively distinct.

Naga: This field of activity causes belching and hiccups. When the air element is agitated, naga becomes active and tries to throw the agitated air out of the stomach, causing vibrations in udana, prana and samana. Naga remains inactive as long as the diet and digestion are healthy. In the state of meditation, naga does not function.

Koorma: This field causes the blinking of the eyes and keeps the eyes healthy, moist and protected. It enables one to see all objects. The eyes shine due to the energy of koorma and one appears impressive. When koorma is under control, the yogi can keep the eyes open for hours, performing trataka. Although koorma operates in a small area, it has a lot of force and during meditation it makes concentration firm and deep.

Krikara: This field causes yawning, hunger and thirst, and assists in respiration. Due to its relation with yawning, its origin is sloth and lethargy. When krikara is controlled with practice, sloth and sleep are overcome, hunger and thirst are controlled, and sweet secretions begin to flow in the mouth. The control of krikara is especially helpful during fasting and samadhi.

Devadatta: This field causes sneezing and aids in respiration. It becomes activated by sharp or irritating smells and causes pain in the nostrils in more intense conditions. In its subtle state, devadatta enables the practitioner to experience divine smells.

Dhananjaya: This field pervades the whole body and is related to the organ of touch. It influences the work of the muscles, arteries and veins, and the skin. The swelling experienced during an injury is due to the motion of dhananjaya. During a tamasic state it reinforces sloth in the body. Dhananjaya is the last prana to leave the body after death and is responsible for decomposition of the body.

Pranayama and prana vidya

Although the ten pranas (major and minor) are identified separately, they work in synchronicity to take every physical action to its rightful conclusion. For example, in the process of metabolizing food, prana helps to take the food down the oesophagus, samana facilitates its digestion, vyana circulates the nutrients, apana eliminates the waste material and udana carries the energy derived from the food for physical work.

The *Prashnopanishad* draws an analogy between the pancha pranas and yajna, likening apana, vyana and prana to the yajna fire, samana to the priest, mind to the host, and udana to the fruit of sacrifice. The pranic process is indeed equivalent to the yajna process: energy is fed, life is infused, and energy is emitted through the combined forces. Therefore, when all the pranas are balanced, the body and mind are in a state of optimized harmony. However, this is not usually the case. Due to overuse and misuse, the pranas of most people are in a state of imbalance.

In the course of daily life, worry and stress use maximum prana, so that the pranic fields become exhausted and discharged. This in turn causes fatigue, depression, and inefficient digestion and circulation. As this vicious cycle continues, the body does not have the strength to walk, work or think, and the smallest disturbance causes nervousness and anxiety. In order to remedy this, the pranas need to be charged constantly, so their functioning is optimized and balance is maintained. This is the first objective of pranayama, which charges and replenishes the pranas through the practices. When the pranas are sufficiently charged, they are awakened.

During the practice of prana vidya, one realizes the awakened pranas. The practitioner becomes intensely aware of each individual prana, its movement and psychic perception. However, one can also begin to appreciate the nature of the different pranas by observing and concentrating on the different actions caused by them. Through the realization of the pranas, consciousness is realized. The sensation of prana in a particular area can become the medium of experience of consciousness or the intelligent principle in that region. As the pranas pervade the gross as well as subtle functions, the deeper their realization the subtler is the perception of consciousness. When the realization of the pranas is sufficiently intense, the yogi can guide these forces and transform their qualities as required.

6

Five Keys

There are five keys that are used to unlock the subtle perception and experience of prana. These keys are: i) psychic breath, ii) psychic passage, iii) psychic centres, iv) psychic sound and v) psychic symbol.

Psychic breath

The psychic breath is the first key to pranic awareness. Psychic breathing is the integration of awareness with the physical breath. The experience of the breath can be both gross and subtle. The basis of the psychic breath is the gross physical breath. The breath moves through the nostrils approximately fifteen times per minute, 900 times per hour and 21,600 times every day, whether one is aware of it or not. The normal experience of breathing is the process of drawing air down into the lungs and expelling it through the nostrils. Guiding this process through willpower and concentration is one aspect of pranayama; the second aspect is psychic breathing.

In the initial stages of psychic breathing, the only requirement is awareness of the natural breath without trying to affect the pattern of the breathing cycle. Once this is achieved, the movement of the breath is experienced in the form of ujjayi pranayama (see Chapter 20: 'Tranquillizing Pranayamas'). The initial process of psychic breathing involves awareness of the deep sound vibration created by the ujjayi breath and its movement during inhalation and exhalation. Ujjayi involves the practice of awareness, concentration and the actual physiological contraction of the throat muscles.

During the practice of ujjayi pranayama, which can also be performed with khechari mudra, there is awareness of the movement and sound of the breath as it passes in and out through the throat. This awareness develops the perception of pranamaya kosha. When psychic breathing is practised with total awareness of the movement and sound of the inner breath in the throat, the mind begins to relax and new forms of experience arise within the personality. During the practice of ujjayi the physiological experience is one of tranquillity, relaxation and one-pointedness. This is the gross experience of ujjayi, and then there is the psychic experience.

As the practice of ujjayi develops, one begins to move the prana. The first manifestation of mahaprana is the prana located in the chest. The first physiological experience that arises from the movement and awakening of prana is in the form of a stream of white light or as a sort of tickling or burning sensation in the throat, chest and lungs. However, as the concentration becomes deeper and more intense, one experiences prana more acutely and the experience changes.

Psychic passage

The second key to pranic awareness is the psychic passage. This refers to any pathway in the body through which aware-ness, breath and prana are directed in one stream of combined force. The psychic passage is not a limited concept; it can be made anywhere to or from any part of the body. Once the passage is visualized, the psychic breath can be moved there, using ujjayi pranayama, and this will bring about an actual pranic transfer. Psychic breathing is an integral part of the science of prana, and it must be mastered to the point where it becomes extremely subtle and spontaneous.

In the practice of prana vidya, many psychic passages are created one after the other, so that prana can be distributed to all parts of the body. Some passages are long and complex routes, and others are short and simple. For the purpose of awakening prana, several important psychic passages must be purified and opened before beginning the actual practice of prana vidya.

Usually the first psychic passage to be opened and experienced is part of the frontal passage, which extends between manipura kshetram at the navel and vishuddhi kshetram at the throat pit. This is the passage used in the first stages of ajapa japa. The full frontal psychic passage extends from mooladhara to ajna, just as the sushumna nadi extends in the spine. The *chakra kshetrams*, trigger points for activation of the chakras in the spine, lie along this frontal passage.

The most powerful psychic passage is the sushumna nadi, which rises straight up through the centre of the spinal column. This is the path through which the awakened kundalini travels from mooladhara to sahasrara. The main chakra points and the experiences of their awakening are situated along this passage. The points located along the spine are known as *chakra sharira*, body of the chakra.

After sushumna, the ida and pingala nadis are the most important psychic channels. However, only pingala is used as a psychic passage. If ida were used in this manner, the mental force would become dominant, which could cause loss of pranic vitality and mental stability.

Ajna chakra is the meeting place of ida, pingala and sushumna nadis, from where the three proceed as one flow of consciousness. After ajna there is no difference between prana and consciousness; there is just cosmic awareness, moving upward.

The practice of prana vidya enables the practitioner to experience the flow and colour of prana as it passes upward through the pingala passage. Sometimes it is seen like the strand of a spider's web, shining and translucent at dawn. One may also see tiny points of luminous light or sparkling jewels suspended on a silver thread. They are the subtle and mysterious chakras located along sushumna. These experiences arise gradually as one purifies oneself through yogic practices. They are an indication that one is making progress and beginning to master the science of prana.

Psychic centres

The third key to awareness of prana is the psychic centres or chakras, vortices of subtle prana located at specific points along the sushumna passage. According to the science of prana, prana is generated at mooladhara, it is stored in manipura, purified at vishuddhi and distributed from ajna. These are the four chakras used in the practice of prana vidya. One needs to become aware of how each chakra influences the activity of pranic energy, and what experience takes place when the various chakras are awakened. With the techniques of prana vidya, the chakras can be awakened quickly if one practises diligently. It will not just happen spontaneously; one needs to stimulate, influence and control prana, and this must be done gradually and with care.

Psychic sound

The fourth key to awareness of prana is the psychic sound. According to yoga, sound manifests within the individual consciousness as well as outside. In order to develop the awareness of psychic sound, one must withdraw the auditory perception so that external sounds are no longer heard. When the attention is completely withdrawn to the centre of the head, one develops the awareness of *chidakasha*, the psychic space within the head. One can then observe any sounds that arise spontaneously within that space.

The experiences of inner sound documented in the classical yogic texts include: buzzing of bees, tinkling bells, conch, flute, *veena* (Indian lute), cymbals, drums and thunder. The psychic sound begins in a very subtle way and the intensity gradually increases. The tinkling of bells or the notes of the veena can actually be heard, even if there are no bells ringing or a veena being played externally. The experience of psychic sound manifests entirely within, without the presence of any outer object or instrument.

63

After bringing the inner sound to one's conscious awareness, a profound throbbing sound may be experienced, as if one were within a deep cavern or tunnel, at the other end of which someone is playing music, drums or a flute. The sound begins at a very low pitch, which gradually increases and then slowly diminishes after some time. At the end of this period one may become aware of the innermost nada, the transcendental sound of *Om*.

Psychic symbol

The fifth key to pranic awareness is the psychic symbol, which is experienced through the practice of concentration. The symbol can be any object on which the mind is fixed. It may be an abstract symbol, a yantra or mandala, candle flame, scene from nature, sun, moon, star, cloud, mountain, lake, flower, sea shell, or anything that attracts one's attention. By concentrating on the symbol, one gradually develops the ability to see it internally as clearly as one sees it externally.

A specific symbol may also be given at the time of mantra initiation as an aid to concentration. The symbol is chosen according to one's personality and astrological sign. Meditation on the psychic symbol prepares the aspirant for higher pranayama practices and enables one to access the inner dimensions of consciousness.

7

Prana and Mantra

An intrinsic relationship between sound and prana under-
lies all creation. At the beginning of creation, when
the first movement arose within the field of dormant consciousness and mahaprana manifested, sound also came into
being. With the first movement of cosmic energy the first
sound manifested, which was *Om*. This transcendental sound
is also called *nada*, the highest level of sound vibration. From
nada emerged *kalaa*, the manifest universe of time, space
and object. In scientific terms, this may be related to the
event of the Big Bang.

In *Tantroktam Devi Suktam* (v. 6) one of the aspects of
Shakti is described as 'Vishnumayeti shabdita', which refers
to the manifestation of primordial energy in the form of
shabda, word. In the *Bible* also it has been said, "In the
beginning was the Word, and the Word was with God." In
order to become manifest, the unmanifest and indivisible
has to take on form. The first form was sound, and it came
into existence through the medium of energy or prana. Due
to the close relationship between prana and nada in the
process of creation, sound is one of the best vehicles for the
transmission of prana shakti at the microcosmic level also.
Therefore mantras, sounds containing psychic force, are
often used in the science of prana.

What are mantras?

Mantras are cosmic sounds, which were discovered in higher states of meditation when yogis explored the different layers of the mind to discover the source of existence. Normally, it is difficult to go beyond the physical level in meditation. With some effort one can contain the agitation of the *vrittis*, waves of the mind, and go up to the mental and intellectual levels. However, very few are able to access the dimension of spirit. Yogis have gone to that level and experienced luminosity, the eternal quality of the spirit. In that state, vibrations are heard which the physical senses are incapable of hearing.

Normally, one hears sounds only within a certain range of decibels; beyond or below that range the frequencies change and cannot be heard. However, in the causal state of consciousness one becomes sensitized and begins to hear and see many things. What one hears are mantras and what one sees are yantras. If one simply makes up some syllables and repeats them – that is not mantra. The mantras that the yogis discovered were sounds vibrating at particular frequencies in each dimension of the personality. They also identified each sound with a particular psychic centre. The mantra *Om*, for example, was identified as the seed sound of ajna chakra, *Ham* of vishuddhi chakra, *Yam* of anahata chakra, *Ram* of manipura chakra, *Vam* of swadhisthana chakra and *Lam* of mooladhara chakra.

In their altered state of observation, the yogis perceived that the chakras are stimulated by chanting a particular sound. This is akin to the effect created when a long rope is tied to a tree trunk and shaken: the wave travels from one end of the rope to the other. Similarly, the ripples of vibration reach and activate the psychic centre when the sound of a frequency is repeated audibly or mentally. Therefore, the yogis combined certain sounds in order to create a particular state of consciousness. In this way mantras such as *Om Namah Shivaya*, *Om Namah Bhagavate Vasudevaya* and others emerged. Mantras became part of spiritual sadhana to awaken different areas of consciousness and develop knowledge and creativity in a particular area of consciousness.

Each mantra has two important qualities, known in Sanskrit as varna and akshara. *Varna* means 'colour' and *akshara* means 'letter' or 'form'. The letters of the Sanskrit alphabet are akshara, which also means 'imperishable'. For once a mantra is uttered, it becomes a part of the eternal akashic record. Every mantra has six parts. First, it has a rishi, who had self-realization through the mantra and gave the mantra to others. Sage Vishwamitra, for example, is the rishi for the Gayatri mantra. Second, every mantra has a metre. Third, it has an *ishta devata* (presiding deity). Fourth, it has a *bija* (seed), which is its essence. Fifth, it has its own *shakti*, energy. Sixth, it has a *kilaka* (pin) which unplugs the *chaitanya* (consciousness) hidden in the mantra. When the plug is removed by constant and prolonged repetition, the chaitanya is revealed.

Most people do not understand the power of mantras and think they can use them in any preferred way. Some use any word or name for their mantra. For example, one may admire a great person and want to make a mantra out of his or her name. One may think of that person as one's guru or God and be filled with great emotional feelings and love for him. One may like to repeat his name; however, that name is merely a sound with an emotional charge, not a mantra charged with prana shakti.

Initiation from a mantra guru is essential to realize the power of a mantra. Recitation of a word or syllable that has been heard or found in a book is not enough. A mantra requires correct phonetic pronunciation, intonation, concentration and creation of the associated mental image or form. Its ishta, bija, shakti and kilaka are a matter of realization, and only one who has realized these aspects can effectively impart its power. Therefore emphasis is placed on initiation. However, there are also universal mantras such as Om or Gayatri, which can be used if one has not received a mantra through initiation.

Prana and mantra

Sound is a form of energy that has frequency, pitch, volume and tone, as well as subtle qualities. Scientifically, sound is vibration at a particular frequency, and it is able to produce physical changes in an organism. Some vibrations can be harmful while others are beneficial. Sound can be concentrated to such degrees of intensity that it can shatter and destroy objects. Holes can be driven into solid metal by using sound alone. It is thought that the great stones of Stonehenge, Easter Island and the Mayan monuments were moved into place using the principles of sound, an accomplishment now lost to modern civilization. The science of sound is also the basis of many esoteric systems. The power of mantra and subtle sound frequencies has been known and used down through the ages by ancient civilizations in order to awaken the inner consciousness and exert an influence upon the external forces of nature.

The principle behind the use of mantra in pranic practices relates to this intrinsic relationship between sound and energy. Every movement of energy manifests sound, and every sound carries energy. The pranas are activated with the chanting of mantras, and the orientation of existing pranic flows are altered or emphasized, so that the mind and perception changes. This brings about harmony in the vibratory field, the pranamaya kosha. Mantras carry a high psychic charge and are able to penetrate deep into the psyche. Thus they are able to influence the vijnanamaya and anandamaya koshas, unlike average words that only affect manomaya, pranamaya and annamaya koshas. Mantras do not work at the level of the conscious mind, but at the level of the deeper mind. Once the experience of harmony begins at deeper levels of consciousness, it percolates down to both the outer and inner spheres. This is the reason why many people experience a sense of elation, inner strength and inspiration while singing kirtan.

In scientific terms, mantra repetition regulates and balances the autonomic nervous system. It facilitates synchronous breathing, directly resulting in cardio-pulmonary resonance, which is indicative of autonomic balance. The 'magical' effect of group chanting or kirtan is due to the fact that during cardiopulmonary coherence the electromagnetic field of the heart is most powerful and pronounced. The powerful and coherent electromagnetic heart field of one person can affect the heart fields of others, leading them to coherent synchrony. During group chanting the electromagnetic fields of all the individuals are both pronounced and synchronized with each other.

The repetition of mantra also arrests the unnecessary movements of prana, so that energy is conserved and mental dissipation is contained. There is greater concentration and the mind can be utilized for higher flights. Therefore, when pranayama is performed with mantra, the practice is more effective. Concentration may be achieved with a numerical count as well, and this is how pranayama practices are usually begun. However, when a mantra is introduced into the practice, the consciousness is raised and concentration assumes a superior quality, so that the whole practice is taken to a different level altogether.

Pranayama and mantra, in fact, make a very powerful combination. Together they are like a missile with an atomic weapon on its head. The missile is the carrier of the atomic weapon; prana is the missile and mantra the atomic weapon on top. When mantras are carried to different parts of the body with the help of prana, they can create actual changes in the physical structure and function. In prana vidya, mantras may be used to transfer prana shakti to others, especially for healing. However, this kind of healing can only be practised by those who have attained *mantra siddhi*, the power and knowledge of mantra, through mantra sadhana. Others will not be able to manifest the power of the mantra effectively for the purpose of healing.

There are many types of mantras of all lengths and descriptions. Tantric mantras are carriers of specific pranic energies and must be used according to certain rules and

69

for particular purposes. They must be learned under the guidance of a tantric guru. There are mantras for bringing down a fever, counteracting poison, removing disease, creating an anaesthetic effect, removing obstacles, conquering enemies, attracting someone, improving health, gaining wealth, sound sleep, marriage, progeny and long life. However, it is necessary to study these mantras very carefully in order to utilize them properly. Universal mantras, such as Gayatri mantra, Durga mantra or Mahamrityunjaya mantra, are sometimes chanted before, during or after healing. A mantra may be chanted for a particular part of the body during contact healing as the hand is passed over the affected part.

Use of mantra in pranayama

Specific mantras may be used in pranayama to create the rhythm of inhalation, retention and exhalation. In this case the count and ratios are maintained by the mental chanting of the mantra. One may use the guru mantra or a universal mantra such as *Soham* or *Om*, for this purpose. However, the best mantra is Gayatri, as it corresponds to the ideal breathing pattern of pranayama.

Gayatri mantra represents cosmic prana. It is comprised of twenty-four syllables which contain the entire form of prana. Inhalation during the repetition of the twenty-four syllables is considered to be the ideal vital capacity. Retention and exhalation are also performed with the same repetition. Not everyone can use the Gayatri in this manner at the beginning of pranayama practice, but the lung capacity expands with regular practice, and then the Gayatri mantra can be comfortably synchronized with the breath.

Gayatri pranayama performed in this way is a complete practice in itself. Omkara or Pranava pranayama is also described in several scriptures as a total practice. The repetition of *Om* may be combined effectively with every pranayama to keep time and to deepen the experience of the practice. Swami Sivananda suggests the use of *Om* in this manner. Bija mantras are also used in pranayama, but for specific sadhanas and always under the instruction of a master. When ajapa japa is practised with ujjayi pranayama, the natural sound of the breath, *Soham* is used as the mantra.

When mantras are used with pranayama, the practice is no longer directed at pranamaya kosha, but achieves a deeper concentration leading to dhyana and samadhi of raja yoga.

Gayatri mantra

The twenty-four syllable basic form of Gayatri mantra as it appears in the *Rig Veda* (3:62:11) is:

ॐ तत्सवितुर्वरेण्यं।
भर्गो देवस्य धीमहि धियो यो नः प्रचोदयात् ॥

Om tatsaviturvarenyam
Bhargo devasya dheemahi dhiyo yo nah prachodayaat.

This can be translated as: "Om. We meditate on the divine light of that adorable Sun of spiritual consciousness. May it stimulate our power of spiritual perception."

In the beginning, one should use the basic form of Gayatri. The inhalation, retention and exhalation must be adjusted according to the mental repetition of the Gayatri. For elementary pranayama, the repetition of one Gayatri mantra represents the duration of one inhalation. During breath retention, the mantra should be repeated twice. While exhaling also the mantra should be repeated twice. For higher pranayama the ratio is gradually increased.

Gayatri is not just a formula or a combination of words. Throughout the Vedas and Upanishads it is said time and again, "Om is nada; Gayatri is prana." Gayatri is created from Om. Om represents the nada of the sound principle. In the order of creation, this sound is further developed, and the developed state of the mantra Om is known as Gayatri. The spiritual teachers say that the original mantra is Om, for it is the universal bija mantra. However, it is a very powerful invocation and sometimes the aspirant is not qualified or

71

prepared for the experiences it can bring. Thus, the wise sages contemplated to discover a milder form of Om, and the Gayatri mantra was revealed to them, which ordinary people could practise without drastic effects.

According to vedic philosophy, prana has three forms. So Gayatri, as the presiding deity of prana, is seen as a little girl, innocent and childish, in the early morning; as a charming young woman in full bloom at noon, and as an old woman, embodying wisdom or *jnana*, in the evening. The colour of Gayatri in the morning is red like the rising sun; at noon she is golden, and in the evening smoky grey. These are the characteristics of prana, represented by the different forms of Gayatri, and this is how Gayatri worshippers may visualize her during their thrice-daily worship.

Some believe that the Gayatri mantra is directed towards the external sun, but ultimately it is directed towards the brilliance of the internal sun. The inner sun must shine so that the consciousness becomes enlightened. In the external firmament, first there is darkness, broken only by the flickering light of stars. Then a dim light shoots forth from the horizon, indicating the break of dawn, and finally the brilliant sun rises, lighting up everything. As it happens in the external horizon, so it is in the inner horizon. Internally also, there is darkness at first. From time to time one sees some visions, which are like stars. Then one experiences traces of light within the horizons of the mind, as the sun is about to come up. That breaking of light is called Gayatri. It represents the sun which illuminates the whole world and also the inner self which illuminates all the planes of existence and consciousness. The external sun only illumines the gross world, but when inner enlightenment takes place all the planes of existence become perceptible.

Gayatri is referred to as the Mother of the Vedas and the Gayatri mantra appears in the *Rig Veda*, the oldest written literature in the library of humankind. Thus, human beings have been chanting the Gayatri mantra for a long time. There is no restriction in the chanting of this mantra, because its effects are benign. In India, children at the age of eight are initiated into the practices of Gayatri mantra, pranayama and surya namaskara in a ritual called *upanayana samskara*. Regular practice of Gayatri mantra helps to harmonize and awaken pranamaya kosha, so that advanced practices of pranayama and other pranic techniques such as prana vidya are more effective.

Omkara pranayama

The Upanishads say that *Om* (or *Aum*) is the primordial sound. Everything has come from *Om* and, at the time of dissolution, everything will revert back to *Om*. The *Mandukyopanishad* (v. 1) states:

ओमित्येतदक्षरमिद ॅ सर्वं तस्योपव्याख्यानं भूतं
भवद्भविष्यदिति सर्वमोङ्कार एव।
यच्चान्यत् त्रिकालातीतं तदप्योङ्कार एव ॥

The word *Om* is the universe. Everything that exists in the past, present and future is *Om*, and that which exists beyond the threefold division of time is *Om*.

While the mantra *Om* is used in different ways in different practices, the scriptures provide specific guidelines on using it for the purpose of pranayama. The *Yoga Chudamani Upanishad* (v. 101–102) describes Omkara or Pranava pranayama thus:

रेचक: पूरकश्चैव कुम्भक: प्रणवात्मक: ।
प्राणायामो भवेदेवं मात्राद्वारशसंयुत: ॥
मात्राद्वादशसंयुक्तौ निशाकरदिवाकरौ ।
दोषजालमबध्नन्तौ ज्ञातव्यौ योगिभि: सदा ॥

The inhalation, retention and exhalation are the Pranava itself. Pranayama should be practised like this for a number of twelve rounds. Twelve rounds through the ida and pingala nadis unfastens the net of impurities. The yogis should know this always.

73

The reference is to synchronization of inhalation, retention and exhalation with the three sounds of Pranava: 'A', 'U' and 'M', in order to align the breath, prana and consciousness and experience their interrelationship. Thus, while inhaling, the 'A' sound should be drawn up the ida passage or left nostril, along with the breath. During this time the 'A' sound should be contemplated along with all of its associations: the conscious state and rajo guna. While retaining the breath, the 'U' sound is contemplated in relation to the subconscious state and sattwa guna. While exhaling, the 'M' sound is directed out through the pingala passage or right nostril, along with the breath. During this time, the 'M' sound is contemplated in relation to the unconscious state and tamo guna. The same process is followed on the right side in order to make one round.

It is recommended that Omkara pranayama be performed for twelve rounds in order to balance the body and mind, and as a preparation for meditation on the Pranava. This prana-yama can also be performed through both nostrils together, as in samavritti pranayama (see Chapter 16: 'Preliminary Breathing Practices'), for meditative purposes. However, in order to purify the nadis it should be done through the alternate nostrils, as in nadi shodhana pranayama (see Chapter 19: 'Nadi Shodhana Pranayama'). Twelve rounds performed through the alternate nostrils will remove all the accumulated blockages and impurities in the ida and pingala nadis, ensuring health, harmony and longevity. Therefore, the Upanishad states that yogis should always know this practice, so they may perform it regularly and derive the benefits.

Bija mantras

The word *bija* means 'seed', which refers to the unmanifest state of existence. Within the seed lies the potential of manifestation. If the seed is sown under conducive conditions, it explodes into a plant. In the same way a bija mantra is a seed, which manifests in various experiences when practised in japa. When the bija mantra becomes manifest, it is called dhwani, shabda or nada. In its manifest state it has vibrations, but there is also a state when it exists without vibration. This unmanifest sound is called bija, and its manifest form is called nada. When a yogi enters into deep meditation and plunges into the unconscious mind, he gains the knowledge of the subtle sounds of bija mantras.

The first bija mantra is *Om* or *Aum*. The three primal sounds, 'A', 'U' and 'M' are the basis of the vocal structure. They combine together to form the sound *Aum*. From this first seed mantra, other seed mantras were derived. The bija mantras are very powerful, for they get assimilated with the mental processes very quickly. The longer mantras are equally good, but they take time to get assimilated. When the mantra *Om* is practised, for example, one enters into a meditative mood very quickly. Another example is the mantra *Hreem*, which has no intellectual meaning, but awakens the pranas and kundalini shakti.

The bija mantras belong to anandamaya kosha and become expressive when the mind has ascended to the unconscious level. They first influence the anandamaya kosha and the effect comes down progressively to the vijnanamaya, manomaya, pranamaya and finally annamaya kosha. The explosion in this case takes place from the depths. With other mantras, the explosion takes place from the mental or pranic level and that influence is raised to the vijnanamaya and anandamaya koshas. Thereafter it again travels back to the physical body. Ultimately the effect is the same, but when the unconscious mind is directly affected, the experiences are fantastic and vivid. When the pranic or mental body are affected, the experiences are mild, like passing dreams. However, if the aspirant is not prepared, he will not be able to handle the strong effect of bija mantras. Therefore, caution must be practised in their use.

Pranayama may be practised with the mental chanting of a bija mantra, if advised by the guru. Specific pranayamas practised with bija mantras are described by Sage Gheranda in the *Gheranda Samhita*. He enumerates three kinds of alternate

75

nostril breathing, and the first two use bija mantras. The first form is intended for purification of the nadis and uses the bija mantras: *Yam*, *Ram*, *Tham* and *Lam*, along with concentration on luminosity of varying degrees and on different *tattwas*, or elements. In the second practice, which he calls *sagarbha kumbhaka*, the bija mantras *A*, *Am*, *U* and *Mam* are used, along with concentration on the related deities (Brahma, Vishnu and Shiva), gunas (rajas, sattwa and tamas), and colours (red, black and white).

Ajapa japa

The word *japa* can be defined as 'continuous repetition of a mantra'. When the suffix 'a' is added to japa, it implies that the process of mantra repetition becomes spontaneous. So, *ajapa* is spontaneous mantra repetition. During meditation, japa is transformed into ajapa in the stage of *dharana*, concentration, where the mantra repeats itself spontaneously, without any effort. As the concentration becomes more and more focused on the japa, one's whole being starts pulsating with the mantra. Japa requires continuous, conscious effort to repeat the mantra verbally or mentally, but ajapa, being spontaneous, requires no effort. Japa comes from the mouth, whereas ajapa comes from the breath and the heart. Japa is the preliminary practice of mantra repetition and ajapa is the perfection of this practice.

The practice of ajapa japa focuses on the natural sound of the breath: the sound of inhalation *So* and the sound of exhalation *Ham*. Ujjayi pranayama is the mode of breathing and different energy channels, or psychic passages, are experienced and activated progressively in the various stages of the practice. Ajapa japa is an indispensable preparatory practice for prana vidya as well as kriya yoga. However, it is also a complete sadhana in itself and leads to the direct experience of samadhi. In order to attain samadhi one has to control and suspend the breath in all other yogic practices, whereas with the practice of ajapa japa, the breathing remains continuous and normal. There is no change even in samadhi.

In the *Bhagavad Gita*, the verse describing the relationship between prana and apana also refers to ajapa (4:29):

अपाने जुह्वति प्राणं प्राणेऽपानं तथाऽपरे ।
प्राणापानगती रुद्ध्वा प्राणायामपरायणा: ॥

Apana is absorbed in prana (by some), and prana in apana by others. By restraining the courses of prana and apana, (the yogi is) wholly occupied in pranayama.

Prana is the ingoing breath, apana is the outgoing breath. *So* represents prana and *Ham* represents apana. Some aspirants merge prana with apana, that is, they join *So* with *Ham*, which then becomes *Soham*. Other aspirants join apana with prana, that is, they join *Ham* with *So,* which becomes *Hamso*. There are other sadhakas who restrain both prana and apana. The *Bhagavad Gita* (5:27–28) also refers to the method of equalizing prana and apana:

स्पर्शान्कृत्वा बहिर्बाह्यांश्चक्षुश्चैवान्तरे भ्रुवो: ।
प्राणापानौ समौ कृत्वा नासाभ्यन्तरचारिणौ ॥
यतेंद्रियमनोबुद्धिर्मुनिर्मोक्षपरायण: ।
विगतेच्छाभयक्रोधो य: सदा एव स: ॥

Shutting out all thoughts of external enjoyments, with the gaze fixed on the space between the eyebrows, having equalized prana and apana that manifest as inhalation and exhalation in the nostrils, he who has brought his senses, mind and intellect under control, such a contemplative soul intent on liberation and free from desire, fear and anger, is ever liberated.

This practice of ajapa japa has been referred to in the scriptures as *viloma ajapa*.

The *Gheranda Samhita* (5:84–96) describes a specific method of ajapa japa and calls it *kevali pranayama*. It says that while a normal person performs the ajapa constantly but unconsciously, the yogi should perform it consciously as a practice. Eight or at least three times a day he should chant the mantra *Soham* to a fixed count while breathing rapidly from both nostrils. The speed of the breath should be double the normal speed, that is, 30 breaths per minute. The number of japa should be gradually increased until the state of *kevala kumbhaka*, spontaneous suspension of breath, is achieved.

In the Upanishads it is said that one should practise *anahad japa*, a japa that never ends. This japa becomes co-extensive with infinity. No such mantra is known; therefore, a method of repeating the mantra is needed so that it does not end. This is achieved through the practice of ajapa japa, where the mantra is adjusted with the breathing process and thus its awareness continues throughout.

Physiology of Respiration and Pranayama

8

Physiology of Breathing

The breath is the thing closest to us. It is tangible, believable, understandable and controllable. The gentle inhalation and exhalation sustains us, calms us, affects our thoughts and is itself affected by our activities, emotions and thoughts. We all experience this daily, yet the breath is often ignored or forgotten. In the practices of pranayama, we become deeply familiar with the breath. A good knowledge of the respiratory system will, therefore, aid and enhance the practices, and help in a better understanding of their physiological parameters. It will also prove indispensable in practising prana vidya, when awareness must be focused on specific internal body parts.

Respiratory structure

The human torso is divided into three parts: the thorax or chest cavity, which houses the heart and lungs; the abdomen, which is separated from the thorax by a thin muscle called the diaphragm, and contains the organs of digestion; and the pelvis, which extends from the hip bones to the perineum, and contains the organs of excretion and reproduction.

The lungs and heart are contained in the ribcage or thoracic cavity, a cage of bones, cartilage and muscles. The lungs themselves are passive. They inflate and deflate only because the walls and floor of the thoracic cavity move, pumping the air in and out of the lungs. The boundaries of the thorax

81

are formed by the twelve thoracic vertebrae of the spine, the sternum in front and the twelve pairs of ribs, which encircle the heart and lungs from the vertebral column at the back to the sternum in front. The thoracic cage protects these vital organs from damage. The spaces between the ribs contain the intercostal muscles, which connect them and give a degree of movement to the whole ribcage. The ribs are articulated at each end, so they can move upwards and outwards like the handle of a bucket.

There are two lungs, one on each side of the chest, separated by the heart and its major blood vessels. Lung tissue is pink in colour in its unpolluted state, because of its many blood capillaries. It is elastic, porous and spongy and, because of the air in its alveoli, it floats on water. The right lung is made up of three lobes or compartments, while the left has only two because the heart takes up room in the left side of the ribcage. The lungs are cone-shaped and consist of an apex, a base, costal surface and medial surface. The apex is rounded and rises into the root of the neck, about 25 mm (1 inch) above the level of the middle third of the clavicle. The structures associated with it are the first rib and the blood vessels and nerves in the root of the neck.

The base is concave and semilunar in shape, and is closely associated with the thoracic surface of the diaphragm. The costal surface is convex and is closely associated with the costal cartilages, the ribs and the intercostal muscles. The medial surface is concave and has a roughly triangular-shaped area, called the hilum, at the level of the 5th, 6th and 7th thoracic vertebrae. Structures which form the root of the lung enter and leave at the hilum. These include the primary bronchus, the pulmonary artery supplying the lung and the two pulmonary veins draining it, the bronchial artery and veins, and the lymphatic and nerve supply.

The area between the lungs is called mediastinum. It is occupied by the heart, great vessels, trachea, right and left bronchi, oesophagus, lymph nodes, lymph vessels and nerves.

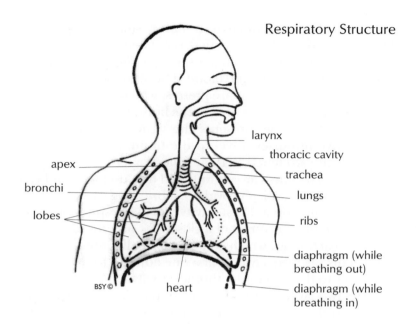

Respiratory Structure

larynx
thoracic cavity
apex
trachea
bronchi
lungs
lobes
ribs

diaphragm (while breathing out)

BSY©   heart   diaphragm (while breathing in)

Inner structure of the lungs

The inner structure of the lungs resembles a tree in which the main trunk is the trachea, the branches are the bronchi and bronchioles, and the leaves the alveoli.

Trachea: The trachea is the windpipe connected to the larynx at the base of the throat. It is a tube formed from cartilaginous rings and muscle tissue, which keep it constantly open. The trachea is lined with tiny hairs called cilia, which have an upward sweeping movement that stops dust, pollen and other minute foreign objects from entering the lungs.

Bronchi: The lower end of the trachea branches into the left and right principal bronchi. The bronchi further divide, like the branches of an upside-down tree, into smaller bronchioles, which traverse the lungs. The larger bronchi retain cartilage and small, smooth muscles, which prevent them from closing, as in the trachea. However, as these bronchial tubes become smaller, the cartilage disappears, leaving only a fibrous muscular coat and the ciliated mucous lining.

Alveoli: The bronchioles terminate in small dilated air-sacs, known as alveoli, which are lined with a network of capillaries. In these alveoli the exchange of oxygen and carbon dioxide takes place between air and blood. The total surface area of the alveoli is around fifty square metres, which is approximately twenty times the surface area of the body. In fact, the alveolar surface of the lungs presents the vastest area from which interceptive impulses travel to the brain, particularly when the lungs are stretched to their fullest extent.

Pleura: The lungs are surrounded by a double membrane, known as pleura, which provides a lubricating surface between the lungs and inner chest cavity during respiratory movements. The pleura consist of a closed sac of serous membrane (one for each lung) which contains a small amount of serous fluid. This sac forms two layers: one adheres to the lung and the other to the wall of the thoracic cavity.

The two layers of pleura, with serous fluid between them, behave in the same way as two pieces of glass separated by a thin film of water. They glide over each other easily, but can be pulled apart only with difficulty, because of the surface tension between the membranes and the fluid. If either layer of pleura is punctured, the underlying lung collapses due to its inherent property of elastic recoil.

Pulmonary arteries and veins: The pulmonary artery originates in the heart and divides into two branches, conveying deoxygenated blood to each lung. Within the lungs each pulmonary artery divides into many branches, which eventually end in a dense capillary network around the walls of the alveoli. The walls of the alveoli and those of the capillaries each consist of only one layer of flattened epithelial cells. The exchange of gases between air in the alveoli and blood in the capillaries takes place across these two very fine membranes. The pulmonary capillaries join up, eventually becoming two pulmonary veins in each lung. They leave the lungs at the hilum and convey oxygenated blood to the left atrium of the heart. The innumerable blood capillaries and blood vessels in the lungs are supported by connective tissue.

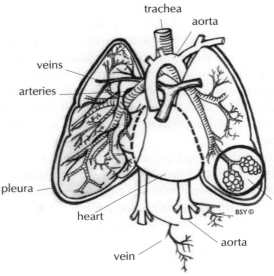

trachea

aorta

veins

arteries

pleura

heart

vein

aorta

BSY©

Respiratory muscles

The expansion of the chest during inspiration occurs as a result of muscular activity, partly voluntary and partly involuntary. The main muscles of respiration in normal, quiet breathing are the intercostals and the diaphragm. During difficult or deep breathing they are assisted by the muscles of the neck, shoulders and abdomen.

The diaphragm and abdominal muscles act like bellows at the base of the thorax, pulling and pushing air into and out of the lungs. Muscular effort is required for both exhalation as well as inhalation. However, only diaphragmatic action is sufficient in resting states and most normal activities. When the abdominal, neck and shoulder muscles are also brought into action, exhalation becomes an active process and the extra force causes rapid exhalation.

Diaphragm: The diaphragm is dome-shaped and consists of a sheet of muscles and tendons attached to the lower ribs, bulging upwards into the thoracic cavity. It forms the dividing barrier between the thoracic and abdominal cavities. The oesophagus, vagus nerve, and main artery and vein to and from the lower body pass through openings in the diaphragm.

Inhalation is produced by contraction of the diaphragm, which flattens out the dome shape and moves it downwards. This increases the volume of the thoracic cavity, creating negative pressure, and consequently draws air into the lungs. Normal exhalation occurs from passive recoil of the ribcage and diaphragm, as these muscles relax and move into their original shape.

The downward pressure on the abdominal viscera from contraction of the diaphragm forces the abdominal wall to extend forward and/or the lower rib cage to expand sideways. The action of the diaphragm also stimulates and massages the abdominal viscera, assisting digestion, assimilation and excretion.

Thoracic muscles: Although the upper chest movement is relatively inconspicuous in quiet breathing, some thoracic muscles play a role. The external and parasternal intercostals (joining adjacent ribs) and the scaleni (connecting the shoulder area and spine) are activated during inspiration to hold the ribs in an expanded position that complements the force of the diaphragm.

There are eleven pairs of intercostal muscles that occupy the spaces between the twelve pairs of ribs. They are arranged in two layers, the external and internal intercostal muscles. The external intercostal muscle fibres extend in a downward and forward direction from the lower border of the rib above to the upper border of the rib below. The internal intercostal muscle fibres extend in a downward and backward direction from the lower border of the rib above to the upper border of the rib below, crossing the external intercostal muscle fibres at right angles. The first rib is fixed; therefore, when the intercostal muscles contract they pull all the other ribs towards the first rib. Due to the shape of the ribs, they move outwards when pulled upwards. In this way the thoracic cavity is enlarged anteroposteriorly and laterally.

The intercostal muscles are stimulated to contract by the intercostal nerves.

Abdominal muscles: The abdominal muscles are the most powerful and important muscles for forced exhalation, but are not used in quiet breathing. Contraction puts inward pressure on the abdominal viscera, which then push the diaphragm up and reduce lung volume. In addition, these muscles may assist expiration by pulling down and deflating the lower rib cage. The important abdominal muscles for respiration are the rectus abdominis, the transverse abdominis, and the external and internal obloquies.

Process of respiration

There are about 15 complete respiratory cycles per minute in normal, quiet breathing. The breath passes from the nasal cavities through the pharynx at the top of the throat and into the larynx, which commences at the point where the oesophagus and the trachea meet. The movement of food, liquid and air is guided by the epiglottis, a cartilaginous flap which closes off the larynx during swallowing. The larynx is made of cartilage and contains the vocal cords, which are responsible for the production of sound. From the larynx, the breath moves down the trachea, through the bronchial system and into the alveoli, where it flows into the capillaries surrounding the alveoli.

Approximately 79 percent of the inhaled breath is nitrogen (which plays no part in the respiratory process), 20 percent is oxygen, and 0.04 percent is carbon dioxide. The exhaled breath contains the same proportion of nitrogen, but the oxygen composition is reduced to about 16 percent, and the carbon dioxide composition increases to about 4.04 percent. Exhaled air is also warmer and more humid, as water vapour is exhaled from the lungs, which can be seen by exhaling over a mirror. As much as 20 percent of body heat can be lost in exhalation.

The oxygen content in air is one of the most important factors for the maintenance of life. It is required for many chemical reactions in which carbon dioxide and water are formed as waste products. The entire process of respiration brings oxygen from the atmosphere into the lungs and bloodstream, and then into all the cells of the body. Thus there are two levels of respiration: the first occurs in the lungs and is called external respiration; the second occurs in the cells and is called internal respiration.

External respiration: The muscles of respiration draw air into the lungs, so that oxygen can be absorbed into the blood and transported to the cells. Oxygen moves into the cell and carbon dioxide moves out of the cell to be carried back to the lungs to be disposed of. This is exchange of gases by diffusion between the alveoli and the blood. Each alveolar wall is one-cell thick and is surrounded by a network of tiny capillaries (the walls of which are also only one-cell thick). The total area for gas exchange in the lungs is 70 to 80 square metres.

Venous blood arriving at the lungs has travelled from all the active tissues of the body, and contains high levels of carbon dioxide and low levels of oxygen. Carbon dioxide diffuses from venous blood down its concentration gradient into the alveoli until equilibrium with alveolar air is reached. By the same process, oxygen diffuses from the alveoli into the blood. The slow flow of blood through the capillaries increases the time available for diffusion to occur. When blood leaves the alveolar capillaries, the oxygen and carbon dioxide concentrations are in equilibrium with those of alveolar air.

The changeover from absorption of gases to elimination of gases takes place at the pause between inhalation and exhalation. The point of exchange is as vital as the exhalation and inhalation. In yogic terms this point is the most important part of pranayama.

Internal respiration: This is exchange of gases by diffusion between blood in the capillaries and the body cells. Gaseous exchange does not occur across the walls of the arteries carrying blood from the heart to the tissues, because

88

their walls are too thick. The concentration of oxygen in the blood arriving at the capillary bed is therefore the same as blood leaving the lungs. Blood arriving at the tissues has been cleansed of carbon dioxide and saturated with oxygen during its passage through the lungs. Therefore, it has a higher concentration of oxygen and a lower concentration of carbon dioxide than the tissues. This creates concentration gradients between the blood and the tissues, and gaseous exchange occurs.

Oxygen diffuses from the bloodstream through the capillary wall into the tissues. Carbon dioxide diffuses from the cells into the extracellular fluid, then into the bloodstream towards the venous end of the capillary.

Lung volume and capacity

Only about 10 percent of the total respiratory capacity is used during each breath in quiet breathing. An average breath during ordinary quiet breathing, known as the tidal volume ('A' in the diagram below), is about half a litre, although the total amount of air which can be inhaled may be as much as 4.5 to 5 litres. This is called the vital capacity ('B' in the diagram). There is always a reserve volume above and below the tidal volume ('C' and 'D' in the diagram, respectively), so that inhalation as well as exhalation may be increased. There is also a certain volume of air which always remains in the lungs, no matter how completely one exhales; this is called the residual volume ('E' in the diagram) and it is just a bit more than one litre.

So, although the vital capacity may be 5 litres, the total lung volume would be about 6 litres. Most of the tidal volume goes to lung areas that exchange oxygen and carbon dioxide with blood, but about 150 ml is dead space from passages that cannot contribute to gas exchange. Dead space volume is relatively constant whereas tidal volume varies greatly with physical exercise, breathing pattern, and other factors. Thus, larger tidal volumes have a smaller proportion of dead space. Dead space can increase significantly with lung disorders.

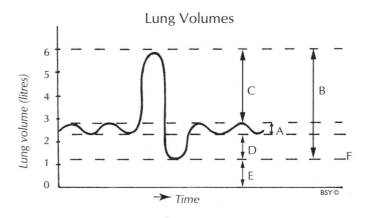

Lung Volumes

A – Tidal volume (0.5 litre); normal quiet breathing
B – Vital capacity (5 litres); maximum inhalation and exhalation
C – Inhalation reserve (3 litres)
D – Exhalation reserve (1 litres)
E – Residual volume (1.2 litres)
F – Resting exhalation level (2.2 litres)

The volume of air that moves into and out of the alveoli per minute is called alveolar ventilation. It is equal to the tidal volume minus the dead space, multiplied by the respiratory rate: (TV – dead space) × respiratory rate = (500–150) ml × 15 per minute = 5.25 litres per minute. All the above values are typical for a young adult male. The volumes are about 25 percent less for an average female, and vary with body size, posture and physical condition. Lung function tests carried out to diagnose and monitor respiratory disorders are based on the parameters above.

If the lungs are not developed properly or are damaged, their volume and capacity is reduced and they cannot perform the function of oxygenating the blood in an efficient manner. Lung volumes can be increased by the practices of pranayama and deep breathing exercises. Lungs which have a good reserve capacity will turn out extra work when extra demand is made on them. It must also be taken into account that the distribution of blood in the lungs is gravity-dependent, and in the upright position there is far more blood in the lower part of the lung than in the upper part. On the other hand, the free flow of gases into and out of the alveoli is greater in the upper portions of the lung. This anomaly can also be dealt with by developing the ability to guide the reflexes in the lungs and changing the breathing patterns.

Respiratory control

The respiratory mechanism is regulated through nervous and chemical control. The quantity of air inhaled and the rate of breaths per minute vary considerably, depending on physical, mental and emotional conditions, as well as influences from the external environment.

Respiratory control structure: The respiratory control centre lies in the medulla oblongata at the base of the brain (see figure below). In the medulla there are inspiratory neurones and expiratory neurones. The neurones in the pneumo-taxic and apneustic centres, situated in the pons, influence the inspiratory and expiratory neurones of the medulla. Motor impulses leaving the respiratory centre pass in the phrenic and intercostal nerves to the diaphragm and intercostal muscles respectively, and activate movements in the respiratory muscles to inhale air. Afferent or sensory impulses travel to the medulla via the vagus nerve due to expansion of the alveoli and smaller bronchioles. Central chemo-receptors situated on the surface of the medulla oblongata and peripheral chemo-receptors situated in the arch of the aorta and in the carotid bodies also respond to changes in the partial pressures of oxygen and carbon dioxide in the blood and cerebrospinal fluid.

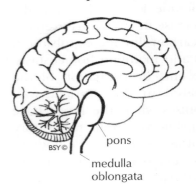

pons

medulla
oblongata

All the major structures of the respiratory system have nerves relating to both the sympathetic and parasympathetic nervous systems. Inhalation brings in oxygen; it is energizing

91

and extroverting. This stimulates the sympathetic nervous system and promotes catabolism (i.e. matter to energy). In yogic terminology it stimulates the pingala nadi. Exhalation throws out carbon dioxide and water vapour; it is pacifying and introverting. This stimulates the parasympathetic nervous system and promotes anabolism (i.e. energy to matter). In yogic terms it stimulates the ida nadi. The rest period between inhalation and exhalation gives stillness and allows the witness attitude to manifest. It also brings about a state of alertness and concentration. At the metabolic level there is utilization of energy and the newly built matter is utilized for different purposes: physical, mental and spiritual. In yogic terms it stimulates the sushumna nadi.

Factors influencing respiration: The rate and depth of respiration are regulated by such factors as extended exercise (where metabolic activity is increased), emotions (e.g. fear or fright), pain or sensory impulses (e.g. when the body is plunged into cold water). Breathing may be modified by the higher centres in the brain by speech and singing, emotional displays such as crying, laughing, drugs, sedatives and alcohol, and sleep. Temperature also influences breathing: in fever respiration is increased due to increased metabolic rate, while in hypothermia it is depressed, as is metabolism. Temporary changes in respiration also occur while swallowing, sneezing and coughing.

Normally, quiet breathing is adequate to maintain arterial oxygen and carbon dioxide levels. However, the rate and depth of breathing increase in strenuous exercise, increasing oxygen uptake and carbon dioxide expulsion in order to meet increased needs and maintain homeostasis. The Hering-Breuer reflex prevents over-inflation of the lungs. Stretch receptors situated in the thoracic wall generate nerve inhibitory impulses when the lungs have inflated. They travel via the vagus nerves to the respiratory centre. Effective control of respiration enables the body to maintain homeostasis of blood gases over a wide range of physiological, environmental and pathological conditions.

Respiratory control: In normal circumstances, nervous control is unconscious. One does not have to think about when to inhale or exhale. However, by changing the pattern of the breath, one can learn to manoeuvre the autonomic nervous system and higher brain function, or in yogic terms, the ida, pingala and sushumna nadis. In other words, by changing the breath pattern one can induce a chosen state of mind. Even though unhealthy breathing habits are likely to be insidious, it is possible to change them because the respiratory motions are controlled by somatic motor neurons. Therefore, it is possible to think the actions of respiration through and control them wilfully.

The ventilation rate of the lungs is normally set to provide oxygen and remove carbon dioxide in accordance with metabolic needs. A better air flow or ventilation of the lungs can be achieved with a slow breathing rate and large tidal volume or fast rate and small tidal volume. When this is achieved though controlled practice, bringing about deep and slow rhythmic respiratory patterns, and changing the habits of faulty breathing, elimination of waste gases is improved, the heart and circulatory functions are regulated and arrhythmic heart beat is rectified. All these induce a sense of relaxation throughout the body-mind complex.

In the practice of nadi shodhana pranayama, when the length of breath is extended from two or three seconds to seven or eight seconds and the air is held longer in the lungs, there is an increased potential for greater gaseous absorption, separation and elimination in the lungs. In the normal breath we find, say, 3.5 mg absorption of oxygen and an output of 2.6 mg of carbon dioxide. In simple regulated breath control practices this ratio can be improved, so that the output of carbon dioxide level is increased to 4.6 mg, that is, almost double the average norm, depending on the technique employed.

It has been found that if the carbon dioxide level in the blood decreases through improved elimination of carbon dioxide, the normal respiratory rate becomes slower.

This condition has an arresting effect on the mental and emotional condition of the mind; it quietens and calms the dissipated mind, creating the essential mental state conducive to control of thought patterns. For the spiritual aspirant this is significant. An understanding of the intimate relationship existing between respiration and states of mind has evolved methods of guided breathing and consequentially altered states of consciousness.

9

Yogic Physiology of the Nose

The nasal passages play a vital role in pranayama practice. Yogis state that the nostrils are control mechanisms for the flow of breath as well as the pranic energy that flows through nadis. The nostrils also have a direct connection to the brain and are doorways to the total mind-body system. Control over the breath in the nostrils allows one to guide the internal environment without the need for external aids such as drugs and chemicals. The internal processes can be influenced by the breath in order to improve health, change states of the mind or attain higher levels of consciousness.

Physiology of the nostrils

The two nostrils allow air to enter and leave the body. They are lined by coarse hairs which act as an initial barrier against dust and other foreign objects. The two nostrils are separated by an osteo-cartilaginous tissue, called the nasal septum. Bones called turbinates protrude from the sidewalls of the two nostrils. They greatly increase the surface area inside the nose, which is exposed to incoming air, and cause eddies in the air, so that dust and foreign particles can settle down. This in turn allows the moist and warm mucous membranes to clean, humidify and regulate the temperature of air entering the lungs. Dust is trapped by the mucus and pushed back into the pharynx by tiny hairs called cilia, which line the mucous membrane of the nose. The cilia have a whip or broom-like movement, sweeping the mucus backwards towards the pharynx.

The inhaled air is humidified by the lachrymal fluid, which is formed by the glands in the eyes and flows continually to the nose through the naso-lacrymal duct. When the lachrymal fluid is in excess, as in crying, infection or irritation of the eyes, it comes out of the eyes as tears. Otherwise, it flows into the nose continuously to humidify the inhaled air. About one litre of this fluid is formed each day. There are blood sinusoids in the mucous membrane of the nose, which warm the inhaled air and condition it to the temperature of the body. There are cavities in the bones of the face, known as para-nasal sinuses, which are connected to the nose. The inhaled air enters these cavities, forming currents, and causing the dust in it to settle down.

This is the 'air-conditioning' function of the nose – purifying, warming and humidifying the inhaled air. Without this initial air-conditioning, the lungs would become dry, clogged with dust, and susceptible to disease. In a temperate climate the estimated energy expenditure to condition inhaled air is equivalent to about one sixth of a person's daily energy output; however, about 30 to 40 percent of this energy is recovered by exhaling through the nose. Higher efficiencies of heat and moisture recovery occur in cold and/or dry environments. It has also been hypothesized that nasal respiration plays an important role in controlling brain temperature, which may have important implications for brain functioning and psychological states.

Link with mooladhara

In yogic philosophy, the nose and the sense of smell are linked via the nadis with mooladhara chakra, the seat of primal instincts, sexual drive, and the abode of kundalini. Dr Sigmund Freud and other investigators have observed a close relationship between the state of the nasal mucous lining and the genital and reproductive function. Other observations have linked general physical and mental health with the condition of the nasal passages and their sensitive mucous membrane. Sometimes nose bleeding accompanies the menstrual period and a heightened sense of smell has also been observed during menstruation.

Apart from the autonomic nervous system, the nerve receptors for smell also lie in the mucous membranes at the top of the nasal cavity. There are approximately five million nerve receptors within the olfactory bulb, which conduct impulses to the portion of the brain lying directly over the nasal cavity. This portion of the brain, the rhynencephalon, is one of its oldest parts. Within it are centres responsible for generating powerful emotional experiences, such as fear, aggression, pleasure, the sexual drive and reproductive cycles. The response to smell is not always easy to explain, because these portions of the brain are concerned with primitive, pre-verbal and emotional images which lie beyond our ability to consciously interpret and intellectualize.

Modern physiology is in complete agreement with yogic philosophy, where the *jnanendriya* (sense) of smell is associated with mooladhara chakra, the centre of instincts, desire for self-preservation and material security. In animals the sense of smell is more highly developed than in human beings. Mooladhara chakra represents the highest of the animal chakras and the lowest of the human chakras.

Yogic philosophy also believes that there is a direct link between mooladhara and ajna chakra, and this too has a physiological interpretation. The olfactory bulb extends back from the eyebrow centre, or *bhrumadhya*, and is the trigger point for ajna chakra. Thus, the situation created during pranayama in the mucous membrane and olfactory nerves may be a part of the psycho-physiological mechanism for the awakening of kundalini in mooladhara and directing it to ajna.

Nostrils and acupuncture

The region of the nasal mucous membrane is also extremely important in the Chinese healing system known as acupuncture. In acupuncture therapy, the *ki* or pranic energy

97

flowing within well-defined meridians or channels of the pranic and etheric body is altered and adjusted by manipulating the system of fluid-filled connective tissue spaces known as meridians within the physical body.

Of the twelve major meridians of acupuncture, six (stomach, bladder, gallbladder, large intestine, small intestine and triple heater) have either their points of entry or exit in the area of the trigeminal nerve enervation which surrounds the nasal mucous membrane.

Interestingly, there is a marked similarity and correspondence between maps of the acupuncture meridians and the descriptions of the course of the major nadis or pranic pathways provided in the ancient Upanishads of India.

Science of swara yoga

Swara yoga concerns the realization of the balance between the dual and complementary polarities of one's essential nature (also see *Swara Yoga: The Tantric Science of Brain Breathing* by Swami Muktibodhananda, Yoga Publications Trust, 2004). According to this system, the flow of prana in ida nadi is equated with the flow of breath in the left nostril, and the flow of prana in pingala nadi is similarly related to the breath in the right nostril. Usually both nostrils do not flow at the same time; one nostril flows for about ninety minutes, then both flow together for a minute or two, and then the flow switches over to the other nostril.

Sushumna, the third principal nadi, is active when both nostrils are flowing equally. This usually occurs only in between the alternating cycles of ida and pingala (in the case of a yogi it occurs more often). When prana is flowing through sushumna, ida and pingala function in perfect balance. At this time the awareness is neither introverted nor extroverted, but remains balanced between the two and the state of meditation, or *dhyana*, dawns effortlessly.

According to the theory of swara yoga, an intimate knowledge of the nature of one's swara and its correlation with the states of mind can lead to efficiency in all that one undertakes. *Shiva Swarodaya*, the principal treatise on swara yoga, states (v. 270):

स्वरज्ञानबलादग्रे निष्फलं कोटिधा भवेत् ।
इहलोके परत्रापि स्वरज्ञानी बली सदा ॥

Millions of other powers are useless before the strength of the swara. One who has this knowledge is always powerful both in this world as the next.

An experimental study done at the Kaivalyadhama Institute, Lonavala, India, has verified that the flow of the breath through each nostril is rarely equal under normal circumstances. Of 204 subjects who were investigated at different times of the day, aged from 10 to 65 years and enjoying good general health, an unequal flow of breath in the nostrils was noted in 174, or 85.5 percent of cases.

Another electro-nasographic study carried out at Kaivalyadhama discovered that changes of electrical potential are continually occurring within the mucous membrane of each nostril. These changes were found to be unequal in the two nostrils, and are believed to be influenced by a subject's psycho-physiological state, as reflected in his breathing. This nasal potential is constantly changing in the same way that the human aura has been seen to change continually when photographed using high-voltage Kirlian techniques.

It has also been observed that the breath which goes through the left nostril has a slightly lower temperature than the breath which goes through the right. This is because the left nostril is related to ida nadi, the flow of mental energy, while the right nostril is related to pingala nadi, the flow of vital energy.

Nasal dominance and nasal airway resistance

What the ancient science of swara yoga describes has become a subject of scientific research in the last century. The nasal flow is termed nasal airway resistance in scientific parlance and the phenomenon of alternating flows is called nasal dominance. However, most of the modern studies have not been able to provide a conclusive statement on the cyclic pattern of nasal dominance, except that the nasal cycle is indeed present as an ongoing physiological phenomenon and may represent the fundamental biorhythms present in individuals. In any case, the phenomenon can be readily verified by personal observation.

The sympathetic nerves control nasal congestion whereas parasympathetic nerves control nasal secretion with some associated influence on blood flow and congestion. Reduced nasal sympathetic vasoconstrictor tone causes congestion, whereas increased sympathetic activity causes decongestion. Reduced parasympathetic tone causes reduced nasal secretion and reduced congestion, whereas increased parasympathetic tone causes increased nasal secretion and increased congestion.

It has been stated by some researchers that the resistance to air flow in nasal breathing may be an efficient passive means of slowing air flow to provide adequate gas exchange at low ventilation rates. It has been observed that underlying the mucous membrane in the nose there is a spongy substance called erectile tissue which fills with blood in much the same way as our sexual organs. There is a condition during sexual arousal called 'honeymoon nose' characterized by chronically clogged nasal passages. The expansion and contraction of this erectile tissue in the nostrils alternates the flow of breath between the left and right sides. The congestion enhances humidifying and warming of inhaled air and may therefore be an efficient passive mechanism for braking the respiratory system elasticity during periods of low ventilation.

Factors affecting nasal dominance

There are a number of factors which alter congestion in one nasal cavity. The first is posture. When lying on one side, the lowermost, or dependent, nostril congests while the uppermost nostril opens. However, if there is no support underneath the axilla (armpit), nasal congestion does not change. On the other hand, pressure under one axilla in the form of a crutch will

100

congest the nostril on that side, opening the opposite one. This is true whether one is upright or lying down. Therefore, it is not gravity alone that is involved, but also the vascular or nervous reflexes. Posture during sleep may play a crucial role in influencing the course of the nasal cycle.

Emotions have also been shown to produce rapid changes in nasal congestion and secretion. In-depth study of a large group of patients repeatedly demonstrated changes in turbinate size and colour in response to varying emotional challenges. Clinical observations of patients with chronic or recurrent nasal congestion found that congestion increased during periods of anxiety, conflict, frustration, resentment and guilt, but decreased during fear and panic. It has also been suggested that increased nasal congestion is associated with a passive, withdrawal response to stressors, whereas decreased congestion occurred in preparation for heightened respiration of an active fight or flight response. Increased ventilation demands can also alter nasal dominance. Nasal resistance can become low and nearly symmetric during exercise, re-breathing with a bag, and breath-holding. Physical factors such as temperature, humidity and irritants are also known to alter nasal congestion.

Many yogic practices, such as nadi shodhana pranayama, jala and sutra neti and the use of the yoga danda, directly influence the balance of breath in each nostril, inducing sushumna nadi to flow and meditation to supervene. Research at Kaivalyadhama Institute has also validated the efficacy of the ancient device of yoga danda, a stick placed under the armpit, which is traditionally used by yogis to manipulate the flow of the breath in the nostrils. The study verified that the breath in the nostril opposite to the yoga danda became markedly freer than that of the nostril of the same side in all subjects, irrespective of age or sex.

The yoga danda is fashioned of suitable length to pass from the ground to the armpit of the meditating individual. The ancient yogis found that by leaning slightly on this rod and applying sustained pressure in one armpit, the flow of

101

breath in the opposite nostril is enhanced. They utilized this principle during meditation practices to maintain a balance between the two nostrils, equalizing the flows of ida and pingala nadis, so that sushumna remains open and successful meditation continues.

For the average person, the brain functions in a balanced, equalized manner only for a few minutes every one and a half hours when the breathing cycle reverses. However, proper use of the yoga danda as well other yogic practices, including pranayama, induce an ongoing balance of both nostrils, enabling yogis who follow this path to maintain longer periods of sushumna flow. In this way meditative awareness may be experienced for hours or days at a time.

Nasal cycles and brain hemispheres

The dual nature of the human psycho-physiological framework is reflected in the very physical structure of man's brain and central nervous system. Neuro-physiological and psychological research studies have demonstrated that the two hemispheres of the brain are actually responsible for different abilities and characteristic modes of expression of human individuality.

The right hemisphere, corresponding to the para-sympathetic nervous system, is responsible for the spatial, artistic, holistic, intuitive and psychic side of perception, which are ida nadi functions. The left hemisphere is responsible for the logical, rational and analytical faculties and sequential and linear modes of thought, which are pingala nadi functions.

The left side of the brain, corresponding to the sympathetic nervous system, has centres for verbal communication: hearing, reading, talking and writing. Formal education takes place more through verbal communication than non-verbal. Hence the left cerebral lobe is referred to as the dominant lobe. The left lobe has the male qualities of competitiveness, selfishness, aggression; while the right cerebral lobe is endowed with the feminine qualities of love, compassion and nurturing.

By balancing ida and pingala nadis, the personality of Ardhanarishwara is created in which the male and female qualities are balanced. In terms of swara yoga, the right side of the brain is activated when the left nostril is flowing, the left side of the brain is activated when the right nostril is flowing, and whenever both nostrils flow equally, every faculty of the human brain is functioning in an optimal and integrated manner as sushumna nadi awakens.

The alternating rhythm of the nasal cycle is necessary for the nervous system as it allows for the sympathetic and parasympathetic systems to operate rhythmically, influencing the behaviour and rhythm of all the other organs in the body and maintaining an inherent balance. The moment the rhythm of the brain is disturbed, the effect spreads through every system of the body. In a mind which is full of anxiety, insecurity or fear, the circuits of the brain are tied in knots. The practice of pranayama restores balance in the ida and pingala nadis and regulates the brain.

Research has also demonstrated the extremely rich and sensitive enervation of the nasal membranes. Studies have shown the presence of twenty times more autonomic nerve fibres within this membrane than in the cerebrospinal (central nervous) system. During inhalation, the flow of air in each nostril stimulates specific unilateral autonomic nerve centres lying within and beneath the mucous membranes, which influence the autonomic processes of respiration, circulation, digestion and so on.

In fact, the whole region of the nasal mucous membrane has been defined as a distinct organ of the autonomic nervous system by some researchers. This means that it responds to various physical and mental situations of arousal, activity, stress and relaxation. In this light, the far-reaching effects of pranayama practices can be understood. Aimed as they are at balancing ida and pingala, the practices thus influence the whole autonomic nervous system, and therefore bring the entire body-mind complex into a state of balance and equilibrium.

Nasal obstruction and nose care

A number of research and clinical studies have pointed to the need for unobstructed, well-functioning nostrils. The work of Dr I. N. Rega, an ear, nose and throat specialist of Bucharest, Romania, deserves comment. In a study of nearly 200 patients suffering from one-sided nasal obstruction, due to distortions and malformations of the median nasal septum present since birth, Dr Rega found that those patients whose breath flowed predominantly via the left nostril suffered a higher than average incidence of a wide variety of respiratory disorders, including chronic mucopurulent sinusitis, middle and inner ear infections, partial or total loss of the sense of smell, hearing and taste, recurrent pharyngitis, laryngitis and tonsillitis, chronic bronchitis and bronchiectasis.

He also found that people with this syndrome were more likely to suffer from a wide variety of more distant disorders, including amnesia, intellectual weakness, headaches, hyperthyroidism (with associated irritability), cardiopulmonary weakness (including palpitations, asthma-like attacks and chronic heart failure), liver and gallbladder problems (varied symptoms), persistently altered cellular constituents of the blood and lymphatic fluid, chronic gastritis and colitis (with symptoms of heartburn, gastric reflux, peptic ulcer and constipation), and sexual and reproductive disorders (symptoms of diminution of libido, menstrual irregularities and diminished virility).

In contrast, patients whose breath flowed predominantly through the right nostril, were found to be predisposed to arterial hypertension and its numerous consequences.

While this study is suggestive rather than conclusive, and is open to criticism in several areas, it largely agrees with the experimental observations of a large number of doctors and physicians, who as early as 1819, were drawing attention to the state of general physical and mental health in relation to the clarity of the nasal passages and their sensitive lining of mucous membrane.

The nose is one of the most vital organs. Apart from its function as an air-conditioner, heater, filter and moisturizer, it has a direct effect on physical, mental, emotional, psychic and spiritual states. The health of the nose can be maintained by yogic practices such as neti and by a healthy lifestyle and diet. This will allow one to practise pranayama efficiently and to balance the sympathetic and parasympathetic nervous systems. The body and mind will then behave as one harmonious unit and the perception will improve. The sense of smell and its related functions on more subtle levels will work optimally, allowing a better relationship with the world and with oneself.

10

What is Pranayama?

Pranayama is a precise science which provides methods to understand the essence of prana and to guide it within oneself as well as the rest of creation. Swami Sivananda says, "He who has grasped prana has realized the very core of cosmic life and activity. He who conquers and controls this essence is able to control his own body and mind, as well as every other body, mind and power in this universe. Thus, pranayama is that means by which the yogi realizes the whole of cosmic life in this little body and tries to attain perfection."

The medium of pranayama is the breath. The practices involve guiding the respiration beyond its normal limit, stretching it, speeding it up and slowing it down in order to experience the full range of respiration on both the gross and subtle levels. Once this has been achieved, prana can be guided further by the practice of prana vidya. In the *Yoga Chudamani Upanishad*, it has been stated (v. 31):

ऊर्ध्वाध: संस्थितावेतौ यो जानाति स योगवित् ॥

One who knows the significance of the ascending and descending of jiva (inhalation and exhalation) is the knower of yoga.

According to the theory of pranayama, the involuntary process of breathing, by which the jiva constantly moves up and down, can be made voluntary by the introduction of awareness. It is possible to attain mastery over the breathing process and harmonize the flow of prana and apana, the two principal flows of energy in the body, through breath awareness and control, coordination of the breath with the mantra, and awareness of the pranic movement within the body. Once this harmony and control is attained through the practices of pranayama, it becomes possible to observe and transcend the gunas, and thus attain liberation.

The understanding of pranayama as a process which begins with the breath but culminates in liberation is emphasized by Sri Shankaracharya also. He says in the *Aparokshanubhuti* (v. 118–120):

चित्तादिसर्वभावेषु ब्रह्मत्वेनैव भावनात् ।
निरोध: सर्ववृत्तीनां प्राणायाम: स उच्यते ॥
निषेधनं प्रपञ्चस्य रेचकाख्य: समीरण: ।
ब्रह्मैवास्मीती या वृत्ति: पूरको वायुरीरित: ॥
ततस्तद्वृत्तिनैश्चल्यं कुम्भक: प्राणसंयम: ।
अयं चापि प्रबुद्धानामज्ञानां घ्राणपीडनम् ॥

Pranayama is the control of all life-forces by realizing naught but Brahman in all things as the mind, etc. The negation of the universe is the outgoing breath. The thought 'I am Brahman' itself is called the incoming breath. The permanence of that thought thereafter is the restrained breath. This is the pranayama of the wise, while the pressing of the nose is only for the unknowing.

Sri Shankaracharya is bringing to attention the fact that while the practices of pranayama do carry a physical component (the 'pressing of the nose' refers to nadi shodhana pranayama), the practitioner who limits himself to this aspect fails to realize the vast scope of pranayama. For pranayama is not merely the science of breath, but the science of universal energy, universal mind, time, space and matter. It is a system through which the vital, pranic energy that holds the universe together is dynamized and redistributed at various levels of existence.

Etymological meaning

The word 'pranayama' has two etymological explanations. It has been interpreted as a combination of the words prana + ayama, and also as a combination of the words prana + yama. The word *ayama* means 'expanding the dimension', so in the first sense pranayama means expanding the dimension of prana. The word *yama* means 'restraint' or 'control', so here pranayama refers to the control or restraint of prana. Both etymological explanations are able to convey the meaning of pranayama.

Prana is a force in constant motion: therefore, if pranayama is understood as prana + yama, then the only way to control a moving force is by stopping it to the extent of complete cessation. Only then is one able to harness its power. This point of complete cessation is *kumbhaka*, or breath retention, whereby the force of prana is held, restrained and directed towards a specific purpose, the awakening of kundalini shakti and union with the divine. However, when pranayama is understood as prana + ayama, it refers to a process of stretching, extending or expanding. In this context, pranayama is the process by which the internal pranic dimension is expanded, increased and held, thereby activating the quantum of prana in the body to a higher frequency.

The scriptures describe seven *ayamas*, or planes of individual existence. The first ayama is bhur loka, the gross physical dimension, perceptible to the mind and senses. The second is bhuva loka in which one perceives dreams and experiences moments of hallucinations. The third is swah loka, perceived in deep sleep. The consciousness traverses these three ayamas in waking, dreaming and sleeping states. When a child is conceived, prana is created in its physical body and gradually extends the area of control to these three fields of human experience, but no further. Normally human perception is confined to these three states and one is not able to perceive the deeper levels of existence.

The four higher dimensions of existence are described symbolically as maha loka, janah loka, tapah loka and satya loka. The gross prana is incapable of penetrating into these subtle dimensions. The purpose of pranayama, therefore, is to refine and transform prana into a subtler force and then extend it into the higher lokas or ayamas. When the pranas are awakened beyond the first three dimensions, then the real purpose of pranayama is fulfilled.

Pranayama for transformation

In the practice of pranayama, prana unites with apana and the united prana-apana is directed upwards to the head. At this time, prana leaves the passages of ida and pingala and travels through the channel of sushumna. When prana passes through sushumna, the light of jnana is kindled and the kundalini is awakened. The mind enters a thoughtless region. All the karmic seeds of the yogi are burnt away. The oblation of the senses is offered into the fire of prana. As the practitioner undergoes this process, the sleeping centres of the brain are awakened.

Usually the brain and the mind are trained through the perceptions available and intelligible to the senses. Yoga, however, has a completely different view of mind control. It says isolate the mind and consciousness from the pathways of sensory stimulation. The brain, mind and consciousness can function independent of the senses. By isolating the brain and mind, the consciousness enters a more powerful state of understanding and realization, and this is the beginning of yoga.

The practice of pranayama has a direct effect on the functioning of the intricate, sophisticated functions of the brain. When the yogis investigated the possibility of an independent method to develop the silent areas of the mind and brain in order to transcend the limiting barriers of the human personality, they discovered pranayama. It is possible to understand this process through modern scientific principles as well.

There are billions of cells in the brain which exist in a chaotic order, without any discipline or unity, shown as random brainwave activity when measured on an EEG machine. These cells are oscillating forms of energy or *shakti*, comprising the totality of brainwave activity. The chaos in the brain and mind is also a result of the millions of archetypes that exist as unorganized geometric patterns and influence one's actions, thoughts, decisions, feelings and awareness as a whole. When the basic elements of the brain move in such a chaotic fashion, so does the thinking process. Pranayama holds the key to blend them together as one pulsating unit.

One cannot discipline or organize the physical brain or bring order into the chaotic elements of the brain without first balancing the nadis. The brain is controlled by the chakras and nadis. Mental balance is not possible unless one is able to balance the ida and pingala nadis through yogic practices. The practices of pranayama are of major importance because they purify and balance the flows of ida and pingala nadis to awaken sushumna nadi and kundalini. Thus the brain cells are stimulated, the brainwaves are streamlined and the archetypes are reorganized. In this way new languages can be learnt, behaviour can be transformed, a culture can be reconstituted, and a civilization can be given a new turn altogether.

According to science, the grey matter of the brain changes during the natural course of human evolution. This process is hastened through the practice of pranayama, and one is able to evolve beyond the natural evolutionary cycle. The benefits of such an event are too numerous to describe, but can be realized only by self-investigation into yoga.

Conscious breathing

Breathing is a unique vital process, which normally functions unconsciously, but one also has the ability to breathe consciously. Other unconscious processes, such as the heartbeat, body temperature and metabolic activity, cannot be controlled by the average person. Unconscious breathing is controlled by the medulla oblongata in the brain stem, a region known as the primitive brain, while conscious breathing comes from the more evolved areas of the brain in the cerebral cortex. In fact, conscious breathing engages the cerebral cortex and stimulates the more evolved areas of the brain.

The regular practice of pranayama over a period of time reinforces cortical control of the breath, a process called telencephalization, where one shifts from unconscious to conscious breathing with profound effects on one's wellbeing. During conscious control of the breath, the cerebral cortex bypasses the respiratory centre in the brain stem. Impulses from the cortex also affect adjoining areas of the brain concerned with emotions. The involvement of the cerebral cortex in conscious breathing causes the cortex to develop and allows the individual to enter higher stages of the evolutionary cycle.

Conscious breathing begins with the awareness: "I am breathing in; I am breathing out." The awareness is an aspect of consciousness and the breath is a vehicle of prana. Thus, in this way, prana and consciousness move together. Awareness of the breath implies that one is simultaneously aware of the consciousness. By the practice of conscious breathing, the witness aspect develops and the expansion of consciousness begins.

Conscious breathing has a calming effect on the mind. Even simple breath awareness, without exerting any control over the natural pattern of the breath, will induce a regular and relaxing rhythm of breathing. This is an effective method of quietening a tense mind. The more complex breathing techniques of pranayama influence the brain even more deeply. There is no system like pranayama that has such an immediate influence on the nervous system, brain and mind.

The first step

The first step in pranayama is to tune into the rhythm of the breath. A smooth, slow rhythm usually indicates a relaxed state of body and mind. Irregular respiration usually means

111

tension. In anxiety the breath is shallow and rapid, in anger short and forceful, in grief arrhythmic and gasping, and in depression, sighing. Irregular breathing is also associated with neuroses and disturbed mental states. It has been observed that exhalation is uneven and incomplete in certain types of neuroses. On the other hand, slow rhythmic breathing creates feelings of relaxation, alpha brain waves and reduced muscle tension.

The rhythms of the breath relate to the brain rhythms, heartbeat, muscle tension, mental and emotional rhythms, hormonal and enzymatic rhythms, sleep and wakefulness, all with varying frequencies and intensities. These rhythms also take place within the external rhythms of day and night, seasons, years and planetary influences. Pranayama leads to the awareness of a rhythmic force within the body and mind. When one becomes aware of the body's vital cycles, they begin to work more optimally. Simultaneously, the mind can be trained to control these forces, thereby opening up areas of consciousness which are beyond the normal awareness and control.

Prana nigraha

Technically, the initial breathing practices are not pranayama, but *prana nigraha*, where one begins to control the breath and the prana. The same practice assumes the form of pranayama when control over the pranas is attained and the pranas have been awakened in the realm of the chakras. In the stage of prana nigraha, one uses the breath as a means to develop and intensify the awareness of pranamaya kosha. The nervous system receives a greater quantum of energy, which is essential to withstand the effects of higher pranayama practice.

Slowly, the pranas are awakened within the physical structure and blockages are removed from the chakras and nadis, thus paving the way for kundalini awakening. According to the *Amritanada Upanishad* (v. 7):

112

यथा पर्वतधातुनां दह्यन्ते मला: ।
तथेन्द्रियकृता दोषा दह्यन्ते प्राणधारणात् ॥

Just as the impurities of mountain minerals are burnt by
the blower, so the stains caused by the sensory organs are
burned by controlling the prana.

The effect of prana nigraha is evidenced by a lightness and
vitality in the body and a calm, relaxed mind, and then
comes the strength and ability to practise pranayama.

Pranayama is kumbhaka

The actual pranayama is *kumbhaka*, the period of breath
retention. The guiding of inhalation (*pooraka*) and exhalation
(*rechaka*) aids in achieving kumbhaka, irrespective of where
it is applied. In nadi shodhana pranayama, for example,
kumbhaka is practised after inhalation and/or exhalation,
but in bhastrika it follows a round of rapid inhalations and
exhalations. In the *Yoga Sutras* (2:49), Maharshi Patanjali says:

तस्मिन्सति श्वासप्रश्वासयोर्गतिविच्छेद: प्राणायाम: ॥

Pranayama is the pause in the movement of inhalation
and exhalation when that is secured.

Yoga Yajnavalkya Samhita (6:25) also equates pranayama
with retention, describing three grades of pranayama,
depending on the periods of breath holding: i) adhama
pranayama (produces sweating), ii) madhyama pranayama
(produces tremors in addition to sweat) and iii) uttama
pranayama (produces levitation).

Kumbhaka is difficult for a beginner, but it becomes easier,
smoother and longer by systematic and regular practice.
Breath retention may come more easily for those who have
followed other yogic practices. The rare few, who are blessed
with an awakened kundalini, may experience *kevala kumbhaka* (spontaneous retention) at their very first attempt at
pranayama. However, it is of paramount importance for all

practitioners that the practice be followed systematically, irrespective of initial experiences. Then only will the full potential of pranayama be experienced. (The following chapter explains the mechanics of kumbhaka, as well as pooraka and rechaka, in detail.)

Units of pranayama

In a systematic practice of pranayama, the first criterion is a balanced ratio of the breath. Timing has a deep effect on the mind and prana. "If one is able to practise five rounds of nadi shodhana with absolute precision in timing, then the laya state of samadhi will come," Swami Satyananda said while explaining the science of pranayama to yoga teachers in Spain during 1979. The ancient yogis who propounded the practices of pranayama were extremely mindful of this fact, and devised various methods to measure the units of pranayama, in the absence of devices such as clocks. Each time unit was called a *matra*. The following physical actions provide a guideline for understanding the notion of matra. Each denotes one matra:

- Twinkling of an eye
- Time taken to pronounce a short vowel
- Time necessary for touching one's knee thrice followed by a clap
- Time occupied by one normal respiration
- Time taken up in pronouncing the sacred syllable *Om*.

As pranayama training was always imparted by a guru to a disciple, the precise balance could be achieved under actual guidance. In modern times, despite the invention of clocks, the measuring of inhalation, exhalation and retention remains a somewhat perplexing issue. Watching a clock or even mental counting can be a distraction while practising. The best way to measure the breath is with the aid of the 24-syllable Gayatri mantra. One repetition of Gayatri mantra provides the proper timing for the inhalation and two Gayatris for the exhalation. The Gayatri is an ideal unit for pranayama, but in case one is unable to chant it in

114

one inhalation, shorter mantras or a simple count may be employed, keeping them uniform (also see Chapter 7: 'Prana and Mantra').

Along with the time unit, the space unit also needs to be taken into consideration. This measures the force with which the inhalation and exhalation are practised. The expelled air current can be felt for a specific distance from the nose, and this was measured with the fingers by the ancients. In regard to the space unit, the air pressure must be uniform, the inhalation and exhalation must be smooth, and the length of exhalation should ideally be double of inhalation, although one may practise equal inhalation and exhalation at the beginning. Overall, one must practise pranayama with utmost mindfulness, follow one's capacity and allow it to build up gradually, for the ratio represents the natural evolution of breath control.

11

Importance of Kumbhaka

The process of respiration has three components: *pooraka*, inspiration; *rechaka*, expiration; and *kumbhaka*, retention. In the classical yogic texts it is said that kumbhaka is pranayama and pranayama is kumbhaka; not pooraka and rechaka, which are natural processes. However, one must remember that inhalation and exhalation are a part of retention. In order to retain the breath, it is necessary to inhale as well as exhale. Therefore, the three components of the breath are also the three parts of pranayama.

Inhalation is described as the active or positive breath, exhalation as the passive or negative breath, and kumbhaka represents the transcendence of duality. Inhalation is the active process of respiration and requires muscular effort to draw air into the lungs. Normal exhalation is passive and does not require muscular effort; rather, the diaphragm and ribcage recoil back into their original places. In pranayama, rechaka is often a slow and controlled process. Generally, it is either the same length or twice the length of pooraka. The main advantage of conscious exhalation is that it develops conscious control over the relaxation response. Slow rechaka is performed spontaneously, for example, when one moans or groans in pain, for this removes pain from the pain centre in the brain. The conscious effort required for slow release of the breath needs the help of the cerebral cortex of the brain. The cerebral cortex sends inhibitory impulses to the respiratory centre in the midbrain. These inhibitory impulses from the cortex overflow into the adjoining area of the hypothalamus, concerned with emotions, and quieten this area. Hence, the soothing effect of slow expiration.

The *Amritanada Upanishad* gives a poetic description of the twin processes of pooraka and rechaka (v. 11–12):

उतिक्षप्य वायुमाकाशे शून्यं कृत्वा निरात्मकम् ।
शून्यभावे नियुञ्जीयाद्रेचकस्येति लक्षणम् ॥
वक्त्रेणोत्पलनालेन तोयमाकर्षयेत्तरः ।
एवं वायुर्ग्रहीत्यः पूरकस्येति लक्षणम् ॥

Raising up the vayu from the akasha (region in the heart) and making the body void (of vayu) and empty, and uniting (the soul) to the state of void, is called rechaka. That is called pooraka when one takes in vayu, as a man would take water into his mouth through the lotus stalk.

Classification of pranayama

The various pranayamas are obtained by modulating the processes of pooraka, rechaka and kumbhaka. The main classical pranayamas are nine: nadi shodhana, bhastrika, kapalbhati (also a shatkarma), sheetali/sheetkari, bhramari, ujjayi, moorchha, surya bheda and chandra bheda. Some of these pranayamas increase heat and some cool the body down. Some pranayamas stimulate, while others harmonize and relax the nervous system. Nadi shodhana is balancing, bhastrika and kapalbhati are activating, and bhramari and ujjayi are relaxing. Sheetali/sheetkari and chandra bheda decrease the inner body temperature; surya bheda and moorchha increase the inner body temperature.

All pranayama techniques alter the normal breathing rate, but some more than others. Bhastrika and kapalbhati speed up inhalation and exhalation. They may be considered as methods of hyperventilation, where prolonged rapid breathing is practised. Similarly, bhramari, ujjayi, sheetali and sheetkari may be regarded as methods of hypoventilation,

117

where reduced or slow breathing, often less than five breaths per minute, is practised.

The hyperventilating techniques come under the classification of vitalizing pranayamas. The rapid and deep breathing increases the alveolar ventilation and stimulates the blood flow in the top of the lungs and those areas where blood circulation is sluggish and even dormant. They have a stimulating effect on the whole body due to the rapid muscular movement and increased metabolic rate induced in all parts of the body. These techniques exercise the lungs and abdomen, and stimulate the nervous system to balance and strengthen itself. They also have a purifying and heating effect on the body and mind.

Hypoventilating techniques are slow and subtle, stretching the capacity of respiration at the other end of the spectrum. They are generally tranquillizing pranayamas, and their effect is more or less opposite to hyperventilation. These techniques reduce the metabolic rate as well as the frequency of brain waves, leading to relaxed meditative states. Thus, one experiences a greater sense of control over the nervous system. Carbon dioxide levels may be slightly increased by these practices, although the oxygen levels remain normal.

The conscious altering of the rate of inhalation and exhalation brings about an improved control of all the above processes. There is a more conscious and efficient absorption of oxygen and elimination of carbon dioxide, as well as improved mental and emotional states. The control of pooraka and rechaka is a preliminary stage in pranayama, designed to improve overall health and vitality, and to prepare the practitioner for later stages. Good health, efficient respiratory function and increased vitality are foundations for the more advanced practices of pranayama, which involve kumbhaka.

What is kumbhaka?

The word *kumbha* means 'vessel', and thus implies holding or retaining something. In pranayama, this term describes the retention of breath. Kumbhaka can be performed after inha-

118

lation (*antar kumbhaka*) and after exhalation (*bahir kumbhaka*). There are two types of breath retention: *sahita kumbhaka*, which is deliberately holding the breath, or *kevala kumbhaka*, where the breath is suspended spontaneously. Kumbhaka is a part of all pranayama practices. In the *Yoga Sutras*, Maharshi Patanjali described pranayama as kumbhaka. The aim of all pranayama practices is to achieve kevala kumbhaka, which is equivalent to the state of samadhi. According to the *Amritanada Upanishad* (v. 13–14):

नोच्छ्वसेन्न च निष्वासेन्नैव गात्राणि चालयेत् ।
एवं भावं नियुञ्जीयात् कुम्भकस्येति लक्षणम् ॥
अन्धवत् पश्य रूपाणि शब्दं बधिरवच्छृणु ।
काष्ठवत् पश्य वै देहं प्रशान्तस्येति लक्षणम् ॥

That is called kumbhaka when there is no expiration or inspiration and the body is motionless, remaining still in one state. Then he sees forms like the blind, hears sounds like the deaf, and feels the body like wood. This is the characteristic of one who has attained much quiescence.

Physiology of kumbhaka

During the practice of kumbhaka the oxygen levels in the body fall and the carbon dioxide levels increase, depending on the speed of metabolism and how relaxed or tense one is. The main effect of kumbhaka is to train the nervous system to tolerate higher levels of carbon dioxide in the body before signals from the primitive brain stem force one to take another breath. Many blood capillaries lie dormant in the brain and become active only when more blood is required. Increased carbon dioxide levels stimulate the brain's capillaries to dilate. In this way, more capillaries in the brain are opened up to improve cerebral circulation.

The brain also stores a certain amount of carbon dioxide, which allows for a more efficient oxygen exchange and carrying capacity of the lungs. Often, when one cannot breathe deeply, it means that the brain's concentration of carbon dioxide is diminished. The lungs are not out of order, but the carbon dioxide concentration of the brain tissues is too low to allow a deeper respiratory process. Nature, it seems, has provided for carbon dioxide storage in the brain in order to activate the respiratory drive and make the oxygen consumption process more efficient. Kumbhaka restores the levels of carbon dioxide in the brain tissues, allowing the system to fully extract oxygen. Additionally, when carbon dioxide is retained in the brain, it increases the capacity for assimilating ions.

Increased carbon dioxide levels in the blood can lead to altered states of consciousness and feelings of expansiveness. It is interesting that researcher J. Wolpe (*Psychotherapy by Reciprocal Inhibition,* Stanford University Press, 1958) recommended what is called CO_2 therapy. He suggested the administration of 65 percent carbon dioxide and 35 percent oxygen for treatment of anxiety based on his experiments, which indicated that one to four of such inhalations will reduce anxiety for several hours or in some cases, for weeks. In another experiment, there were three control groups of highly anxious subjects. One inhaled a carbon dioxide mixture, the second hyperventilated and the third inhaled only air. The anxiety levels became significantly lower in the first group. They also showed a trend toward reduced anxiety after a 24-hour period, not found in the other two groups.

Kumbhaka, in this light, may be called a self-administered CO_2 therapy. However, its effect is beneficial up to a certain optimum level only. Beyond this, it becomes distinctly harmful and may even cause disorientation and hallucination. Hence, it is always stressed that the practice of kumbhaka must be undertaken only under the guidance of an experienced teacher. Metabolic levels and brain activity must be adjusted to produce optimum conditions; only then it will become beneficial.

Another aspect of kumbhaka is that it trains one to control the part of the brain ruling the involuntary processes. One can move the hands, but not the hypothalamus. However, through the practice of kumbhaka, the brain can be trained to act according to one's demands. One can stop its functions or accelerate them. This is how many yogis have been able to stop the heart for a number of days and revive it again. The heart is not an independent organ; it is controlled by a higher centre in the hypothalamus of the brain. With control of the brain, one can automatically control the coronary behaviour, body temperature, digestive system, and so on. In the advanced stages of kumbhaka the period of breath retention can be extended for long durations until all the vital functions appear to cease. In this way the breath may be suspended for days at a time. Yogis have been buried underground in this near-hibernation state, known as *bhu samadhi*, for days at a time.

Kevala kumbhaka

Spontaneous retention is called *kevala kumbhaka*, where the breath suspends without any conscious effort on the part of the practitioner. This form of breath suspension is not aided by exhalation and inhalation and is unconditioned by place, time and number. Kevala kumbhaka can happen to anyone, anywhere, any time, even if one does not practise pranayama. There is no risk involved, because this retention is created by a natural state in the body. When kevala kumbhaka occurs, a point of light arises at the mid-eyebrow centre and spreads throughout the space of consciousness. The whole frontal brain becomes illumined, as though it were daybreak, and one emerges from the darkness that is normally seen behind the closed eyes. It has been said in the *Hatha Yoga Pradipika* (2:73):

प्राणायामोऽयमित्युक्त: स वै केवलकुंभक: ।
कुंभके केवले सिद्धे रेचपूरकवर्जिते ॥

Perfection of isolated retention is freedom from inhalation and exhalation. This pranayama spoken of is verily kevala kumbhaka.

During kevala kumbhaka, the yogi exists on a plane higher than reason, beyond the boundaries of concentration. Swami Sivananda says, "(Through kevala kumbhaka) a yogi comes face to face with facts which ordinary consciousness cannot comprehend. This is achieved by proper training and manipulation of the subtle forces of the body, causing them to push the mind upward into higher planes. When the mind is raised into the superconscious state of perception, it begins to act from there and experiences higher knowledge. Such is the ultimate object of pranayama, which is achieved through control. He who knows pranayama and kevala is the real yogi."

One who has mastered kevala kumbhaka can hold the breath for as long as he likes. He has perfected hatha yoga and attained the state of raja yoga. Many *siddhis*, psychic powers, manifest to the one who has mastery of kevala kumbhaka. He remains unaffected by pain, his excretions and sleep are diminished, and his body and mouth do not give off bad odour. He is lean and thin, but his countenance glows. The *Yoga Shastra of Dattatreya* states (v. 146–147):

केवले कुम्भके सिद्धे रेच-पूरक-वर्जिते ।
न तस्य दुर्लभं किंचित् त्रिषु लोकेषु विद्यते ॥

There is nothing unobtainable in the three planes of existence for him who has achieved kevala kumbhaka without rechaka and pooraka.

The *Hatha Yoga Pradipika* echoes the same notion (2:74):

न तस्य दुर्लभं किंचित्त्रिषु लोकेषु विद्यते ।
शक्त: केवलकुंभेन यथेष्टं वायुधारणात् ॥

Nothing in the three planes of existence is unobtainable by him who has mastery of kevala kumbhaka and can retain the breath as desired.

Kumbhaka and samadhi

During kumbhaka the quantum of prana increases as the body, breath and mind are brought into a state of stillness. The stillness allows prana and consciousness to intensify, as in a pressure cooker – the intensity of energy and heat go up because they are not released from the body. This pressure is sustained while kumbhaka is maintained, allowing prana and consciousness to flow unimpeded throughout pranamaya kosha.

The expansion of prana also has a substantial effect on the mind. There is greater mental power and the awareness becomes acute. The capacity of the mind increases due to the stillness, as there are no fluctuations or disturbances. Just as light is transformed into a laser beam, the mind becomes totally focused and one-pointed. At this stage there is total cessation of the mental patterns. The dissipation of the mind ceases and the mental perception and the pranic structure sever their connection with the physical body. There is a total experience of intensity: intensity of stillness, intensity of mind, intensity of prana and intensity of practice. This intensity of practice enables one to hold the concentration and focus, and leads on to the path of samadhi.

The process can also be described physiologically. In kumbhaka the carbon dioxide levels in the brain increase. In reaction, the neurons begin firing nerve impulses in the brain to signal the body to breathe. Transmission of a nerve impulse involves more than one neuron; it needs a synapse (the point where an impulse passes from one neuron to another) and neurotransmitters, which are synthesized nerve cells. The longer the kumbhaka is held, the more nerve impulses are generated and transmitted.

While kumbhaka is maintained, this constant firing of impulses builds up an immense amount of nervous energy in the brain, forcing the creation of new neuronal pathways and the activation of dormant centres. The brain is literally illumined and awakened. In addition, the corpus callosum, a thin sheet of membrane between the two hemispheres of the brain, is activated during the practice of kumbhaka. These nerve fibres permit the passing of information between left and right hemispheres, which means that the whole brain can function and perception is not limited to one mode of processing.

In the *Yoga Sutras*, Maharshi Patanjali refers to this potential of kumbhaka to illumine the dormant centres of the brain when he says (2:52):

ततः क्षीयते प्रकाशावरणम् ॥

Thereby the covering of light disappears.

As the dormant potentials of the brain are exploded, the practitioner is propelled into greater understanding of the depths and dimensions of his being, which are beyond those of ordinary experience. Part of this expansion of awareness gives the ability to experience prana as a subtle force, manifesting in different ways, which explains the light that is visible in chidakasha during kumbhaka.

While such immense activity is taking place in the internal spheres, the external activities completely cease. To the onlooker the yogi is as still as a rock but, in fact, he is traversing spheres beyond the reach of the reasoning mind. However, if the yogi enters darkness instead of illumination, it is better to stop the practice. This indicates *jada samadhi*, a state of external and internal cessation where no evolution comes about. Temporary suspension of all the faculties takes place, usually accompanied by an inability to penetrate through it unaided.

Kumbhaka and kundalini

The process of kumbhaka can be viewed from yet another perspective to understand how it helps in the awakening of kundalini. During the practice of kumbhaka certain events take place in the body. The temperature of the body changes, the skin resistance changes, the brain wave frequencies become lower and the coronary function becomes nominal. At this time, certain enzymes or hormones are released into the bloodstream from the pituitary gland. As a result, the use of oxygen is replaced. When the use of oxygen is withdrawn, a sort of suffocation is expressed by the organs of the body.

Mooladhara chakra is the seat of the kundalini shakti. Usually the kundalini remains dormant in mooladhara, but during kumbhaka, the temperature in mooladhara rises. When the consumption of oxygen dwindles to nothing, the kundalini feels intense suffocation. As the brain waves are lowered, a surge takes place in mooladhara and this is the awakening of kundalini.

This can be explained in another way. During inhalation, the prana vayu flows upward from manipura to vishuddhi. During exhalation, apana vayu flows downward from manipura to mooladhara. Kumbhaka, however, brings about a fusion of apana and prana with samana, creating an intense pressure at manipura, which is the storehouse of prana. The merging of these three pranas into one mighty force activates the other two flows of udana and vyana. With the five pranas activated and the total awareness focused at manipura, kundalini is simultaneously awakened. This is the culmination of pranayama. The upward flow of prana and the downward flow of apana attain a state of equilibrium and remain suspended. The breath is held spontaneously, either externally or internally, without any trace of activity on any level of existence. The *Hatha Yoga Pradipika* states (2:41):

विधिवत्प्राणसंयामैर्नाडीचक्रे विशोधिते ।
सुषुम्नावदनं भित्त्वा सुखाद्विशति मारुतः ॥

By systematically retaining the prana, the nadis and chakras are purified. Thus the prana bursts open the doorway to sushumna and easily enters it.

Guidelines for kumbhaka

In order to develop kumbhaka the practices of pranayama should be followed systematically. The diet should be regulated and constipation removed, so that toxins do not form in the body. Sexual moderation should also be observed by the practitioner, as this act produces certain toxin-forming hormones.

When practising kumbhaka, the breath should be retained without fear or shaking of the body. After completing the retention, exhale slowly and steadily, without any anxiety. Will power may be used to retain the breath, but the air should not be forced to remain inside by continuing the inhalation. One must not push one's limits. During the practice, prescribed ratios of inhalation, exhalation and retention should be followed.

During kumbhaka concentration can be achieved by focusing on a symbol, and the best symbol is light. While holding the breath, the light should be visualized at the eyebrow centre. If one is unable to visualize the light, trataka can be practised on a candle for some time prior to the practice. If the inner space becomes dark after practising kumbhaka, it is a negative symptom. However, if it becomes more and more illumined, it is a positive symptom.

The practice of kumbhaka should be undertaken when the ratios of inhalation and exhalation have been mastered. The nadis are purified in this way and become fit for sustained kumbhaka. The *Yoga Chudamani Upanishad* (v. 93) says that kumbhaka should be practised when the exhaled breath extends for twenty-six *angulas* (finger-widths). This distance can be measured easily by raising both hands in front of the face, so that the palms face downward with the fingers straight.

12

Benefits of Pranayama

> The physical body that is exposed to the processes of yoga
> is freed from old age, disease and death.
>
> *—Shvetashvatara Upanishad*

Pranayama initiates a process in the physical body whereby
the energy molecules and the mental forces which interact
with one another in life and consciousness are transformed.
When the molecules of mind are transformed, higher
qualities such as love, compassion and unity arise. Matter is
energy and, therefore, the physical body can be transformed
into energy. The physical body is not merely a bundle of
bone, marrow, nerves and mucus. One must re-analyze and
re-define what the body is and how far its transformation can
be effected.

Can this body be turned into light particles? This must
be considered in terms of science, not in terms of belief
or faith. If this physical body can be transformed, if the
molecules can undergo a state of metamorphosis, how is that
achieved? The answer is that the body is rendered extremely
subtle and pure through the process of yoga and accordingly
transformed. Pranayama is a key method. When the yogic
texts state that through pranayama one can control one's
circumstances and character, and harmonize the individual
life with cosmic life, they are referring to the power of
pranayama to bring about such an intrinsic transformation.

The aspirant who practises pranayama in a sustained manner will find that every aspect of the being, at every level, is gradually being impacted. As one advances in the practices, the structure, the skin and the smell of the body begin to change. One is always full of fresh energy, and the senses are calmed and their outgoing tendency diminishes. Impurities are removed not only from the physical and pranic bodies, but also from the mental, psychic and causal bodies. As a result, the intellectual capacity increases, and the mind and thoughts become more powerful. As prana flows freely through all the levels of being, the negative tendencies begin to drop off almost automatically. The small things that could earlier spin one out of control dissolve into nothing, and the connection with and experience of cosmic prana becomes stronger and steadier.

Awakening of vital energy

The one essential benefit of pranayama is that it allows one to increase one's level of vital energy, thus strengthening the force of the different systems active within, resulting in better overall health. The practices connect the individual with the very source of energy so that one's physical and mental energies do not get depleted. This brings about continuous alertness and a sense of wellbeing, dynamism and vitality. The purpose of pranayama is not to learn how to breathe or even to breathe better, but to awaken the inherent energy, the power or prana, within.

The process of energization through pranayama can be understood from another perspective. Pranayama creates static electricity in the body which helps to recharge the positive ions breathed in from the environment and convert them into negative ions. The effect is the same as that created by rain and thunderstorm. Hot and sultry weather makes one feel lethargic, but the air becomes fresh and clean with rain and one feels energized and dynamic. Rain and thunderstorm charge the positive ions in the environment and convert them into negative ions. Similarly, pranayama generates static electricity in the body in very minute quantities and there is a feeling of improved energy and dynamism.

Physical benefits

When the rishis discovered the science of pranayama, they did not have yoga therapy in mind, although the practices have innumerable physical benefits. The therapeutic aspect of pranayama is an incidental by-product. The main objective of pranayama is to balance the interacting processes of the pranic and mental forces for awakening the higher centres of human consciousness. Nevertheless, the practitioner of pranayama will experience many benefits at the physical level. These effects have been documented scientifically, and it has been observed that pranayama influences almost all the organs and physiological systems, as indicated below.

Respiratory system: Pranayama exercises the muscles of respiration and the lungs through the processes of deep, rapid or slow breathing. The chest is opened to its fullest extent and the lungs are stretched to the utmost. This strengthens the respiratory muscles and makes the lungs more elastic, resulting in a healthier process of respiration.

During pranayama one does not absorb a larger quantity of oxygen. In fact, the amount of oxygen absorbed during a round of pranayama is less than the amount absorbed during normal respiration. The average person inhales about 7,000 cc of air in one minute during normal inspiration; during pranayama, one inhales about 3,700 cc in one minute. The total intake of air being smaller in pranayama, the absorption of oxygen is also smaller. However, the practices allow more time for oxygen to mix with the blood flow and for the system to eliminate waste through the breath and blood. The training given to the respiratory organs and muscles during the pranayama practice prepares them to work efficiently all through the day. With a more efficient respiratory apparatus, a larger quantity of oxygen is absorbed throughout the day than it normally would be.

Digestive and eliminatory system: Similar benefits are received by the organs of digestion, absorption and elimination. The stomach, pancreas, liver, bowels and kidneys are all exercised in pranayama through the massage given to them by the diaphragm and the abdominal muscles. This happens in normal respiration as well, but during pranayama the movement of the muscles and the resulting massage is greatly accentuated. All the associated muscles and nerves are toned up and rendered healthier. Constipation is removed and all the organs function better. Absorption also becomes more efficient with a well-functioning digestive and eliminatory system so that the blood is enriched with nutritive elements.

Cardiac system: In 1968, the Bihar School of Yoga was asked by the Health Ministry of the Government of India to conduct research on coronary diseases and yoga. About one thousand patients suffering from cardiac disorders such as angina, myocardial infarctions and other cardiac diseases were referred to yoga and pranayama practices. At the end of the study period, it was found that the practice of pranayama had helped each and every patient, but especially those suffering from angina and ischemia. Many other research studies have verified that pranayama is extremely beneficial for the heart. The practices minimize the stress put on the cardiac system by day-to-day life. Breathing with slow, deep and long breaths gives rest to the heart. Many heart conditions can be managed through pranayama.

Nadi shodhana pranayama in particular exercises the whole cardiac system. In this practice the ratio of 1:2 maintained between inhalation and exhalation has a direct relationship with the systolic and diastolic periods of the cardiac rhythm. When the heart is damaged, the ratio between the systolic and diastolic periods often becomes 2:1, 3:1 or even 5:1; however, with regular practice of nadi shodhana, the correct rhythm can be restored. One can observe from the pulse that the heart rate speeds up with inspiration and slows down with expiration. Breathing with the ratio of 1:2 relaxes the coronary muscles without reducing the supply of oxygen to the brain and body tissues. However, the effect of relaxation is nullified by further lengthening the exhalation, for example, breathing with the ratio of 1:4, because the brain accelerates the heart rate in reaction to a decreased supply of oxygen in the blood.

During the practices of pranayama, the muscles of the heart are also gently massaged, allowing for good circulation. In bhastrika and kapalbhati, vibrations spread to the entire circulatory system, including the veins, arteries and capillaries, making them function more efficiently.

Pranayama gives proper training to the coronary behaviour and this has another connotation for the spiritual aspirant. When the practitioner enters the state of meditation having practised pranayama, there is no stress on the heart, and the body is able to withstand the higher states of consciousness without any adverse effect.

Endocrine system: The endocrine glands influence the behaviour, reactions, interpretations, and even the so-called natural responses. Pranayama harmonizes, purifies and neutralizes the secretions of these glands and thereby influences thought and behaviour. The overall health of the endocrine system is largely dependent on the quality of the blood and its distribution to the glands. During pranayama, especially the vitalizing practices, the circulation of the blood becomes very rapid and the quality of the blood is also rendered very rich. The richer and more liberal blood supply brought to the endocrine glands enhances their functionality and the regulated breathing helps to balance the system.

The effects of pranayama on the endocrine system are most striking in relation to the pineal gland. This mysterious gland, located behind the third ventricle of the brain in the region of the ajna chakra, normally begins to decay with the onset of puberty. The pineal gland acts as a check for the pituitary gland, which is responsible for controlling the growth and functions of the other endocrine glands. If the pituitary gland is not regulated from an early age, an imbalance arises between the physical and mental development and the emotions mature before they can be handled. Therefore, in India, children from the age of seven or eight begin the practice of pranayama in order to maintain the activity of the pineal gland for a longer period, so that the transition from childhood to adulthood is smooth.

Nervous system: The brain, spinal cord, cranial and spinal nerves benefit from a richer and more liberal blood supply received through pranayama. In addition, the actions of the diaphragm and the abdominal muscles during extended inhalation pull up the lower part of the spinal column. If jalandhara bandha is integrated into the pranayama practice, the upper part of the spinal column is also pulled up. The pulling up of the vertebral column as a whole tones the roots of the spinal nerves and gives a strong peripheral stimulus to the whole nervous system. If pranayama is combined with all the three bandhas, the high intra-thoracic, intra-pulmonary and intra-abdominal pressures gives peripheral stimulus to the different nerve plexuses situated in the abdomen and thorax.

Respiration also controls fluctuating moods, which are subtle behaviours of the mind. The neuronic memory of the brain influences the projection of moods. However, the neurons fire more rhythmically and the electrical interactions between the different brain centres become more regulated when one breathes slowly and deeply in a systematic and coordinated manner. The wild fluctuations of the brain waves are streamlined and there is a balance between the two hemispheres of the brain. This is seen on the EEG as emissions of longer alpha waves and reduction of beta waves. The alpha waves bring harmony to the brain as well as the coronary, respiratory and circulatory systems. People suffering from high blood pressure are benefited by influencing the alpha wave behaviour of the brain.

Pranayama is also practised to bring the mind under control, and for this purpose the round is usually begun from the left nostril, which represents ida nadi or the mental energy. In contrast, the rotation of awareness in yoga nidra is begun from the right side to first subdue pingala, the vital energy and heat in the body. By practising pranayama systematically for a few years, a gradual transformation is brought about in the structure of the nervous system. Ultimately, there comes a moment when one closes the eyes, goes in and achieves meditation.

Greater concentration

In the *Yoga Sutras* (2:53), Maharshi Patanjali says:

धारणासु च योग्यता मनस: ॥

The mind becomes fit for concentration (by the practice of pranayama).

The cumulative effect of pranayama is that the mind becomes steady like a candle flame in a still room. The disturbing energies are removed and the prana moves in the ether principle. The velocity of the mind is slowly decreased, but its power is increased. Rajas and tamas are subdued and the tossing of the mind is arrested. The mind becomes one-pointed and achieves *dharana*, concentration, and *dhyana*, meditation.

The advantage of stepping into meditation through pranayama is that the mind remains dynamic and does not slip into a state of hypnosis. Some forms of dhyana yoga may induce hypnosis, if practised for too long. Pranayama prevents this, and also keeps the mind from becoming distracted during meditation. Usually, during meditation the mind wanders and ponders upon daily interactions and passions. One may bring it back to the meditation, but again and again it dissipates. When pranayama is combined with the practice of meditation, this wandering tendency of the mind is overcome, because the process of pranayama stills the mind and makes it one-pointed.

Experience of higher consciousness

The practices of pranayama develop the quality of human consciousness and should be adopted with this attitude.

Control over the mind is achieved by regular and systematic practice, so that one is able to handle the involuntary processes of the body, brain and mind. This means that one is now the master of oneself and one's destiny. At the physical level, the high pressure and stimulation exerted on the nervous system during the practices of pranayama cause the consciousness to be internalized, so that super-sensory perceptions become possible. Once the physical structure is changed, the mental substance automatically undergoes a change.

At the pranic level, the awakening of prana shakti becomes a bridge to cross over from the gross to subtle experience of yoga. Planes of consciousness that had previously remained in darkness are illumined as prana flows into them. The practitioner is able to penetrate these higher dimensions of existence experientially. The *anahad nada*, subtle inner sounds, are heard distinctly and the mind evaporates at this time. The practitioner of pranayama does not have to fight with the wild and untamed mind; it becomes calm and controlled by itself.

As prana circulates into the dark areas of the brain and mind, one's evolution is catalyzed and a higher intelligence manifests. The kundalini is awakened and the practitioner does not need to learn meditation. The meditative state arises by itself, and a new realm of consciousness opens. One is born into a radiant area of experience; such is the great science of pranayama.

Changes in the relationship with gravity

The classical yogic texts state that by concentrating on the tip of the nose during kumbhaka, one will control prana. By concentrating on the navel during kumbhaka, all diseases will be cured. If one concentrates on the toe of the foot, one will attain lightness of the body. When the yogi can perform kumbhaka for three hours, he will be able to balance himself on his thumb. This last statement relates to the fact that one's relationship with gravity changes by the practice of pranayama. One may not realize this, but it can be measured by scientific instruments.

The relationship with gravity is one of attraction. By the practice of pranayama, this attraction loses its intensity and the laws of gravity no longer operate in full scale. This brings about the experience of weightlessness, which may eventually culminate in levitation. During or after the practice of pranayama, it is not unusual to feel a sense of lightness. Sometimes one may experience the feeling of soaring or swinging. Normally, this is only a feeling; the body remains on the ground. However, if the body were to actually rise from the ground and levitate slightly, the nervous system would be significantly impacted. The quality of sleep, dreams and thinking are based on a certain relationship with gravity. If that principle were changed, the quality of thinking and feeling would also undergo change.

The relationship with gravity is also responsible for the natural tendencies of attachment and rootedness, which cause one to fear death and cling to life. Hence, when the equation with gravity changes, dispassion arises naturally and the fear of death diminishes. For the spiritual aspirant overcoming the fear of death is an important achievement. In the *Yoga Sutras* of Maharshi Patanjali, fear of death or *abhinivesha* is listed as one of the five basic *kleshas*, or causes of pain. These kleshas have to be dissolved before enlightenment takes place. In the *Hatha Yoga Pradipika* (2:39), it is also said:

ब्रह्मादयोऽपि त्रिदशा: पवनाभ्यासतत्परा: ।
अभूवन्नंतकभयात्तस्मात्पवनमभ्यसेत् ॥

Even Brahma and other gods in heaven devote themselves to practising pranayama because it ends the fear of death. Thus it (pranayama) must be practised.

Today very few practitioners experience the siddhis attributed to the mastery of pranayama in the yogic texts, such as becoming as small as an atom or as large as a mountain. However, the adept is bound to attain some extraordinary attributes. His countenance will become striking, so that he stands apart in a crowd. The body will become lean, strong and healthy, and fat will be reduced. The voice will become sweet and melodious. There will be lustre in the face, and the eyes will sparkle. The appetite will become keen; excrements and urine will decrease. He will require fewer hours of sleep to rejuvenate him. Accordingly, the *Shiva Samhita* (3:44) states:

अरोगित्वमदीनत्वं योगिनस्तत्त्वदर्शिनः ॥

The yogi (who has achieved success in kumbhaka) acquires a disease-free and sorrow-free state.

Karmic purging
Pranayama gives purity, and the light of knowledge shines forth. There is no purificatory action greater than pranayama. The karma that covers the light and binds one to repeated births becomes ineffective and is eventually destroyed by the perfection of pranayama. The *Shiva Samhita* (3:49) says:

पूर्वार्जितानि कर्माणि प्राणायामेन निश्चितम ।
नाशयेत्साधको धीमानिहलोकोद्भवानि च ॥

The wise practitioner surely destroys all his karma, whether acquired in this life or in the past, through the regulation of breath.

Then it adds (3:51):

पापतूलचयानाहोप्रदहेत्प्रलयाग्निना ।
ततः पापविनिर्मुक्तः पश्चात्पुण्यानि नाशयेत् ॥

As the fire of annihilation burns away everything, pranayama destroys the multitude of sins. After freeing the yogi of all sins, it then destroys all his virtuous actions.

This describes the state wherein the yogi rises above the play of opposites and rests in his own Self, in supreme contentment.

13

Research on Breath and Pranayama

Medical science has done a significant amount of research on the effects of pranayama over the last few decades. Once translated as 'breathing exercises', pranayama is now recognized by scientists throughout the world as a means of invigorating, enhancing and accelerating the revitalizing processes in the body. Studies have been published on pranayama research undertaken in countries such as Australia, Russia, Turkey, Germany, USA, India and others. Some of the studies are summed up here to indicate modern understanding of an ancient science propounded through intuition and depth of experience.

Breathing

Worldwide surveys have found that most people do not breathe correctly. The majority of the population do not breathe enough to fulfil the needs of the body and brain. Breathing affects almost all the functions of the body, including the heart. Investigations have been carried out on yogis who could stop their heart at will. It was found that when the heart stopped, the breath stopped as well, but the yogis continued to live.

In 1977, such an experiment was conducted on a 102-year old yogi. He was buried underground for nine days, and after six days he was declared clinically dead. The electrodes that were recording his pulse rate indicated that his heart had stopped, which meant that his brain was being deprived of oxygen. On the ninth day, he emerged from the 'grave' in perfect health as testified by the medical doctors and scientists attending the demonstration.

This may not be a great spiritual feat, but it is certainly a scientific feat and guideline. Through the breath the involuntary processes of the body, brain and mind can be mastered. Control over these processes enables one to direct the major course and destiny of one's life and death. Now it is also established that conscious breathing is registered in the frontal brain (responsible for evolution and higher awareness), while spontaneous breathing is recorded in the primitive brain, once again validating the accuracy of yogic discovery.

In research that Stephen Elliott[1] carried out in Texas, USA, it was documented that the breath rate has a direct relationship with the heart rate. The average pattern of breathing significantly influences the general state of the heart. It can induce hypertension or relaxation, and impacts the overall health and longevity of an individual. He concurred that those who habituate themselves to slow, deep abdominal breathing (through practices such as pranayama) are healthier. Elliott came upon his findings after several years of personal yogic practice and established the circular relationship between breath and states of mind. With the help of electromyography, the shift towards autonomous balance with relatively slower, deeper and synchronous breathing was verified.

All over the world, sports institutes have also been researching the effects of breathing on performance. Among the initial researchers, Bowerman and Brown (1971) suggested that the breathing should be steady and rhythmic for athletes to master speed. They recommended learning to exhale in patterns that coincide with foot strikes, and suggested puffing the cheeks just before exhaling (in other words, kumbhaka) to enhance carbon dioxide/oxygen exchange in the lungs. Bramble and Carrier (1983) also observed that the higher the performance levels of runners, the greater the tendency to exhale rhythmically, in synchronicity with their footsteps.

Thomas Miller, a physical trainer, carried out a research in which he administered standing, high cadence/intensity bike interval training to two groups of matched, experienced runners. In his book *Programmed to Run*, he explained how one group was taught breathing skills while the other group did only physical training. Post-training testing results showed that although both groups had similar physiological characteristics, the 'breathers' stayed on the treadmill longer and improved more in the 10-km time trials than did their peers. In other words, the focus on their breathing helped them become more efficient than the runners who focused on effort instead. The breathers were also seen to possess greater awareness of their circumstances (such as increases in elevation on the treadmill) and could adjust the breathing to sustain their speed longer.

Pranayama as therapy

The yogis who expounded on the practices of pranayama knew that a sustained and systematic practice would relieve the practitioner of various diseases. In the *Hatha Yoga Pradipika* (2:17), it has been said, "Hiccups, asthma, coughs, headache, ear and eye pain, and various other diseases are due to disturbances of the vital air." It is also known that the yogis who live in the Himalayas survive on very little food and water, and are able to withstand the extreme cold without any traditional methods of insulation.

In the former Soviet Union, research was conducted on yogic practices from this point of view. Scientists researched the effects of pranayama on resistance and immunity, not only to external or internal agents, but also to the influences of the planets. Astronauts were sent into space after being trained in pranayama, and it was found that they were able to endure the altered external environment much more easily than those who had not received the training. It was concurred that the practice of pranayama improves the resistance of all the systems that are required to defend the body from extraneous factors.

Numerous other studies on pranayama have established that the practices reduce stress and hypertension, normalize blood pressure (both high and low), alleviate heart disease, increase vitality and lung capacity, and balance the relationship between the brain hemispheres. It has also been found that pranayama results in a synchronous flow of alpha, delta and theta waves, which harmonizes brain and heart activity.

Pranayama practices combined with asanas and/or relaxation practices have produced significant, and in some cases remarkable, improvements in chronic diseases in controlled experiments. Heart disease[2] and hypertension[3] have received the most attention. There have also been significant results for chronic lung disease[4].

The stress reduction benefits of slow, deep, diaphragmatic breathing suggest that pranayama practices are a valuable component of integrated treatment programs. A study by A. L. Scopp[5] found that treatment with both yogic breathing practices and a physical relaxation procedure produced significantly lower state and trait anxiety than either the breathing or relaxation treatments alone.

Research on nadi shodhana

Nadi shodhana pranayama is one of the most important practices in yoga. In 2002, the Yoga Research Foundation (YRF), Munger, India, undertook a research project to study some of the basic psycho-physiological effects of nadi shodhana pranayama on healthy subjects. Twenty-two resident students of BSY in the age group of 19 to 62 years were studied for a period of six months. The students practised nadi shodhana with the ratio of 1:1 (count of 10:10) and then 1:2 (count of 10:20), doing ten rounds daily. The parameters of the research were: performance speed in repetitive mathematical task, breath holding time (BHT), peak expiratory flow, systolic and diastolic blood pressure, pulse rate, effects on swara and pranic experiences.

140

Overall, it was found that performance speed in repetitive mathematical task increased in the whole group and BHT and peak expiratory flow showed improvement all throughout. It is interesting that the older age group showed more benefit from BHT as compared to the middle or younger age group. BHT being an indicator of health of cardiac and respiratory systems, it is likely that the older age group, which is more prone to blockages in the vascular system, benefited more from the purifying action of nadi shodhana pranayama. The overall cardiovascular effect showed stimulation during early phases as the subjects were trying to achieve a predetermined pattern of breathing. As their bodies got adjusted to this pattern, balance in the autonomous nervous system became manifest. In terms of swara, significant change was recorded in the balanced flow in the two nostrils. Pranic experiences at ajna were more noticeable as compared to those at mooladhara.

In another study conducted by YRF in 2007 on 30 hypertensive adults in Bhopal in association with the national corporate organization Bharat Heavy Electricals Ltd. (BHEL), it was found that the practice of nadi shodhana pranayama for one month (ratio of 1:1 without kumbhaka) brought down both systolic and diastolic blood pressures. The systolic BP came down by 10 mmHg on an average by the end of two minutes and continued to fall during and after the practice (total 14.5 mmHg). The diastolic BP showed parallel changes with total fall of 4.2 mmHg. This indicated that the sympathetic overtone in the subjects was reduced through the practice.

Research on ujjayi

YRF also conducted a study in 2006 in Bhopal on the effects of ujjayi pranayama. Twenty-two asthmatics, eleven hypertensives and seven healthy adults practised ujjayi for over one month for five minutes every day. The asthmatics gained the most from the practice. Oxygen saturation or the amount of oxygen assimilated into blood increased from 0.75 percent up to five percent (maximum), the average being two percent – a significant percentage clinically.

Ujjayi pranayama creates positive airway pressure due to constant partial contraction of the glottis and prevents closure of smaller bronchi towards the end of exhalation. This is especially helpful in asthmatics to improve oxygenation and empty the lungs more fully (minimizing air trapping), thus allowing the next inhalation to be more effective. The slower rate of breathing encourages laminar or steady flow in contrast to the turbulent flow during a bronchospasm, reducing airway resistance to the airflow so there is less work for the respiratory muscles. The asthmatic has to spend less energy for the act of breathing and the level of fatigue experienced during acute asthma is reduced. For these reasons, ujjayi is very useful during an actual attack of asthma.

For the hypertensives, practice of ujjayi resulted in a significant fall in systolic BP (by 20 mmHg) and diastolic BP (5 mmHg) which continued for two minutes after the end of practice.

Research on bhramari

Bhramari provided the basis for a clinical research project carried out in 1993 by Munger Hospital, India, in cooperation with Bihar School of Yoga. Dr. Vibha Singh examined 448 pregnant women over one year. All underwent the same treatment (medical check-ups, dietary advice, pre-birth instruction, etc.) with the exception of 112 women, who practised bhramari 1–2 times a day for 5–10 minutes during their entire pregnancy and continued to do so in the first phase of the actual birth. The report[6] produced the following results for the bhramari group:

- Normal blood pressure for all, compared to 25% in the control group with high blood pressure (high blood pressure is a normal occurrence during pregnancy)
- Lower number of miscarriages (2% compared to 8%)
- Fewer premature births (2.6% compared to 5%)
- 25% shorter labour
- Generally little pain during labour

142

- Only one case (1%) of Caesarean section compared to 4% in the control group
- None of the newborns suffered from lack of oxygen (0% against 12%)
- Greater average weight for the newborns (3325 g compared to 2850 g).

The results indicate that the regular practice of bhramari during pregnancy alleviates anxiety and stress. The hormone balance of the women is better regulated, which promotes the birth of healthy children.

In another study conducted by Dr. Singh, bhramari provided multiple benefits in surgical patients, showing shorter healing time, less infection, reduced requirement of anaesthetic and fewer post-operative problems overall.

There is ample evidence that bhramari works as a stress reducer. The vibrations of the humming sound influence different parts of the brain, eliminating anxiety and promoting a calm state of mind. Bhramari also stimulates the hypothalamus, the pineal and the pituitary glands.

The reason behind the tranquillizing effects of bhramari is pointed out by an experiment conducted by dermatologist A.B. Lerner and his colleagues in 1959 at the Yale School of Medicine, USA[7]. They were looking for a cure for melanoma, skin cancer caused by an excess of melanin, and found that the pineal gland secreted a hormone, now known as melatonin, which inhibits melanin formation. However, what they also found was that the injection of this hormone put the laboratory animals to sleep. Melatonin is a natural tranquillizer produced by the body, like endorphins, which are painkillers. As bhramari stimulates the pineal gland, it is able to create its signature effects.

Research on kapalbhati and bhastrika

Normally, hyperventilation would have an adverse effect on the body, causing dizziness and other symptoms. Studies have shown, however, that when yogic rapid breathing techniques such as bhastrika and kapalbhati are performed, these negative symptoms do not manifest. In a research paper, Wenger and Bagchi[8] noted that the pattern of heart rate, finger temperature and pulse volume were different during kapalbhati than during normal hyperventilation. Kuvalayananda and Karambelkar[9] also noted that mean carbon dioxide concentrations of alveolar air after kapalbhati were similar to resting levels, not lower as occurs with hyperventilation. In a study conducted by YRF at Munger in 2004, it was found that when 21 healthy adults practised bhastrika (five rounds in progressive stages for five weeks) the post-practice pulse rate and BP readings showed a downward trend. This was especially true when bhastrika was performed with external retention and bandhas.

Frostell, Pande and Hedenstierna[10] found that the average arterial carbon dioxide partial pressure was slightly (14%) reduced but within the normal range during a predominantly thoracic variation of bhastrika. All research indicates average tidal volumes during kapalbhati of about 35 to 55 percent of the average resting tidal volume. It is concurred that carbon dioxide concentration in expired air is lower during yogic rapid breathing than during normal breathing because total ventilation increases more than carbon dioxide production.

It has also been found that the heart rate accelerates during the first 20 to 40 seconds of the yogic rapid breathing practices and then levels off at the faster rate. The degree of heart rate increase varies with the intensity and type of rapid breathing.   For a healthy adult, bhastrika and kapalbhati provide significant exercise for the respiratory muscles with only a mild to moderate overall body work output. The average oxygen consumption rates during kapalbhati have been 1.1 to 1.8 times higher than while sitting quietly[11]. It has also been reported that average oxygen consumption increases as duration of rapid breathing increases from one to five minutes. Research[12] found that bhastrika at about 4 breaths per second, maintained continuously for 30 to 60 minute periods, increased oxygen uptake compared to sitting quietly by a factor of three, which was about 23 percent of maximal aerobic capacity and an over 200-fold increase in respiratory work. Likewise, the high heart rates observed[13] during bhastrika are consistent with moderate rather than mild work loads. The YRF (2004) study observed that when external retention was practised after the rapid breathing of bhastrika, oxygen saturation decreased. When external retention was combined with maha bandha, the effect was profound and oxygen saturation decreased up to 54 percent (maximum).

These practices can prove to be useful for persons with chronic obstructive lung disease when performed under expert guidance, because their activities can be limited by respiratory muscle endurance. However, they should use caution with rapid breathing, as it has been found that indiscriminate practice can exacerbate a condition. The YRF study, when it used a pulse oxymeter in the fourth week of the experiment, found that the changes in the pulse rate and oxygen saturation of blood during the various phases of bhastrika (including external kumbhaka and maha bandha) were very rapid. This confirms the repeated advice to practise caution, for such fluctuations will tax a weak heart, and an individual with heart, circulatory, respiratory and brain disorders may not be able to tolerate them. Similarly, when an organ is damaged, the fall in oxygen supply can further deteriorate its function.

It has also been recorded that while practising kapalbhati, bhastrika, surya bheda and moorchha pranayamas, there is awakening of extra electrical impulses in the central autonomous system, resulting in extra activity in the brain. The electrical voltage becomes at least 20 times higher than normal. In yogic terms, this indicates the awakening of sushumna. This is supported by the YRF (2004) study, which showed a change of swara to sushumna in most cases after the practice.

Research on kumbhaka

Breath retention can initiate powerful parasympathetic and sympathetic reflexes. The net psycho-physiological effects depend greatly on various physical and psychological parameters

145

during the retention. It has been noticed that increased blood carbon dioxide concentrations from kumbhaka cause opening of the nasal airways. In an inactive person the heart rate commonly decreases by roughly 10 percent, if the breath is held after maximum inhalation[14]. The heart rate shows little change if the breath suspension is after normal exhalation, and it increases or shows little change if suspension is after maximum exhalation[15]. These and other studies also verify that the breath can be held much longer after inhalation than after exhalation.

Exhalation pressure against the closed airway during breath holding causes sympathetic activity and increases the heart rate; whereas inhalation pressure causes parasympathetic activity and can reduce the heart rate[16]. Strong exhalation pressure can increase the heart rate by over 30 percent above the baseline rate. Control of pressure in the lungs requires deliberate effort because respiratory system elasticity leads to exhalation pressure if the respiratory muscles are relaxed after inhalation. Thus, the slowing of the heart rate from kumbhaka can be cancelled unless tension is maintained in the respiratory muscles.

Kumbhaka also causes vasoconstriction and decreased blood flow to the limbs, but a well-maintained flow to the brain and heart[17]. The reduced peripheral blood flow is accentuated by exhalation pressure during kumbhaka[18]. Psychological factors can override or enhance the responses to kumbhaka. Mental distraction or preoccupation during kumbhaka can attenuate or eliminate the cardiovascular responses[19].

Schmidt[20] observed large rhythmic swings in heart rate and blood pressure during advanced pranayama practices by a subject with over five years of experience. Heart rate during nadi shodhana (at the ratio of 1:4:2, with about one breath per minute) increased to about 120 beats per minute during kumbhaka and quickly decreased to about 60 bpm during the slow exhalation. Blood pressure in the left brachial artery decreased to about 55/30 mmHg (systolic/diastolic) during kumbhaka and quickly increased to about 150/65 mmHg during the slow exhalation. The baseline resting heart rate was about 70 bpm and blood pressure about 105/50 mmHg.

It has also been observed that the experience of enhanced energy, mental and physical balance, calmness and mental clarity associated with the pranayama practices increases greatly after several years of practice. The beginners following the same techniques do not show such strong physiological changes.

Research has also been conducted on health threats of kumbhaka on people with abnormalities. It has been found that breath retention can induce a variety of cardiac arrhythmias[21], but these appear to be a health threat only for people with significant pre-existing heart abnormalities[22]. Thus, the yogic precaution that kumbhaka techniques should be introduced gradually and only with proper guidance appear to be scientifically valid, particularly in the absence of a thorough heart examination. The techniques appear to pose no threat when done properly and introduced gradually for normal subjects.

Research on kumbhaka with bandhas

When kumbhaka is performed with bandhas the heart rate for relatively inexperienced subjects increases only slightly or shows no change. In one experiment it was noted that the average heart rate increased about 8 percent during full inhalation kumbhaka with jalandhara bandha compared to the average baseline rate[23]. The six subjects had about seven weeks of experience with the bandha. The average heart rate showed no change from the baseline rate during uddiyana bandha in a study with 39 subjects with less than eight months training[24].

In another study, which included moola bandha, the average heart rate increased by about 10 percent with 28 subjects[25]. Similar heart rate responses were found in subjects with no previous experience and in subjects with at least six months training. However, certain individuals may show a striking heart rate decrease during kumbhaka. The heart rate of a healthy 21-year old male slowed to 34 beats per minute while doing kumbhaka with uddiyana bandha after three weeks of practice[26]. Heart rate was normal before and after the practice.

Radiological and direct observation indicated that the expanded chest during the practice of mahabandha (combination of jalandhara, uddiyana and moola bandhas) avoided physical pressure on the heart and blood vessels, and maintained blood flow to and from the head[27]. The researchers also reported that the shape of the heart indicated good venous return. Contraction of the abdominal muscles greatly increases venous return and cardiac output[28]. In fact, pilots discovered early in aviation that undesirable effects of G-forces could be alleviated in part by tightening of the stomach muscles and taking a deep breath, thus enhancing venous return to the heart.

Conclusion

More research is required to validate pranayama scientifically and help understand how it aids wellbeing. Some of the studies mentioned here are preliminary and often research is hampered by lack of funding and access to practitioners and equipment. Innovators have tried to develop new methods of measuring subtle changes and processes, but it is also important that the various strands are collated. When science uses the experience handed down by yogis for thousands of years it is tapping into a vast resource that may uncover new insights into life and how it works.

References

[1] Elliott, Stephen & Edmonson, Dee, *The New Science of Breath – Coherent Breathing for Autonomic Nervous System Balance, Health, & Well Being*, RN.

[2] Ornish, D., Brown, S., Scherwitz, L.W., Billings, J.H., Armstrong, W.T., Ports, T.A., McLanahan, S.M., Kirkeeide, R.L., Brand, R.J., & Gould, K.L. (1990), 'Can Lifestyle Changes Reverse Coronary Heart Disease?' *The Lancet*, 336, 129–133.

Ornish, D., Gotto, A.M., Miller, R.R., Rochelle, D., McAllister, G, et al. (1979). 'Effects of Vegetarian Diet and Selected Yoga Techniques in the Treatment of Coronary Heart Disease', *Clinical Research*, 27, 720A.

Ornish, D., Scherwitz, L.W., Doody, R.S., Kesten, D., McLanahan, S., Brown, S.E., DePuey, G., Sonnemaker, R., Haynes, C., Lester, J., McAllister, G.K., Hall, R.J., Burdine, J.A., Gotto, A.M. (1983), 'Effects of Stress Management Training and Dietary Changes in Treating Ischemic Heart Disease', *Journal of the American Medical Association*, 249, 54–59.

[3] Irvine, M.J., Johnston, D.W., Jenner, D.A., & Marie, G.V. (1986), 'Relaxation and Stress Management in the Treatment of Essential Hypertension', *Journal of Psychosomatic Research*, 30, 437–450.

Patel, C., Marmot, M.G., Terry, D.J. (1981), 'Controlled Trial of Biofeedback-Aided Behavioural Methods in Reducing Mild Hypertension', *British Medical Journal*, 282, 2005–2008.

Patel, C., North, W.R.S. (1975, July 19), 'Randomized Controlled Trial of Yoga and Bio-Feedback in Management of Hypertension', *The Lancet*, 93–95.

[4] Kulpati, D.D.S., Kamath, R.K., Chauhan, M.R. (1982), 'The Influence of Physical Conditioning by Yogasanas and Breathing Exercises in Patients of Chronic Obstructive Lung Disease', *Journal of the Association of Physicians of India*, 30, 865–868.

Tandon, M.K. (1978), 'Adjunct Treatment with Yoga in Chronic Severe Airways Obstruction', *Thorax*, 33, 514–517.

[5] Scopp, A.L. (1974), 'Anxiety Reduction through Breathing and Muscle Relaxation Training: Cognitive and Affective Concomitants', Unpublished doctoral dissertation, Duke University.

[6] Singh Vibha, 'The Role of Bhramari in Pregnancy', *Yoga*, January 1995.

[7] Lerner, A.B., Case, J.D., Heinzelman, R.W., 'Structure of Melatonin', *Journal of American Chem. Soc.*, 81:6084, 1959.

[8] Wenger, M.A., Bagchi, B.K. (1961), 'Studies of Autonomic Functions in Practitioners of Yoga in India', *Behavioural Science*, 6, 312–323.

[9] Kuvalayananda, S., Karambelkar, P.V. (1957c), 'Studies of Alveolar Air-III: Carbon Dioxide Concentrations in Resting Alveolar Air', *Yoga-Mimamsa*, 7(2), 79–86.

[10] Frostell, C., Pande, N.N., Hedenstierna, G. (1983), 'Effects of High-Frequency Breathing on Pulmonary Ventilation and Gas Exchange', *Journal of Applied Physiology*, 55, 1854–1861.

[11] Gore, M.M., Gharote, M.L. (1987), 'Immediate Effect of One Minute Kapalbhati on Respiratory Functions', *Yoga-Mimamsa*, 25(3&4), 14–23.

Karambelkar, P.V., Bhole, M.V. (1988), 'Respiratory Studies during Kapalbhati for 1, 2, 3 and 5 Minutes', *Yoga-Mimamsa*, 27(1&2), 69–74.

Karambelkar, P.V., Deshapande, R.R., Bhole, M.V. (1982), 'Some Respiratory Studies in Respect of Kapalbhati and Voluntary Hyperventilation', *Yoga-Mimamsa*, 21(1&2), 54–58.

Miles, W.R. (1964), 'Oxygen Consumption during Three Yoga-Type Breathing Patterns', *Journal of Applied Physiology*, 19, 75–82.

[12] Frostell, C., Pande, N.N., Hedenstierna, G. (1983), 'Effects of High-Frequency Breathing on Pulmonary Ventilation and Gas Exchange', *Journal of Applied Physiology*, 55, 1854–1861.

[13] Hoffman, K., Clarke, J. (1982), 'A Comparative Study of the Cardiac Response to Bhastrika', *Research Bulletin of the Himalayan International Institute*, 4(2), 7–16.

[14] Lin, Y. (1982), 'Breath-Hold Diving in Terrestrial Mammals', *Exercise and Sport Sciences Reviews*, 10, 270–307.

[15] Angelone, A., Coulter, N.A. (1965), 'Heart Rate Response to Held Lung Volume', *Journal of Applied Physiology*, 20, 464–468.

Kawakami, Y., Natelson, B.H., DuBois, A.B. (1967), 'Cardiovascular Effects of Face Immersion and Factors Affecting Diving Reflex in Man', *Journal of Applied Physiology*, 23, 964–970.

Openshaw, P.J.M., Woodroof, G.M.F. (1978), 'Effect of Lung Volume on the Diving Response in Man', *Journal of Applied Physiology*, 45, 783–785.

Song, S.H., Lee, W.K., Chung, Y.A., Hong, S.K. (1969), 'Mechanisms of Apneic Bradycardia in Man', *Journal of Applied Physiology*, 27, 323–327.

[16] Craig, A.B. (1963), 'Heart Rate Responses to Apneic Underwater Diving and to Breath Holding in Man', *Journal of Applied Physiology*, 18, 854–862.

Paulev, P. (1968), 'Cardiac Rhythm during Breath-Holding and Water Immersion in Man', *Acta Physiologica Scandinavica*, 73, 139–150.

Paulev, P., Honda, Y., Sakakibara, Y., Morikawa, T., Tanaka, Y., Nakamura, W. (1988), 'Brady- and Tachycardia in Light of the Valsalva and Mueller Manoeuvre (Apnea)', *Japanese Journal of Physiology*, 38, 507–517.

Sharpey-Schafer, E.P. (1965), 'Effect of Respiratory Acts on the Circulation', *Handbook of Physiology*, Sec. 2. Circulation: Vol. III, 1875–1886, American Physiological Society.

Song, S.H., Lee, W.K., Chung, Y.A., Hong, S.K. (1969), 'Mechanisms of Apneic Bradycardia in Man', *Journal of Applied Physiology*, 27, 323–327.

[17] Brick, I. (1966), 'Circulatory Responses to Immersing the Face in Water', *Journal of Applied Physiology*, 21, 33–36.

Elsner, R., Franklin, D.L., Van Citters, R.L., Kenney, D.W. (1966), 'Cardiovascular Defence against Asphyxia', *Science*, 153, 941–949.

Heistad, D.D., Abboud, F.M., Eckstein, J.W. (1968), 'Vasoconstrictor Response to Simulated Diving in Man', *Journal of Applied Physiology*, 25, 542–549.

[18] Paulev, P. (1969), 'Respiratory and Cardiovascular Effects of Breath Holding', *Acta Physiologica Scandinavica*, Suppl. 324, 1–110.

[19] Ross, A., Steptoe, A. (1980), 'Attenuation of the Diving Reflex in Man by Mental Stimulation', *Journal of Physiology*, 302, 387–393.

Wolf, S. (1978), 'Psychophysiological Influences on the Dive Reflex in Man', in P.J. Schwartz, A.M. Brown, A. Malliani, A. Zanchetti (Eds.), *Neural Mechanisms in Cardiac Arrhythmias*, 237–250, New York: Raven.

Wolf, S., Schneider, R.A., Groover, M.E. (1965), 'Further Studies of the Circulatory and Metabolic Alteration of the Oxygen-Conserving (Diving) Reflex in Man', *Transactions of the Association of American Physicians*, 78, 242–254.

[20] Schmidt, T.H. (1983), 'Cardiovascular Reactions and Cardiovascular Risk', in T. M. Dembroski, T.H. Schmidt, G. Blumchen (Eds.), *Bio-behavioural Bases of Coronary Heart Disease*, 130–174, Basel, Switzerland: Karger.

[21] Lamb, L.E., Dermksian, G., Sarnoff, C.A. (1958), 'Significant Cardiac Arrhythmias Induced by Common Respiratory Maneuvers', *American Journal of Cardiology*, 2, 563–571.

Olsen, C.R., Fanestil, D.D., Scholander, P.F. (1962), 'Some Effects of Breath Holding and Apneic Underwater Diving on Cardiac Rhythm in Man', *Journal of Applied Physiology*, 17, 461–466.

Whayne, T.F., Killip, T. (1967), 'Simulated Diving in Man: Comparison of Facial Stimuli and Response in Arrhythmia', *Journal of Applied Physiology*, 22, 800–807.

[22] Paulev, P. (1969), 'Respiratory and Cardiovascular Effects of Breath Holding', *Acta Physiologica Scandinavica*, Suppl. 324, 1–110.

[23] Bhole, M.V. (1979), 'Some Studies of Jalandhara Bandha during Breath-Holding in Beginners', *Yoga-Mimamsa*, 19(4), 27–35.

[24] Oak, J.P., Bhole, M.V. (1984), 'Pulse Rate during and after Bahya Kumbhaka with Different Conditions of the Abdominal Wall', *Yoga-Mimamsa*, 22 (3&4), 71–76.

[25] Gopal, K.S., Anantharaman, V., Balachander, S., Nishith, S.D. (1973), 'The Cardiorespiratory Adjustments in Pranayama with and without Bandhas, in Vajrasana', *Indian Journal of Medical Science*, 27, 686–692.

[26] Monjo, P.D.V., Gharote, M.L., Bhagwat, J.M. (1984), 'Effect of Kapalbhati and Uddiyana Bandha on Cardia Rhythms', *Yoga-Mimamsa*, 23 (1), 41–62.

[27] Gopal, K.S., Lakshamanan, S. (1972), 'Some Observations on Hatha Yoga: the Bandhas', *Indian Journal of Medical Science*, 26, 564–574.

[28] Guyton, Arthur C. (1986), *Textbook of Medical Physiology* (7th ed.), Philadelphia: W. B. Saunders.

Pranayama Practice:
I: Pre-Pranayama Training

14

Conscious Breathing

A yogi measures the span of life by the number of breaths, not by the number of years.

—*Swami Sivananda*

Breathing is a natural process and the normal rate is 15 breaths per minute, 900 breaths per hour and 21,600 breaths per 24 hours. When the breathing rate is increased, longevity is decreased. At the rate of fifteen breaths per minute one will live up to 75 or 80 years. At the rate of ten breaths per minute the lifespan is lengthened to about 100 years. The lifespan is shortened when the breathing rate is above 15 breaths per minute, as in the case of a dog that lives for 10 or 15 years. Quick, shallow breathing is an ageing factor as well as being detrimental to physical and emotional wellbeing, integration and balance. One should become conscious of the breath and learn to maintain the normal breathing rate of fifteen breaths per minute. If one relaxes the body, stops worrying, and becomes aware of the breath for a minute or so, the breathing rate will drop down to fifteen.

Incorrect and irregular breathing often reflects various disturbances in the body and mind. One is familiar with the disruption in the breathing pattern associated with pain or powerful emotions. A sob of grief, a startled gasp, and the deep trembling breaths of anger are well known examples of how emotion affects the breathing. This process also works the other way around. Correct breathing profoundly improves one's physical and mental wellbeing. Therefore, the first prerequisite of pranayama is conscious breathing, whereby it becomes possible to correct the breathing habits. In order to develop conscious breathing, one must free the mind from emotional tension.

The breath is perhaps the only physiological process that can be either voluntary or involuntary. One can breathe consciously and control the breathing process or one can breathe reflexively or unconsciously. If the breath is unconscious, it falls under the control of primitive parts of the brain, where emotions, thoughts and feelings of which one has little or no awareness become involved. However, the moment one starts to breathe consciously, the frontal brain registers the breath, allowing control of the different hemispheres of the brain.

Natural breath awareness

The breath should become a part of one's constant awareness. The first step towards achieving this is to simply become aware of the breathing process. Without awareness, nothing can be achieved in regard to the breath. Although the breathing process continues twenty-four hours a day, one is neither aware nor in control of this vital process. The following techniques can be used to develop increased awareness of the breathing process.

Counting the breath

Sit comfortably or lie in shavasana and practise *kaya sthairyam*, complete body stillness, for a few minutes.

Become aware of the natural breath.

Do not try to change the breathing pattern; just become aware of the natural incoming and outgoing breath.

Observe this natural process that has been occurring throughout your life, and which has always been taken for granted. You breathe day and night, yet normally you are unaware of even one breath.

Be aware now of each and every breath.

Do not interfere with the natural rhythm of your breathing; simply witness each respiration.

Become increasingly conscious of the breath; let yourself relax into its continual, smooth ebb and flow.

Come closer to the breath and observe how it is flowing.

Is the breath fast or slow, shallow or deep, regular or irregular?

Is there any gap in between breaths? Are you sometimes gasping for breath?

Do not modify or control the breath in any way.

Just observe each breath as a silent witness and make a mental note of how you are breathing.

Keep your awareness on each and every inhalation and exhalation, without missing a single breath.

Say to yourself mentally, "I am aware that I am breathing in; I am aware that I am breathing out." Continue in this way.

Now count your breath backwards from 27 to zero.

Mentally say, "I am aware that I am breathing in; I am aware that I am breathing out, 27. I am aware that I am breathing in; I am aware that I am breathing out, 26," and so on.

Continue counting in this manner until you reach zero.

If you lose count at any point begin again from 27. The object is not to reach zero, but to keep your awareness fixed on every breath. Each number must register in your conscious awareness.

Awareness of the breath enables you to relax, but when you lose this awareness there is tension. So count without losing awareness and without making any mistakes.

When you reach zero, end the practice.

Leave the awareness of the breath and become aware of the body.

Gradually extrovert the awareness and slowly open the eyes.

Mechanics of breathing

Sit in a comfortable position and practise kaya sthairyam for a few minutes. Alternatively you may lie in shavasana and relax the whole body.

Become aware of the natural breathing process without altering the breath in any way.

Be totally aware of the spontaneous and rhythmic flow of the breath.

Now, focus the awareness on the breath in the nostrils.

Be aware that you are breathing through the nostrils.

Feel the breath entering the nostrils and flowing up the nasal passages.

The breath feels cool as it enters the nostrils upon inhalation, and warm as it flows out of the nostrils upon exhalation.

Continue observing this process as a detached witness.

Now feel the passage of air in the throat behind the nostrils.

Be aware of the sensation created by this movement of the breath.

Feel the breath at the back of the mouth.

Feel the breath flowing down and up the throat passage.

Feel the air passing down the throat as you inhale and up the throat as you exhale.

Next, focus the awareness at the chest.

Be aware of the lungs expanding with each inhalation and contracting with each exhalation.

As you inhale, feel the oxygenated breath flowing into the lungs and becoming absorbed.

As you exhale, feel the carbon dioxide being gathered up and expelled by the lungs.

Be aware of the expansion and contraction of the ribcage with each breath.

Do not force these movements; let the entire process be spontaneous.

Bring your awareness down to the diaphragm, a sheet of muscle separating the lungs from the abdominal organs.

Become aware of the movement of the diaphragm. Feel

it moving downward as you inhale, and upward as you exhale.

Take your awareness into this movement.

You will notice that the movement of the diaphragm is also producing a rhythmical motion in the abdominal region.

Become aware of the whole breathing process from nostrils to abdomen.

Be aware of each component in the action of breathing.

Continue in this way for some time.

End the practice and leave this awareness of the breathing process.

Bring your awareness back to the whole body.

Become aware of the external surroundings and then open your eyes.

Heightening breath awareness

The above practices create an initial awareness of the breath. The following practices deepen this awareness, enhance sensitivity to the respiratory system and develop an awareness of total breathing. This prepares one to experience the subtleties of the breathing process, so that the effects of pranayama can be understood.

Respiratory system awareness

Lie down in shavasana or sit in a comfortable posture. Make sure that the spine and head are in one straight line, with the shoulders, back, neck and arms relaxed.

Be aware of the whole body and of relaxation.

Now become aware of the area from the abdomen to the nose. Focus the awareness on this region only and try to feel it as one unit.

This is the area of respiration from the abdomen up to the nose.

Develop the awareness of the breath in this area.

Now bring the awareness to the nose and to the breath in the nostrils.

Mentally see the hairs in the nasal passages that form a filter for the dirt and dust.

See the sensitive mucous membrane that lines the nasal cavities and warms and moistens the incoming air, making it acceptable to the lungs.

Feel the breath passing over the hairs and the mucous membrane with its nerve connections to the brain, which subtly influences the whole nervous system.

Now bring the awareness to the sinus cavity, behind the nose.

Inside the sinus cavity there are scroll-like bones and intricate airway passages. Feel the breath flowing through this cavity.

What do you smell as you inhale? Intensify this awareness of smell.

Travel from the nasal chambers down into the throat.

The opening of the throat is above the soft palate at the back of the mouth.

The throat leads to the pharynx, which stretches down to the larynx, where the vocal cords are situated.

Feel the breath passing up and down the back of the throat, through the vocal cords and trachea or windpipe.

Follow the breath down the windpipe into the chest.

Just behind the breastbone, in front of the oesophagus, the trachea divides into two tubes called bronchi, one entering the left lung and the other entering the right lung.

Each bronchial tube divides itself into several tree-like branches or bronchioles, which again divide into smaller and smaller tubes.

Visualize the air flowing down the trachea, dividing at the junction of the bronchi and branching out further into smaller and smaller bronchioles.

Clustered around these smallest of tubes are tiny air sacs known as alveoli.

Intertwined with the alveoli are minute blood vessels.

All this forms a spongy substance, called the lung.

Feel the breath reaching these air sacs and being absorbed.

The oxygen in the breath is filtered through these air sacs into the blood vessels, which carry this enriched blood to the heart to be pumped to all parts of the body.

The blood vessels also bring impure blood, loaded with carbon dioxide, to be exhaled with the breath from the lungs. Visualize this exchange also.

For the next few minutes follow each inhalation from the nostrils to the lungs, then the exhalation from the lungs to the nostrils.

Become intimately attuned to every detail of the breath, from the flow of air in the nasal passages to the exchange of oxygen and carbon dioxide in the alveoli.

Now extend your awareness even further. Breathing also occurs in each and every cell of the body.

Feel the oxygenated blood flowing from the lungs into the heart and then being pumped to every portion of the body, to the deepest internal organs and the furthest extremities.

Expand the awareness into every cell.

Experience the respiration to its fullest extent, both external and internal.

End the practice and switch back to normal breathing.

Bring the awareness back to the body.

Slowly become aware of the external environment.

Sensitizing the lungs

The following two methods stretch the chest cavity, allowing for greater movement of the lungs. They are useful for chest development, preparation for pranayama, or to develop greater awareness of the movement of the lungs inside the ribcage. The first technique develops awareness of expansion in each lung separately.

Technique 1: awareness of each lung separately

Sit in vajrasana with the head and spine in one straight line. Interlock the fingers behind your neck and bend from the waist to the right side as far as is comfortable, without hunching the shoulders or bending forward.

161

Hold this position while inhaling and exhaling deeply for 10 breaths.

Feel the predominant use of the left lung in this position. Become conscious of the movement in the left lung only. Inhale returning to the upright position and exhale while bending to the left side, as far as is comfortable.

Hold this position for 10 deep breaths. Feel the predominant use of the right lung.

This may be repeated 3 times on each side.

BSY ©

Technique 2: expanding the lungs

Lie on your back with the legs folded in padmasana or any cross-legged position.

Bring the arms over the head, holding the elbow of each opposite arm. The arms should be flat on the floor.

Try to bring the knees as close as possible to the floor, stretching the pelvis.

In this position the spine becomes arched, giving a stretch to the chest, allowing maximum lung expansion.

Breathe slowly and deeply with awareness of each breath, feeling the expansion in the lungs.

Increase your awareness of the breath in the lungs.

Continue deep, regular breathing for 3–5 minutes.

15

Basic Breathing Methods

After learning to breathe consciously, it is necessary to learn to breathe completely, utilizing the full capacity of the lungs. There are three basic mechanisms of breathing: (i) abdominal or diaphragmatic, (ii) thoracic or chest and (iii) clavicular or shoulder breathing. Diaphragmatic breathing occurs when the action of the diaphragm increases and decreases the size of the thoracic cavity, whereas thoracic and clavicular breathing are produced through expansion and contraction of the ribcage. The normal breathing of an average person is a combination of thoracic and clavicular breathing. A combination of all three is known as full yogic breathing, which is a prerequisite of pranayama.

Diaphragmatic or abdominal breathing

The diaphragm separates the lungs from the abdominal cavity. In normal breathing it hardly moves, but during deep breathing it extends downward into the abdomen on inhalation and upward on exhalation, promoting the most efficient type of breathing. Less effort is expended in diaphragmatic breathing to obtain the same quantity of air. Infants and small children use their diaphragms exclusively for breathing. Chest breathing occurs only later after the bony structure of the chest matures.

Diaphragmatic breathing should be cultivated during daily life until it becomes a spontaneous habit. Nowadays, however, few have the ability to breathe with the abdomen due to tension, unhealthy habits, poor posture and tight clothing. A complete revolution in the state of physical and mental wellbeing can be obtained by mastery of this technique. Diaphragmatic breathing is particularly recommended for those suffering from chronic, obstructive lung disease. The simplest way to relax any mental tension is through abdominal breathing, as it promotes parasympathetic cardiovascular dominance. Of course, during strenuous activities, such as heavy physical work or competitive sport, greater lung capacity is required to absorb more oxygen, and then fuller breathing is required. However, in most daily situations, simple abdominal breathing is sufficient.

In abdominal breathing there is a slight movement of the lower ribcage due to abdominal expansion, but this should not be forced by the ribcage muscles. The motion of the diaphragm massages the abdominal organs and tones the muscles of the abdominal wall, thus improving digestive, metabolic and excretory functions. During abdominal breathing less strain is placed on the heart. While practising in the upright position, the effect of gravity on the abdominal organs assists the downward movement of the diaphragm.

As diaphragmatic breathing exerts a pull from the bottom of the lungs, rather than from the sides, as with thoracic breathing, the fresh air is more evenly distributed throughout the lungs. With less efficient types of breathing, pockets of stale air remain in the lobes of the lungs. In diaphragmatic breathing the tidal volume is larger and the proportion of ventilation wasted as dead space is minimized. In addition, enhanced ventilation of the lower lungs increases efficiency of gas exchange, because of greater blood flow in the lower lungs due to gravitational forces.

The base of the heart and lungs are attached to the upper surface of the diaphragm, while the liver, spleen, stomach and pancreas lie immediately beneath it and are attached to the lower surface. Increased diaphragmatic movement improves blood circulation in these organs, thus improving their performance. It also assists in the return flow of blood from the lower part of the body to the heart, which is important for cardiac output and efficiency, and helps to drain the sub-diaphragmatic lymphatic system. The vagus nerve, a parasympathetic nerve, connecting the abdominal organs, heart and lungs to the brain is also said to be massaged and toned.

X-ray observations of diaphragmatic movement have shown that relaxed, pleasant thoughts and sensations increase its movement considerably while the breath becomes slower and deeper. A wide amplitude of diaphragm movement results in slow, deep breathing while a narrow range of movement results in shallow, rapid respiration. Not only do relaxed thoughts allow muscle relaxation and greater diaphragmatic movement, but slow, relaxed breathing also calms the mind. One of the mechanisms by which this may occur is through the release of endorphins. Deep breathing has been observed to release endorphins into the bloodstream. The endorphins are potent brain chemicals, neuro-modulators, which help cope with pain and are part of the mechanism for dealing with and eliminating fear and anxiety.

The first step in re-learning proper breathing is to master abdominal breathing. Some may find it difficult at first, but with practice it becomes automatic and natural. Abdominal breathing should be practised first in shavasana, then in a sitting or standing position.

Natural abdominal breathing

Lie in shavasana and relax the whole body.
Allow the breath to become spontaneous, regular and even.
Let it be natural, not forced or controlled in any way.
Take the attention to the diaphragm and visualize it as a sheet of muscle beneath the lungs. The best place to focus the awareness is at the bottom of the sternum.

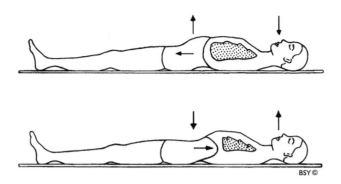

BSY©

While breathing in, visualize this dome-shaped sheet of muscle flattening and pushing downward on the abdominal organs below it. At the same time, the breath is being drawn into the lungs.

While breathing out, the diaphragm relaxes. Feel it moving upward again to resume its dome-shaped position beneath the sternum, pushing the air out of the lungs and releasing the pressure on the abdominal organs.

Increase the awareness of the movement of this interface between the chest and abdomen. Feel how its rhythmic motion produces spontaneous abdominal breathing.

Do not force the breath in any way; there should be no tension in the abdominal or chest muscles. If any tension is felt, allow it to melt away.

Diaphragmatic breathing is not produced by the abdominal muscles.

The movement of the diaphragm should feel natural and comfortable, without any resistance.

Continue natural, abdominal breathing for some time.

Now place your right hand on the abdomen, just above the navel, and the left hand over the centre of the chest.

With abdominal breathing, you will feel your right hand moving up with inhalation and down with exhalation.

There should be no tension in the abdomen.

Do not force the movement of the abdomen.

166

Your left hand should not move with the breath. Try to feel the expansion and contraction of the lungs by means of the breath.

Continue for a few minutes, until you feel that only the diaphragm is moving with the breathing process.

Controlled abdominal breathing

Lie in shavasana and relax the whole physical body.

You may place one hand on the abdomen, above the navel, if you wish.

Begin abdominal breathing and feel the abdomen moving up and down.

At the same time, the abdominal and chest muscles should remain totally relaxed.

Breathe out slowly and completely, using the diaphragm.

Feel that the movement of the diaphragm is responsible for the abdominal movement.

As you breathe out, feel the abdomen and navel moving inward towards the spine.

At the end of exhalation, the diaphragm will be totally relaxed, arching upward into the chest cavity without any contraction of the abdominal muscles.

Hold the breath out, without any strain, for a second or so.

Breathe in slowly and deeply from the diaphragm.

Try not to expand the chest or move the shoulders.

Feel the abdomen expanding and the navel rising.

Fill the lower lobes of the lungs as much as possible, without expanding the ribcage.

Hold the breath in, without effort, for a second or two.

Then, with control, exhale slowly and completely, pushing all the air out of the lungs.

Again feel the navel moving toward the spine.

At the end of exhalation the abdomen will be relaxed, the navel depressed toward the spine.

Hold the breath out for a short time, then inhale.

Repeat the whole process.

Continue the practice for 50 breaths or up to 10 minutes.

167

Thoracic breathing

Thoracic breathing is a method of producing expansion and contraction of the ribcage. In thoracic breathing this is achieved by the sets of muscles attached to the ribs and other structural parts of the body, as well as muscles acting between the ribs themselves. To inhale, certain groups of these muscles act to pull the ribcage upward, forward and outward, expanding the thoracic cavity and drawing air into the lungs. Exhalation occurs by the passive recoil of the ribcage as these muscles relax. Another set of muscles compresses the ribcage even further than this starting position, if complete expulsion of air from the lungs is required.

Thoracic breathing is a less efficient type of breathing than abdominal breathing, but is required during increased physical activity, when a greater volume of air must be drawn into the lungs. In comparison with abdominal breathing, more muscular effort is required to perform thoracic breathing for the same quantity of air. Thoracic breathing is often associated with situations of mental stress and tension, as its function is to assist the lungs to gain more oxygen in a stressful situation. However, the tendency to continue this kind of breathing often remains long after the stressful situation has disappeared, creating bad breathing habits. In fact, research has found that over 20 percent of the normal population tends towards habitual thoracic breathing.

Thoracic breathing is inefficient, because it brings the bulk of air into the middle lobes of the lungs, which are poorly supplied with blood. The alveoli towards the outer lung surface tend to expand more than is optimum, while the central alveoli do not open out properly, which creates uneven gas diffusion. If the outer alveoli open wider than is preferable, as occurs in certain disease states such as asthma and emphysema, they can also lose their elasticity. Then they remain in a fixed, open position with very little excursion for taking in air. The chest appears large and barrel shaped, but the lungs do not move well during respiration. Therefore, thoracic breathers need to take occasional deep breaths that will fill their lungs from top to bottom.

In relation to the cardiovascular system, thoracic breathing brings about reduced parasympathetic tone and increased sympathetic dominance, which are expressed in increased heart rate and cardiac output, muscle vasodilation, decreased blood flow and oxygen supply to the heart and brain, and increased likelihood of major heart abnormalities. The reduced carbon dioxide concentration in the blood is a key physiological factor underlying these effects.

Some people actually 'freeze' or immobilize the diaphragm and use the upper body to breathe in an attempt to hold back sexuality, fear, aggression and other powerful feelings. Since these emotions are associated with mooladhara, swadhishthana and manipura chakras, stiffening the diaphragm serves to isolate the associated feelings in the lower body, pushing them out of awareness. However, intentional thoracic breathing in supportive settings can also be used to induce and release strong emotions and tension as a form of therapy.

Thoracic breathing should be practised for control over the full range of breathing capacity. It is also necessary in order to perform yogic breathing and certain pranayamas. The following techniques are intended as a guide.

Thoracic breathing with passive exhalation
Lie in shavasana and relax completely.
Let the breath find its natural rhythm.
Maintain unbroken breath awareness.
Concentrate on the sides of the chest.
Discontinue any diaphragmatic breathing.
Inhale by slowly expanding the ribcage.
Feel the movement of the individual ribs outwards and upwards, drawing air into the lungs.
Expand the chest as much as possible.
Exhale by relaxing the chest muscles.
Feel the ribcage relax back to the starting position, forcing the air out of the lungs.
Breathe slowly and deeply with total awareness.

Forced Breathing

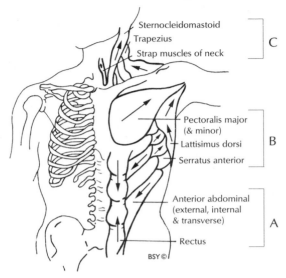

Sternocleidomastoid
Trapezius
Strap muscles of neck
C

Pectoralis major
(& minor)
Lattisimus dorsi
Serratus anterior
B

Anterior abdominal
(external, internal
& transverse)
Rectus
A

BSY ©

A: Forced abdominal movements; B: Forced chest movements
C: Forced clavicular movements

Do not use the diaphragm to assist either inhalation or exhalation.
Continue thoracic breathing, pausing slightly for a second or two after inhalation and exhalation.
Count 50 breaths.

Thoracic breathing with forced exhalation

Lie in shavasana and relax the body completely.
Commence thoracic breathing as above.
Practise for a few minutes.
Complete the next exhalation and then contract the ribcage, even beyond the natural position. You will notice that some air still remaining in the lungs after the last exhalation has just been forced out. Some abdominal tension is required to achieve this.
Now the lungs feel completely empty.

170

Commence the next inhalation, expanding the ribs naturally, and then expand them further into a full thoracic inhalation.

On the next exhalation, again compress the ribs beyond their natural resting position, forcing out all the air.

Continue with forced inhalation and exhalation, maintaining a slow steady rhythm in the breath.

Try to fully appreciate the difference between passive and forced exhalation while practising thoracic breathing.

Continue the practice, pausing for a second or two after each inhalation and exhalation.

Count 50 breaths.

Clavicular breathing

Clavicular or shoulder breathing ventilates the upper lobes of the lungs. This type of breathing takes very little effort and is commonly performed during sedentary activities. As a component of yogic breathing, it is the final stage of total ribcage expansion. It is performed after the thoracic inhalation has been completed in order to absorb a little more air into the lungs. In this type of breathing the upper ribs and collarbone are pulled upwards by the muscles on either side of the neck and throat. In daily life it occurs during such conditions as sobbing or an asthma attack.

The following practice helps to develop the mechanism of clavicular breathing, so that it can be used efficiently when required.

Clavicular breathing with thoracic breathing

Lie in shavasana and relax the whole body.

Commence thoracic breathing with passive exhalation and continue for a few minutes.

Then inhale fully, expanding the ribcage.

When the ribs are fully expanded, inhale a little more until expansion is felt in the upper portion of the lungs, just below the collarbones, which also move up slightly.

The maximum ribcage expansion takes place at this point.

171

Exhale slowly, releasing the upper chest first.
Relax the rest of the ribcage back to the normal position.
Continue for a few more breaths.
Change back to normal breathing and end the practice.

There is no need to practise shoulder breathing on its own. Just practise it long enough to be able to perform it in combination with yogic breathing.

Clavicular Action

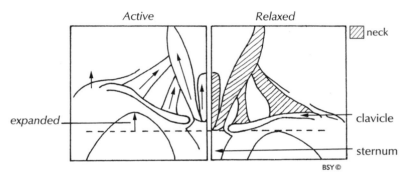

Paradoxical breathing

The gasping breath or the paradoxical breath is another method of breathing outside the domain of the three natural methods of breathing. It manifests when the need to stimulate the sympathetic nervous system is most intense. One inhales so deeply and quickly that the abdominal wall moves in during inhalation rather than out. This is what occurs in a state of shock. For example, if one takes an ice-cold shower on a winter morning the mouth will probably open and suck air in with a gasp at the first contact with the water.

This is called paradoxical breathing because the abdominal wall moves in rather than out during inhalation, and out rather than in during exhalation. Paradoxical breathing stimulates the sympathetic nervous system even more than thoracic breathing. If one were to breathe in this way for even

172

10–15 breaths, one will immediately get nervous and jumpy, for it gives an immediate jolt of adrenaline causing the fight or flight reaction. It is usually seen only in a state of acute anxiety.

Yogic breathing

In daily life one is subjected to a wide variety of situations that demand appropriate physical and mental responses. This can be observed in the changing intensity of the breathing patterns described above. The practice of yogic breathing enables one to experience the complete range of each breathing mode. This increases ventilation, as the lungs are completely filled with air and all the lobes are expanded, and bestows the numerous benefits of deep, fully-controlled breathing. As one exerts more control over the breathing process, it becomes possible to control the finer details of the mental process.

In yogic breathing, while inhaling, the lower lobes of the lungs are filled first, extending the diaphragm downward into the abdominal cavity and pushing the abdominal muscles outward. This is followed by thoracic breathing, which fills the middle lobes of the lungs, and creates an outward and upward movement of the ribcage. The inhalation is completed with clavicular breathing, which fills the upper lobes of the lungs, using the accessory muscles in the neck and shoulder girdle to further lift the ribcage.

The exhalation is the exact reverse of this process, with a combination of diaphragmatic and thoracic compression of the lungs to complete the expulsion of air. Contraction of the intercostals moves the ribcage inwards and relaxation of the abdominal muscles allows the abdominal contents to move upwards against the relaxed diaphragm muscle, producing the final expulsion of air. The lungs are stretched to maximum capacity on both inhalation and exhalation. Inhalation commences in the lower lobes of the lungs and is completed in the upper lobes. In exhalation the process is reversed. All the stale air is expelled with each outgoing breath and the next inhalation brings fresh air to all the lobes of the lungs.

The purpose of yogic breathing is to gain control over the breathing process, correct poor breathing habits and increase the oxygen intake, when necessary. Proficiency in yogic breathing means that all aspects of the breathing mechanism have come under the control of the conscious mind and can be controlled at will. This does not mean that yogic breathing should be practised at all times. During most pranayama techniques, yogic breathing is recommended. However, in pranayama it is not necessary to extend the breath into the clavicular region. The combination of abdominal and thoracic breathing is optimum and produces a comfortable rhythmic wave of inhalation and exhalation.

Advantages of yogic breathing

In yogic breathing the lungs expand vertically as well as horizontally. The vertical expansion is promoted by increased diaphragmatic movement. During normal breathing the upward and downward movement of the diaphragm is approximately one centimetre, whereas in yogic breathing this movement may be as much as three to four centimetres. The sitting postures adopted during pranayama also promote greater expansion of the lungs in a vertical axis.

Normal, quiet and unconscious breathing moves half a litre (500 ml) of air into and out of the lungs (tidal volume). About a quarter of this volume (150 ml) is unused and occupies the spaces of the trachea and bronchi, which are merely air passages in which no exchange of gases occurs. Therefore, in normal breathing only a very small volume of fresh air actually enters the alveoli in the lungs with each breath. In yogic breathing a much larger quantity of air reaches the lungs and inflates more alveolar tissue. During one full inhalation up to five litres of air may be taken in. Thus, more oxygen is made available for gas exchange with the blood.

The increased vertical movement of the diaphragm also opens the alveoli of the lungs more evenly, particularly at

174

the central, basal and apical areas of the lungs. Due to this even expansion, a greater expanse of alveolar membrane becomes available for gas exchange. The larger the surface area available, the more efficient is the gaseous exchange. In horizontal expansion, some alveoli may remain closed and collect secretions, causing them to become prone to disease. The possibility of this is reduced in yogic breathing.

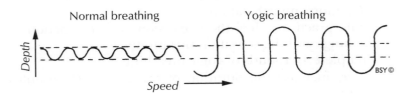

Yogic breathing

Lie down in shavasana and relax the whole body.

Inhale slowly from the diaphragm, allowing the abdomen to expand fully.

Breathe slowly and deeply so that little or no sound is heard.

Feel the air filling the bottom lobes of the lungs.

After full abdominal expansion, expand the chest outwards and upwards.

At the end of this movement, inhale a little more and feel the air filling the upper lobes of the lungs. The shoulders and collarbones should move up slightly.

This completes one inhalation.

The whole process should be one continuous movement, each phase of the breath merging into the next without any obvious demarcation point.

The breathing should be like the swell of the sea with no jerking or unnecessary strain.

Now start to exhale.

First relax the collarbones and shoulders.

Then allow the chest to relax downward and then inward.

Next, allow the diaphragm to move back up into the chest cavity.

Without straining, try to empty the lungs as much as possible by pulling the abdominal wall down towards the spine, while simultaneously contracting the ribcage further, in a smooth, harmonious movement.

This completes one round of yogic breathing.

Continue breathing in this manner.

Hold the breath for a second or two at the end of each inhalation and exhalation.

While practising, feel the expansion and contraction of the lungs and the sensation this produces.

Complete 10 rounds of yogic breathing.

Slowly increase the duration of practice to 10 minutes daily.

Do not strain the lungs in any way.

Once the technique has been mastered in shavasana, practise in the sitting position.

Awareness of the components of yogic breathing

Sit in vajrasana, siddhasana or any comfortable cross-legged posture.

Begin to practise full yogic breathing.

Place the hands lightly on the abdomen and inhale.

Feel the abdomen expanding forward.

Exhale and relax.

Repeat 5 times.

Next, place the hands on the front of the lower ribcage with the fingertips touching.

Inhale from the abdomen and continue this inhalation into the chest.

Be aware of the distance between your fingertips while inhaling and exhaling.

Repeat 5 times.

Now put your hands on the back of your ribcage and inhale. Be aware of the expansion of the chest cavity from behind.

176

Exhale and relax.

Repeat 5 times.

Finally, rest your hands just under the collarbones and inhale. While inhaling feel the collarbones and upper chest gently rising.

Exhale and relax.

Repeat this process 5 times.

16

Preliminary Breathing Practices

Each of the three elements of pranayama: pooraka, rechaka and kumbhaka, can be controlled in various ways. More benefit can be obtained from pranayama practices by increasing the degree of control over each of the elements of breathing. Breath control means altering:
- Duration of inhalation, exhalation and retention
- Depth of inhalation and exhalation
- Force of inhalation and exhalation.

Duration refers to the time taken to perform a complete inhalation, exhalation and retention. Depth refers to the degree of expansion or compression of the lungs during inhalation and exhalation. Force refers to the amount of muscular effort applied to produce inhalation and exhalation or to maintain retention.

As the pranayama practice becomes more advanced, an extended duration of breathing and retention is required. It is necessary to progress comfortably, without strain or the need to take interim breaths. Hence, along with duration, the depth of breathing should be increased in order to meet oxygen requirements. At the same time, the force of the breath should be correspondingly minimized to decrease oxygen consumption and tension in the body. The following techniques are suggested to gradually extend breathing capacity.

Deep breathing practice

This practice should be performed for a few minutes daily in the fresh air of early morning. Each deep breath consists of a full inhalation and a long steady exhalation through the nose. The breath should be inhaled and exhaled slowly to full capacity. During inhalation, observe the following guidelines:

- Take the standing position with the hands on the hips. The elbows should point outward to the side, and not backward.
- Lengthen the chest upwards. Press the hip bones downward with the hands. This will form a vacuum, allowing the air to rush into the lungs of its own accord.
- Keep the nostrils wide open, but do not use the nose as a suction pump. The nose should be a passage for the inhalation.
- No sound should be produced during inhalation. Correct breathing is soundless.
- Stretch the chest upward without arching the back. Lift the shoulders up, but do not force them back. Keep the head straight.
- Keep the abdomen relaxed; do not draw it inwards.

During exhalation, observe the following:

- Allow the ribs and upper trunk to sink down gradually. Draw the abdomen upwards slowly.
- Keep the head, neck and trunk in a straight line. Do not arch the back or bend forward.
- Contract the chest and exhale slowly through the nose without producing any sound. Expiration takes place by relaxing the respiratory muscles. The chest lowers by itself as the air is expelled.
- Do not retain the breath after inhalation. When inhalation is complete, begin exhalation at once.
- When one round of three deep breaths is over, take a few normal breaths and then start the second round. During the pause, stand still in a comfortable position with the hands on the hips.

Do 5 rounds during the first week and increase one round every week.

This technique was recommended by Swami Sivananda:

"Standing erect, arms flowing open, chest wide, raise yourself gradually upon your toes, inhaling continuously and deeply all the time. Fill your chest with pure air. Then gradually exhale and slowly bring down your heels and your arms."

Viloma Pranayama (reverse breath)

In viloma pranayama the breathing is interrupted throughout inhalation and/or exhalation. In normal breathing, inhalation and exhalation flow smoothly and evenly. *Viloma*, meaning opposite, here indicates interruption of the natural flow of breath. This practice develops control over the breath flow and is an easy method of extending the breath duration. It may be used as a preparation for nadi shodhana and bhastrika.

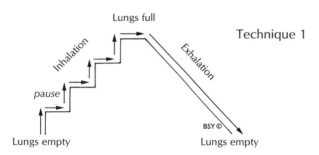

Technique 1: interruption of inhalation

Lie down in shavasana or sit in any comfortable posture. Relax the whole body and practise breath awareness for a few minutes.

Practice slow, deep breathing with awareness of each inhalation and exhalation. Let the breathing become stabilized.

Begin inhalation with a series of short pauses: inhale–pause, inhale–pause, inhale–pause. Continue in this way until the lungs are full.

The diaphragm and abdomen should remain firm after each pause.

Imagine that you are breathing up a set of stairs. This visualization may make the practice easier for you.

On completion of the interrupted inhalation, exhale slowly and smoothly until the lungs are empty. Do not strain.

Practise 11 rounds, then relax and breathe normally.

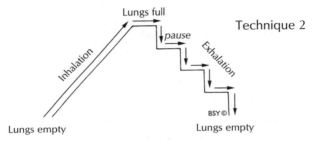

Technique 2

Technique 2: interruption of exhalation

Practise in the same way, except that inhalation is smooth and full.

Exhalation is interrupted by a series of pauses until the lungs are completely empty.

The number of pauses depends on the individual capacity.

Practise 11 rounds, then relax and breathe normally.

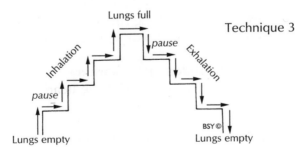

Technique 3

Technique 3: interruption of inhalation and exhalation

This practice combines both interrupted inhalation and interrupted exhalation.

Inhale with a series of pauses until the lungs are full.

181

Then exhale with a series of pauses until the lungs are empty.

Try to control the abdomen, but do not use force.

Take a normal respiration between each round.

Practise 11 rounds.

Practice note: The number of pauses may vary in the three techniques, but will normally be from three to five. More control of the breath can be obtained by increasing the number of pauses. Increasing the force of the breath can also be done. Short forceful breaths will prepare the lungs and musculature for the practices of bhastrika and kapalbhati.

Rhythmic breathing

The breathing rhythm is never constant, but continually changes in response to the demands placed upon the body and mind. During different activities, such as sleeping, eating, walking, riding a bicycle or reading, the rhythm and duration of the breath vary. Different mental states are also reflected in the breathing pattern. Throughout the day the rhythm of the breath is constantly changing, usually without one's knowledge. Rhythmic breathing produces a calming effect and can be used to stabilize the mind during periods of tension and turmoil. Both body and mind respond positively to rhythmic breathing. The following techniques induce conscious control of the breathing rhythm. They are all based on an equal duration of inhalation and exhalation (1:1 ratio).

Technique 1: with abdominal breathing

Sit in a comfortable asana with the head and spine erect or lie in shavasana.

Close the eyes and relax the whole body.

Practise body awareness for a few minutes.

Become aware of the natural breath. Be aware that you are breathing in and out. Do not alter or control the breath in any way.

Observe the natural breathing pattern and see whether one breath is longer or shorter than the next. Maybe the inhalation is longer than the exhalation. Increase the awareness of each breath.

Be aware of how rhythmic or arrhythmic the natural breathing pattern is. With this knowledge you will be able to establish a regular pattern.

Commence deep abdominal breathing. Inhale to the count of 4 and exhale to the count of 4. You may also count by mentally chanting the mantra Om 4 times on inhalation and 4 times on exhalation.

Relax the throat so that the breath flows freely through the respiratory passage.

Let the breath be smooth, even and regular.

Continue the practice for 5 minutes.

Return to normal breathing. Become aware of your body and surroundings, and slowly open your eyes.

Technique 2: with yogic breathing

Sit in a comfortable asana with the head and spine erect or lie in shavasana.

Practise body awareness for a few minutes, allowing the breath to become steady.

Be aware of the natural flow of the breath.

Commence yogic breathing. Inhale first from the abdomen then expand the cavity of the chest, filling the lungs. Exhale in the reverse order.

The breathing should be relaxed and comfortable, without strain.

Count the time it takes to complete one inhalation.

Then exhale for the same duration as the inhalation. You may also count by mentally repeating the mantra Om.

Be aware of the duration of each breath.

Let the air flow freely through the throat.

Do not use excessive force.

Continue the practice for 5 minutes.

After completing the practice, return to normal breathing. Become aware of your body and surroundings, and slowly open your eyes.

183

Technique 3: synchronizing the breath and heart rhythm
Sit in a comfortable asana or lie in shavasana.
Practise body awareness for a few minutes, allowing the body and breath to stabilize.
Become aware of the breath and heartbeat, and observe these two rhythms for a few minutes.
Focus the attention on the heartbeat. If the heartbeat is difficult to locate, feel the pulse at one wrist.
Commence yogic breathing, counting 4 heartbeats for every inhalation and exhalation. This ratio of four to one is the normal heartbeat to breath ratio.
If you are sensitive, you may be able to detect a change in the heart rate between inhalation and exhalation; the heart beats more slowly during exhalation.
You may also perceive a general slowing down of the heart rate as relaxation is induced by the rhythmic breathing. A slower heartbeat means that the breath becomes even slower.
Continue to observe this relationship for five minutes.
After completing the practice, open your eyes and release the asana.

Technique 4: extending breath duration (1:1 ratio)
Assume a comfortable asana or lie in shavasana.
Practise kaya sthairyam for a few minutes, becoming steady in the posture.
Let the breath become regular and even.
Begin to practise abdominal breathing, inhaling for the count of 4 and exhaling for the count of 4.
Continue this for a few minutes longer.
Now increase the count, inhaling to the count of 5 and exhaling to the count of 5.
Maintain abdominal breathing.
As this ratio becomes comfortable, increase the duration of inhalation to the count of 6 and exhalation to the count of 6. Continue breathing using the abdomen only.
As each ratio becomes stabilized, increase the inhalation and exhalation by a count of one, up to the count of 8.

184

Do not strain on any account.

Feel the abdominal breath becoming slower, deeper and lighter.

If you cannot reach the count of 8:8, maintain the count you can perform comfortably.

Be aware of the subtle nature of the breath.

Commence yogic breathing with the ratio of 6:6.

Allow this ratio to become stable.

Increase the duration of inhalation and exhalation by one count.

Do not constrict the throat.

As each count becomes stabilized, increase the ratio by one until you reach the count of 10:10. If this ratio is beyond your capacity, maintain a comfortable count.

As the inhalation and exhalation become longer, feel the breath becoming lighter and deeper. Feel the lightness of the breath in the nostrils.

Continue for a few minutes more.

Discontinue yogic breathing and switch back to normal breathing.

Bring the awareness back to the physical body, to the external sounds, and open your eyes.

Extended exhalation

Inhalation is an active movement, whereas exhalation is a passive movement of relaxation, a state of repose. The heart beats more slowly during exhalation than during inhalation. By slowly lengthening the exhalation, the state of relaxation arises, bringing many benefits to the physical and mental levels. While extending the exhalation, the abdominal muscles are contracted, which has a strengthening effect. Extended exhalation also lessens pain, as in crying and sobbing, which produce slightly extended bursts of exhalation. This is nature's way of dulling pain, both physical and mental. The following practice will help in times of stress as well as in the practices of classical pranayama with advanced ratios.

185

Extending exhalation (1:2 ratio)

Sit in a comfortable posture with the head and spine straight, or lie in shavasana.

Relax the whole body.

Become aware of the natural breath.

Be aware of breathing in and breathing out.

Continue in this way for a few minutes.

Begin abdominal breathing.

Feel the breath becoming rhythmical.

Mentally count to 4 on inhalation and on exhalation.

When this smooth, even rhythm is established, count to 4 on inhalation and to 5 on exhalation.

Extend the count of exhalation to 6, 7 and 8.

Practise 5 rounds with the 4:8 ratio.

Repeat the process with yogic breathing.

Practice note: The ratio of 1:2 is sufficient to move on to other pranayama techniques.

Kumbhaka

There are three types of breath retention: *antaranga kumbhaka* or internal retention, *bahiranga kumbhaka* or external retention, and *kevala kumbhaka* or spontaneous retention. The last occurs when the breath automatically ceases and no effort is applied.

Kumbhaka exists in normal respiration, but only for a split second and it is not conscious or controlled. This section gives several preliminary practices to develop the awareness of kumbhaka, so that it will be familiar when required in the pranayama techniques. Each stage should be mastered before proceeding to the next.

Advice and precautions: Seek competent guidance before attempting the practices of kumbhaka. These techniques should be approached slowly, moving systematically and comfortably through each stage. Kumbhaka should not be practised by people with high blood pressure, cardiovascular problems, vertigo, cerebral diseases and mental defects. The previously described techniques of inhalation, exhalation and rhythmic breathing should be perfected before starting internal retention (antaranga kumbhaka). Again, internal retention should be mastered before proceeding to external retention (bahiranga kumbhaka). If the body or mind feels tense in any way, it means that one has exceeded one's natural capacity. One should then stop and go back to the previous stage. By practising slowly, the foundation will become solid.

Technique 1: internal retention (1:1:1)
Sit in a comfortable position or lie in shavasana.
Relax the whole body.
Practise yogic breathing for a few minutes.
Begin counting to 4 on inhalation and on exhalation.
Continue for a few minutes. There should be no tension in the body or mind.
Now begin internal retention.
Inhale for a count of 4, hold the breath inside for a count of 2 and then exhale for a count of 4.
If you feel any strain, go back to normal breathing.
Continue for 11 rounds.
When this practice becomes comfortable, extend the count of internal retention to 3, and then to 4.
This is a 1:1:1 ratio.
Practise 11 rounds and gradually increase to 21 rounds.
If the breathing is rhythmic and the body and mind are relaxed, the practice is correct.

Technique 2: extended internal retention and exhalation (1:1:2 and 1:2:2)
Practise the ratio of 4:4:4, allowing this ratio to become stabilized.
Gradually extend the exhalation to a count of 8.
This is the ratio of 1:1:2.
Breathe normally in between each round if the feeling of breathlessness arises.
Return to the ratio of 4:4:4 whenever strain is felt.
When the ratio of 4:4:8 is comfortable continue the

practice without normal breathing in between. Practise 11 rounds and slowly increase to 21 rounds. When the ratio of 4:4:8 becomes comfortable, the count of inner retention can be increased slowly to the count of 8. Then practice with the ratio of 4:8:8.

Samavritti Pranayama (equalizing breath)

The word *sama* means 'equal', 'even' or 'perfect'; *vritti* literally means 'movement' or 'action'. In samavritti pranayama the respiration is divided into four equal parts. The inhalation, internal retention, exhalation and external retention are of equal duration, making the ratio 1:1:1:1. This practice produces an even and rhythmic flow of breath. However, external retention is difficult to master. The practitioner should be aware of any internal signals arising during the practice, and release any tension forming in the body or mind before continuing the next round. The mastery of samavritti pranayama enables one to undertake the classical pranayama practices.

Technique I

Sit in a comfortable position and relax the body and mind.

Become aware of the natural breath and its spontaneous rhythm.

Commence yogic breathing.

Count to 4 on inhalation, count to 4 on internal retention, and to 4 for exhalation. Continue in this way for a few minutes.

Now, after exhalation, hold the breath outside for the count of 4.

Take several normal breaths in between each round.

When the feeling of breathlessness or gasping for inhalation subsides after external retention, dispense with the normal respiration in between rounds.

Practise 11 rounds.

Technique 2

Resume the practice with the ratio of 1:1:1:1.

Mentally imagine a square. Feel that the inhalation is ascending the left side of the square.

On internal retention the awareness travels across the top of the square from left to right.

While exhaling, descend the right side of the square.

On external retention, take the awareness across the bottom of the square from right to left.

This is one round.

Practise 11 rounds and gradually increase to 21 rounds.

When 21 rounds can be completed without exhaustion, slowly increase the count of the ratio by one until the count of 10:10:10:10 is reached.

Practice note: The techniques described above should not involve any strain. If the practitioner feels shortness of breath, dizziness or fainting, he should stop the practice and consult a yoga teacher. The breath should not become over-extended at any stage of the practices. The need to take extra breaths during or at the end of the round indicates that the practitioner is over-extending his capacity and should go back to a previous stage that feels more comfortable. The breathing capacity extends slowly with practice. The ratio should be increased weekly or monthly, giving the lungs and muscles time to adapt to each stage. The practitioner should not proceed to a further stage until he can perform the present stage comfortably.

17

Awareness of the Subtle Breath

Yoga is a science and pranayama is an application of this science. The breathing techniques alone, as a purely mechanical operation, create an appropriate effect on the body, mind and spirit. However, it has been observed that the effect of these techniques can be greatly amplified when they are applied with sensitivity and awareness of their subtle influences, and with a deeper understanding of the relationship between the body, energy and mind. Application of a technique without awareness will produce results; however, the process becomes more efficient with awareness, and the inner knowledge begins to awaken.

By developing the sensitivity of the breath from the gross to the subtle levels, one understands the secrets of the intimate relationships in the cycles of life. Once this knowledge awakens, self-mastery follows. In daily life, most things are mechanical and automatic. One eats, works and plays, experiences anger, jealousy and joy, without awareness of what one is doing or feeling. This lack of awareness is carried over into the yogic sadhana also. Many practitioners perform as many practices as possible in the allotted time, so they can finish in time for breakfast. But what do they accomplish? Where is the awareness?

The following techniques are methods of increasing sensitivity to the subtle levels of the breath, the flows of swara and the pancha pranas. These practices are intended to awaken an insight into the aspects of breath, prana, body and mind, which are normally beyond the mundane awareness. Although they may be regarded as preliminary techniques, they can also be practised at any level of sadhana.

Awareness of swara

Swara is the flow of breath in the nostrils. One can easily know which nostril is flowing by blocking one nostril at a time, and observing which flow is stronger. A detailed examination of the breath in the nostrils will give quite specific information about one's psycho-physiological state. The aspects to be examined include:

• Distance the breath extends beyond the nostrils
• Predominance of either the right or left nostril
• Direction in which the breath flows into and out of the nostrils.

The observation techniques described below will show that these three aspects are quite variable. When the swara is observed over a long period, it will yield a wealth of information. These techniques can be practised at any time and during any situation. It is suggested that one observe the swara throughout a range of activities and experiences; for example, sitting, eating, talking, walking, exercising, working, relaxing, meditating, feeling anger, sorrow, happiness, depression, exhilaration, contentment, stress and so on. The breath may be checked before, during and after each of these situations. The practitioner should relate his observations to what he already knows about the ida/pingala system, various tattwas and the pancha pranas. This can become a very involved sadhana in itself.

Technique 1: observation of swara

Sit in any comfortable position.

Focus the awareness on the natural breath in the nostrils.

Place the back of the hand in front of the nostrils. Try to determine how far the exhalation flows out beyond the

191

nostrils by feeling the breath on the hairs on the back of the hand.

Observe the breath and determine its length.

The natural length of the breath is between 7–12 finger-widths (*angulas*) from the nostrils. During states of emotion and excitation the breath can extend to 36 finger-widths. During extreme physical exertion, it may extend to 100 finger-widths.

The next step is an even more subtle observation. Try to determine the direction in which the exhaled air leaves the nostrils, using the back of the hand.

Observe whether the exhaled breath flows from the centre of the nostrils (signifying the predominance of *prithvi tattwa*, the earth element), upwards (signifying the predominance of *agni tattwa*, the fire element), downwards (indicating *apas tattwa*, the water element), from the sides (indicating *vayu tattwa*, the air element), or in a diffused flow, without any predominant direction (indicating *akasha tattwa*, the ether element).

At this stage one need not contemplate what each flow signifies; simply be aware that they exist.

Go on witnessing the breath flow.

Observe the various flows of swara minutely.

Practice note: A more sensitive measurement can be made by holding a small down feather or a cotton thread in front of the nostrils. By observing the direction of the emerging breath over a period of time, one will see that the breath emerges at various angles at different times, and even at differing angles from each nostril. This is a perfectly normal occurrence.

Technique 2: Akasha Pranayama (space breath)

Sit in a comfortable meditative posture, preferably siddhasana, siddha yoni asana or padmasana.

Practise kaya sthairyam for a few minutes, and then observe the breath until it becomes silent and steady.

Perform nasikagra drishti, gazing down at the nose tip.

Become aware of the breath at the nostrils.

Continue breath awareness with nasikagra drishti for approximately 5 minutes.

Now close the eyes and be aware of the breath entering and leaving the nostrils. Imagine a fine membrane at the entrance of the nostrils over which the air passes as it enters and leaves the body.

Continue the awareness of the breath flowing over this interface.

Now extend the awareness beyond the nostrils and visualize different movements made by the breath in the air outside the nostrils upon inhalation and exhalation.

While breathing out feel the outer air being displaced by the expelled air.

While breathing in feel the outer air being drawn inside the nostrils.

Maintain this awareness for a few minutes, keeping the breath silent.

Slowly make the breath lighter. This should not involve any tension or constriction of the nasal passages.

Apply less force and extend the duration of the breath.

Feel the breath simply entering and leaving the body, effortlessly and soundlessly.

The breathing should become so light that it feels as if there is no disturbance of the air beyond the nostrils during either inhalation or exhalation.

At this point the breath will be completely silent. The experience at the mental level will be that of *akasha* (space).

Continue soundless breathing and feel the mind becoming silent and calm.

Get ready to end the practice. Gradually return to body awareness.

Switch back to normal breathing. Slowly open the eyes.

Balancing the swara

During the natural oscillation of the breath between the left and right nostrils, relating to ida and pingala nadis, a balanced flow through both nostrils exists only for a matter of minutes. However, this period of balance can be extended by altering the breath in the nostrils, so that they remain equalized. The following techniques influence the breath flow to bring about this balance. Alternatively, these practices may be used to increase the flow of breath in either nostril, depending on whether one requires more vital energy (right nostril) or mental energy (left nostril).

The body and mind have their own self-regulating mechanisms. One should not assume that because one works at a desk all day, the left nostril should remain dominant during that time. Sometimes, however, one becomes locked into a state of ongoing mental turmoil (left nostril), or competition and aggression (right nostril). At such times, these techniques may be used to change the dominant swara and divert the energies. Mostly these methods are applied during spiritual practice to maintain a balanced flow in sushumna. At the time of sunrise and sunset either the left or right nostril becomes dominant, depending on the phase of the moon. This is a time of intense swara activity and it is not advised to alter the flows during this period.

Padadhirasana (breath balancing pose)

Sit in vajrasana with the body upright and straight, and the head facing forward.

Place each hand under the opposite armpit, with the thumb upward.

Close the eyes and breathe normally with awareness of the breath in the nostrils.

Continue for 5–10 minutes.

This may be practised for extended periods of time for spiritual purposes.

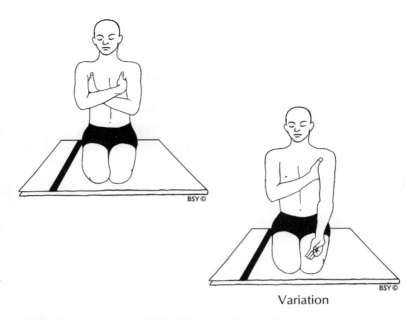

Variation

Variation: changing the flow in the nostrils

Sit in vajrasana, as above.

In order to increase the flow of breath in the right nostril, place the right hand under the left armpit, with the thumb upward.

Place the left hand on the left thigh in chin mudra.

Alternatively, to increase the flow of breath in the left nostril, place the left hand under the right armpit.

The right hand is placed on the right thigh in chin mudra.

Close the eyes. Breathe naturally with the awareness on the breath in the nostrils.

Let the weight of the arm create the necessary pressure in the armpit; no extra pressure is needed.

Continue for 5–10 minutes, or for as long as necessary, until the flow is well established in the required nostril.

Danda Kriya (stick action)

Sit in a comfortable meditative asana and allow the breath to become steady.

In order to increase the flow of breath in the left nostril, place a *yoga danda* (T-shaped stick) under the right armpit, so that it creates a slight pressure under the arm.

To increase the flow in the right nostril, the danda is placed under the left armpit.

Adjust the pressure under the armpit to increase or decrease the flow in the nostril accordingly.

Practice note: This practice requires a yoga danda, long enough to fit snugly under the armpit, when seated in a meditative posture.

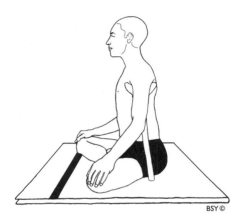

BSY©

Variation: two dandas

Place one danda under each arm.

Alter the pressure under the armpit by leaning the body slightly to the right or left, as required, to maintain the balanced flow.

Practise for as long as necessary.

Practice note: This practice requires the use of two dandas or, alternatively, one danda may be moved from the right to the left armpit to adjust the flow in the nostrils as required. The use of a yoga danda has the added advantage of giving support to the body during extended periods of meditation or pranayama, although this should not be depended upon.

196

Lying on the side

To increase the flow of breath in the right nostril, lie on the left side.

The right knee should be bent, touching the floor, with the right foot tucked behind the left knee.

To increase the flow in the left nostril, practise lying on the right side.

Alternate nostril breathing

Sit in a comfortable meditative asana.

Become aware of the flow of breath in the nostrils.

In order to increase the flow of breath in the right nostril, inhale through the left nostril and exhale through the right.

To increase the flow in the left nostril, inhale through the right nostril and exhale through the left.

Practise for 5–10 minutes, observing the change in the swara.

Acupuncture point

Sit in any comfortable position.

Pinch the fleshy portion of the hand between the thumb and index finger until you find a point which gives a slightly painful sensation.

To open the right nostril, press the point on the right hand, and on the left hand for the left nostril.

Maintain steady pressure or gently massage this point for 5–10 minutes.

Practice note: This technique applies pressure to the acupuncture meridian relating to the large intestine, which runs through the point described to the respective nostril.

197

Mental control of swara
Sit in a comfortable meditative asana.
Become aware of the breath in the nostrils.
If the flow in the left nostril is stronger, concentrate on the breath flowing in the right nostril. This may be assisted by visualization.
After some time, the flow of breath in the right nostril will increase.
The breath flow in the left nostril may also be increased in the same way.

Practice note: This technique should be regarded as an experiment in mental control over the body. The concentration required to produce this effect could be used more constructively in other techniques.

Prana Mudra Pranayama (invocation of energy)

Prana mudra pranayama develops the awareness of the seven chakras: mooladhara, swadhisthana, manipura, anahata, vishuddhi, ajna and sahasrara, and the subtle movement of energy associated with their activation. This practice is also known as shanti mudra, or attitude of peace. This attitude of the whole being is one of supplication to receive the radiations of the sun and the heavens, both physical and imaginary. It can be practised at sunrise, facing the sun, if desired. However, this is unnecessary because the practice actually awakens the prana shakti from within. Prana mudra develops personal strength, confidence and an inner glow of health. It is an excellent pre-meditative technique, but can also be performed at any time.

Technique

Stage I: Sit in a comfortable meditative pose. Make sure the spine and head are in a straight line.
Close the eyes and place the hands in the lap in bhairava mudra.
Exhale as deeply as possible, contracting the abdominal muscles to expel the maximum amount of air from the lungs.

198

Stage 1

Stage 2

Stage 3

Stage 4

Stage 5

BSY©

199

While retaining the breath outside, perform moola bandha with awareness of mooladhara chakra.

Retain the breath and the bandha for as long as is comfortable.

Stage 2: Release moola bandha and slowly inhale, expanding the abdomen and drawing the maximum volume of air into the lungs.

Simultaneously raise the hands until they are in front of the navel.

The hands should be open with the palms facing inward.

The fingers should be pointing towards each other, but not touching.

The upward movement of the hands should be coordinated with the abdominal inhalation.

Relax the arms, hands and fingers.

While inhaling from the abdomen, feel the prana being drawn upward from mooladhara to manipura chakra in the spinal column.

Stage 3: Continue the inhalation, expanding the chest.

Simultaneously raise the hands until they are directly in front of the heart.

Feel the pranic energy being drawn upward from manipura to anahata chakra while inhaling. You may even feel a pulse beat in the heart area.

Stage 4: Inhale a little more air into the lungs, raising the shoulders.

Feel the prana being drawn up from anahata to vishuddhi chakra and then spreading like a wave to ajna chakra.

Coordinate the hand movement with the breath, raising the hands in front of the throat.

Stage 5: Retain the breath inside and stretch the arms and hands to either side in an arc.

In the final position the hands should be level with the ears with the palms turned upwards towards the heavens.

While spreading the arms feel the movement of prana from ajna to sahasrara.

Concentrate on sahasrara and visualize an aura of pure light, emanating from the head.

Feel your whole being radiating vibrations of peace to all beings.

Retain this position for as long as is comfortable without straining the lungs.

Stage 6: While exhaling, return to the starting position.

Repeat all the stages in the reverse order.

Feel the prana moving progressively back down through the chakras until it reaches mooladhara at the end of exhalation.

Perform moola bandha and concentrate on mooladhara chakra.

Relax the whole body, breathing slowly and deeply.

Repeat 5–10 rounds.

Practice note: The awareness should move in a smooth and continuous flow, in coordination with the breath and the raising and lowering of the hands from mooladhara to sahasrara and back to mooladhara. When the practice is perfected, the breath may be visualized as a stream of light, ascending and descending the sushumna nadi within the spine.

Awareness of pancha pranas

The pancha pranas are the five energy flows which comprise the pranic body: prana, apana, samana, udana and vyana. The following practice is a variation of prana mudra pranayama with awareness of the five pranas instead of the seven chakras.

Variation: Prana Mudra Pranayama with awareness of pancha pranas

Perform stage 1 as described above. Develop the awareness of apana in the lower abdominal region.

In stage 2, while raising the hands, feel the transformation from apana to samana at the navel area.

During stage 3, continue raising the hands from samana to the region of prana in the chest region.

In stage 4, raising the hands from the chest to the throat and head, be aware of prana moving into the region of udana.

In stage 5, be aware of the diffusion of vyana throughout the body and all around, as the hands and arms are spread to either side.

Remain aware of the whole body enveloped in and radiating pure light, while simultaneously being aware of the flows of the five pranas within the physical body. In stage 6, exhalation follows the reverse movement of the arms, bringing the awareness down through the five pranas to the starting position.

Hasta Mudra Pranayama (hand gesture breath)

The four techniques described here utilize specific hand positions known as *hasta* or hand mudras. The concept of mudras and details of mudra techniques are described in Appendix C. From the pranic point of view, they represent a linkup of specific nadis in the body (in this case, the fingers), by which prana is redirected to different areas. These mudras are subtle techniques and their effects may not be immediately noticeable without awareness and sensitivity.

These pranayama techniques using hand mudras ventilate the lower, middle and upper lobes of the lungs and influence other vital organs indirectly. The pancha pranas are also activated by these practices. They are also therapeutic pranayamas, as they relieve disorders related to specific areas of the body. All four should be practised together in the sequence described, although for therapeutic purposes only the relevant practice need be applied.

Technique 1: Chin Mudra Pranayama (gesture of conscious breath)

Sit in vajrasana or any other asana with the spine straight.
Place the hands on the thighs in chin mudra with the palms upwards.
Inhale through both nostrils then retain the breath inside.

202

Exhale, and retain the breath outside.

Try to maintain the ratio of 1:1:1:1 throughout the round, using a comfortable count.

Continue for up to 27 rounds.

Benefits: This practice ventilates the lower lobes of the lungs and stimulates the region of apana below the navel.

Technique 2: Chinmaya Mudra Pranayama (gesture of pure wisdom breath)

Sit in vajrasana or any other asana with the spine straight. Place the hands in chinmaya mudra with the palms downwards on the thighs.

203

Inhale through both nostrils then retain the breath inside. Exhale, and retain the breath outside.

Try to maintain the ratio of 1:1:1:1 throughout the round, using a comfortable count.

Continue for up to 27 rounds.

Benefits: This practice ventilates the middle lobes of the lungs. Energy is directed to the area of samana and prana between the navel and the throat.

Technique 3: Aadi Mudra Pranayama (primary gesture breath)

Sit in vajrasana or any other suitable posture with the spine straight.

Place the hands on the thighs in aadi mudra with the backs of the hands upwards. Do not clench the thumb tightly.

Inhale through both nostrils then retain the breath inside. Exhale, and retain the breath outside.

Try to maintain the ratio of 1:1:1:1 throughout the round, using a comfortable count.

Continue for up to 27 rounds.

Benefits: This practice ventilates the upper lobes of the lungs, moving energy to the region of udana in the neck and head.

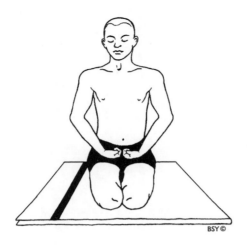

Technique 4: Brahma Mudra Pranayama (gesture of supreme spirit breath)
Sit in vajrasana or any other suitable asana with the spine straight.

Practise brahma mudra with the knuckles of the hand together and the thumbs away from the body.

Inhale through both nostrils then retain the breath inside.

Exhale, and retain the breath outside.

Try to maintain the ratio of 1:1:1:1 throughout the round, using a comfortable count.

Continue for up to 27 rounds.

Benefits: The practice revitalizes the whole body through the stimulation of vyana.

This completes the four mudra pranayamas. By practising each for 27 rounds, one will perform 108 rounds, which comprise the total practice.

205

Pranayama Practice:
II: Classical Pranayamas

18

Guidelines for Pranayama

Pranayama can be practised by all people, regardless of age and physical condition. However, the practices should be learned individually from a master or qualified teacher and not selected at random. Every individual has a different physical and mental constitution, which a qualified teacher is able to assess. Specific pranayamas, rounds and ratios are prescribed according to these criteria. These subtleties cannot be gauged without the maturity of practice and understanding. The *Hatha Yoga Pradipika* states (2:16):

प्राणायामेन युक्तेन सर्वरोगक्षयो भवेत् ।
अयुक्ताभ्यासयोगेन सर्वरोगसमुद्भव: ॥

All diseases are eradicated by the proper practice of pranayama; all diseases can arise through improper practice.

The lungs, heart and nerves are normally strong and gain added strength with regulated and sensible pranayama practice. However, if the practitioner overdoes it or performs unsuitable practices, the body may be weakened and the inner organs damaged. Pranayama also accentuates whatever is in the mind, whether positive or negative. So, by wrong or excessive practice, one's mental quirks and even nervous tics could become exaggerated.

When pranayama is improperly practised, problems may arise without any warning signals, so extra care is required.

209

Every practice should be treated with respect and caution. There should be no violent respirations, no extended kumbhaka beyond a comfortable measure, no forcing of the breath, body or mind. The practitioner should not attempt to perform an advanced pranayama which is beyond his present capabilities. In this way comfortable progress will be assured and one will be able to achieve full benefit from the wonderful science of pranayama.

The *Yoga Chudamani Upanishad* states (v. 118):

यथा सिंहो गजो व्याघ्रो भवेद्वश्य: शनै: शनै: ।
तथै सेवितो वायुरन्यथा हन्ति साधकम् ॥

Just as the lion, elephant and tiger are brought under control slowly and steadily, similarly the prana should be controlled, otherwise it becomes destructive to the practitioner.

Patience and perseverance are necessary in spiritual life, and this is especially true for pranayama. The practitioner should not be frustrated if he cannot attain a certain ratio or number of rounds; it may take months or even years to perfect one pranayama alone. The regular practitioner is progressing all the time, although the progress cannot be seen objectively. So there is a tendency to think that nothing is happening; however, one should be assured that the practice is developing on both the gross and subtle levels.

Preliminaries: In order to qualify for pranayama, one must first master yoga asanas. In order to reap the full benefit of asanas, one must undergo the process of shatkarmas. The physical body is a combination and permutation of the five elements: earth, water, fire, air and ether. Shatkarmas purify these elements, so they do not interfere with the activities of prana. The effect of asanas and pranayamas increases substantially when the body is relieved of toxins. The body becomes sensitive and responds to the changes that an asana or pranayama demands from it.

The inner body of a pranayama practitioner needs to be pure. Adverse effects may be experienced if one practises

210

pranayama without removing the energy blocks and toxins accumulated on account of an irregular lifestyle. For example, fermentation of mucus will immediately interfere with pranic activities. The practice of shatkarmas gives a good flushing to the mouth, nose, stomach, intestines, and indeed the whole body. Neti kriya cleans the nasal passages and kunjal kriya removes mucus and hyperacidity from the stomach.

When shatkarmas are followed by asanas, the pranas are able to penetrate each and every nerve, cell and pore of the body. The practitioner will reap enormous benefits by following a routine of shatkarmas, asanas and pranayamas, even if he has completely neglected the body for years. However, if one has led a simple and balanced lifestyle, and maintained purity of the body, then one can start directly with pranayama.

Diet: The practitioner of pranayama should choose a balanced diet that is suitable to his constitution. There is no one diet that is right or wrong for everyone. As the saying goes, "One man's food is another man's poison". Food can be classified into three basic groups: (i) tamasic – which creates lethargy, dullness; (ii) rajasic – which creates excitement, passion and disease, and (iii) sattwic – which bestows balance, good health and longevity. Fresh and natural foods are sattwic; packaged and refined foods are tamasic and should be avoided.

A diet of grains, pulses, fresh fruit and vegetables, and a small amount of dairy products is most beneficial. For non-vegetarians, a small portion of meat, fish or eggs may be added. The diet must also be adjusted to avoid constipation. Overall, the principle of moderation should be followed. The *Gheranda Samhita* states (5:16):

मिताहारं विना यस्तु योगारम्भं तु कारयेत् ।
नानारोगो भवेत्तस्य किंचिद्योगो न सिध्यति ॥

One who takes up yoga practices without observing moderation of diet obtains no benefit; rather, he gets various diseases.

211

The ayurvedic principle in regard to diet is: fill half the stomach with food, one quarter with water and leave one quarter empty. Given the opportunity most people overeat, when they could manage better on one balanced meal per day. Excessive eating satisfies the senses and the mind, but it places pressure on the diaphragm and lungs, and full-depth respiration becomes difficult.

Place: Pranayama should be practised in a clean environment to minimize the effects of pollution. One may practise in the open air or in a well-ventilated, clean and pleasant room. One should never perform pranayama in a foul-smelling, smoky or dusty room. Ideally, the place of practice should be somewhat isolated, away from people, noise and interruptions. Avoid practising in the sun or wind. The soft rays of the early morning sun are beneficial, but when they become stronger, they are harmful and the body will become overheated. Practising in a draught or wind may cause chills and upset the body temperature.

Cleanliness: Personal cleanliness is necessary for pranayama practice. If a full bath is not possible, one should wash the hands, face and feet with water. Bathing helps to wake up properly before commencing sadhana. However, one should not bathe immediately after pranayama; one should wait for at least half an hour.

Time of practice: Early morning is the best time to practise pranayama. At the time of *brahmamuhurta* (between four and six am) the vibrations of the atmosphere are in their purest state. The body is fresh and the mind has very few impressions, compared to its state at the end of the day. Most pranayamas should not be done in the heat of the day (unless a special sadhana is given by the guru). The yogic texts advise four periods for the practice of pranayama: sunrise, noon, sunset and midnight, but this is for advanced practitioners only.

Pranayama should not be practised after meals. One must wait for three hours after a meal before practising. An empty stomach ensures that the prana vayus are not concentrated in the digestive process and can be used to initiate more subtle activities. At the same time, pranayama should not be practised when one is very hungry.

Sequence: Pranayama should be performed after asanas and before meditation practices. After doing asanas, the practitioner may rest for five minutes and then begin pranayama. A few rounds of pranayama may also be practised just before japa and meditation. The mind becomes one-pointed and the body feels lighter after pranayama, and then meditation is more enjoyable.

The seat: Natural fibres such as cotton or wool are best to sit on for the practice of pranayama. It is not advisable to sit on or wear materials made of synthetic fibres, as they repel negative ions and attract positive ions. Positive ions are not conducive to pranayama or to good health because they act as a shield, obstructing the flow of negative ions into the body.

Posture: The ability to sit comfortably in a meditation asana is a requisite for the successful practice of pranayama. The correct posture enables efficient breathing as well as stability of the body during the practice. Both concentration and technique are hampered by poor posture. The chest, neck and head must be in one vertical line during the practice, so that the spinal cord remains straight. One should not allow the body to become crooked or to collapse. The body should not bend forwards or backwards or to the right or left. By regular practice, mastery over the pose will come by itself.

The best postures for the practice of pranayama are padmasana, siddhasana, siddha yoni asana and swastikasana. When one advances in the practice, prana moves through the body at a terrific speed. This movement must be supported by total immobility of the body, which these postures maintain. As the body produces more energy, it effectively turns into an electrical pole. The left side carries cool energy and the right warm energy, representing the negative and positive poles. The additional energy produced by the practice can escape through the earth connection. Therefore, a closed circuit must be created to ensure that the energy remains within the body. This circuit

213

is made by the four meditation postures and strengthened by the application of mudras and bandhas. This may not apply to a beginner, but if one wants to advance in pranayama, then expertise in the meditation asanas is imperative. In the beginning however, one may sit in sukhasana (comfortable pose), especially if one is overweight.

Starting nostril: When alternate nostril breathing is used in nadi shodhana or bhastrika, usually the practice is begun from the left nostril. However, if the left nostril is blocked, one may begin with the right nostril. In the course of the practice the blocked nostril will become free and open.

The nose: Respiration begins with the nose and the breath in the nostrils is closely related to many subtle balances in the body-mind system; therefore, attention should be paid to ensuring its efficient operation. The practice of pranayama is obstructed by chronic or acute nasal disabilities. All breathing should be through the nose except where otherwise specified. The nasal cavity should be regularly cleaned by jala neti for efficient operation of the nostrils. This will increase sensitivity to the action of the breath and prana. Nasal blockages caused by colds and allergies respond positively to this regular cleaning.

Flaring the nostrils: The practitioner should be aware of the nostrils throughout the practice of pranayama. Conscious breathing allows the air to enter the nostrils more easily, evenly and in greater volume. Control of the nostrils allows them to contribute to a greater receptivity of the entire respiratory system. Conscious control of the nostrils will develop with practice.

Normally the nostrils barely move, if at all, during respiration. Ideally, however, the nostrils should expand outwards while inhaling and relax back to their natural position while exhaling. Flaring the nostrils is an important aspect of pranayama, particularly in bhramari, samavritti and nadi shodhana pranayamas. This simple practice alone will effectively facilitate the absorption of prana in the body, while increasing the air intake by up to ten percent.

Breathing: The breathing should become very subtle during the practice of pranayama. The gross breath can be felt at a distance of 2–36 finger-widths from the nose. The subtler breath extends for a shorter distance. The practitioner should breathe in such a way that the breath does not extend beyond two finger-widths during exhalation, and retention does not make one exhale forcefully. The internal retention should be adjusted, so that one does not gasp while breathing out.

The speed of inhalation and exhalation should also be consistent and uniform. When one is tired, for example, the tendency is to inhale deeply and slowly and exhale quickly. When one is not tired, one may inhale more quickly and exhale slowly. This inconsistency in the breath creates uneven waves, which disturb the mind. There must also be uniformity in the breath. If a speedometer were placed inside the nose, one would see that the breath is never uniform. This is particularly noticeable after internal retention. During one exhalation, there may be up to ten different speeds. The breath should be smooth and uniform, without stops, jerks or tremors.

Ratio of inhalation, retention and exhalation: The practitioner must adjust the inhalation, retention and exhalation so that the feeling of suffocation or discomfort is not experienced at any stage of pranayama. One should never feel the necessity of catching a few normal breaths between any two successive rounds. The period of exhalation should not be unnecessarily prolonged; otherwise the following inhalation will be done in hurried manner and the rhythm will be disturbed. The *Yoga Chudamani Upanishad* states (v. 119):

युक्तं युक्तं त्यजेद्वायुं युक्तं युक्तं प्रपूरयेत् ।
युक्तं युक्तं प्रबध्नीयादेवं सिद्धिमवाप्नुयात् ॥

The breath should be inhaled slowly with awareness. The breath should be retained properly with awareness. The breath should be exhaled slowly and carefully. Thus perfection is attained.

In order to progress in pranayama, the inspiration and expiration must be properly trained before attempting retention. The ratio of inspiration and expiration should be 1:2 and the breath should be subtle, slow, continuous and unbroken. Breath retention should only be practised for as long as comfortable. This is important as the lungs are very delicate organs and any strain can easily injure them. Some people twist their facial muscles while performing retention, indicating that they are going beyond their capacity. This must be observed and avoided.

Breath retention should be so regulated that one can perform the required number of rounds without strain. The practitioner must have good control over the lungs at the end of retention, so that he can exhale smoothly in proportion to the inhalation in the ratio of 1:2. The retention of the breath should be related to the exhalation and not merely to one's capacity. Breath retention should be practised when both nostrils are flowing, so that both hemispheres of the brain are developed equally.

Bandhas: Advanced practitioners should practise retention along with the three bandhas: jalandhara bandha (chin lock), uddiyana bandha (abdominal lock), and moola bandha (perineal lock). When the breath is retained inside, jalandhara and moola bandha are practised. When the breath is held outside, all three bandhas are practised (see Appendix D). The practice of bandhas with pranayama builds up a negative pressure, which redirects the prana generated to the upper part of the body and head, creating an intensity not experienced otherwise.

Time unit: The use of a time unit is necessary to maintain the ratio. The practitioner may use a mental, numerical count to begin with. However, when the technique becomes comfortable, one should switch over to a mantra, such as Aum, Gayatri or the guru mantra as per one's inclination. Gayatri and Aum are the best mantras for pranayama. When one has advanced in the practice, one need not count or keep any unit. One will become established in the ratio naturally through force of habit.

216

Fatigue: One should not continue pranayama practice when fatigued. There must always be joy and exhilaration during and after the practice. One should come out of the practice fully invigorated and refreshed.

Illness: Pranayama should not be practised during illness. One should suspend the practice at this time and rest until health is restored. When recommencing the practice, one should not start at the same level where one left off. Instead, one should revert to a previous stage of practice where the program can be continued at a comfortable level. If suffering from any disease, one should inform the teacher or guide before commencing any course of pranayama practice.

Pregnancy: Pranayama provides many benefits during pregnancy. Women are more sensitive and responsive to prana while nurturing new life within the womb. The enhanced breathing ensures a plentiful supply of oxygen to the placenta. Techniques such as bhastrika and kapalbhati are useful during labour. Bhramari has also proved to be useful (see Chapter 16: 'Research on Breath and Pranayama'). Balancing pranayamas help the mother maintain equilibrium between her own needs and those of the child. However, the practice should always be well within the range of the mother's capability, and no practice should be forced. Kumbhaka and uddiyana bandha are restricted during pregnancy.

Possible side effects: When practising pranayama for the first time, a few symptoms may be experienced by normally healthy people, such as itching, tingling, burning, heat or cold, lightness or heaviness. The pulse may become rapid and there may be slight dizziness or pain. Sometimes, aspirants experience pain at the dorsal region. These symptoms do not indicate incorrect practice, but that the body is trying to adjust to the practice. However, if the reactions persist, one should have the technique checked.

Traditional texts on pranayama also describe effects such as trembling, perspiring, shaking, etc. that refer to a high stage of practice. A half-hour practice will not result in these symptoms. Those who practise pranayama as a sadhana for three to five hours daily may experience them. Nevertheless, if perspiration appears during the practice, one should not wipe it with a towel, but rub it back into the body with the hands. The body should not be exposed to chill or draughts during or after the practice.

Regularity: One of the most important disciplines for the practitioner of pranayama is regularity. This means developing a regular lifestyle as well as being consistent in the practice of pranayama itself. There will be no progress if one jumps from one practice to another every day. In the beginning one should ask the teacher to create a capsule of daily pranayamas, which one should improve to a high degree through regular practice.

Pranayama practices will progress over a period of time. Beginners need to practise the preliminaries in order to go on to the more advanced levels. Regularity in practice is essential for increasing the physiological capability as well as adjusting the body and mind to the increased pranic force. This is a slow and steady process, and the practitioner should never try to hurry.

Pranayama should be practised every day at the same time and in the same place. This builds up positive, spiritual vibrations in the place, and the regularity creates inner strength and willpower. The practitioner should follow the general guidelines for pranayama, but also allow intuition and common sense to prevail from time to time.

Advice for pranayama sadhana: The pranayama usually taught by yoga teachers is only preparatory. The main purpose of pranayama is to evolve the psychic and causal bodies. Therefore, pranayama sadhana as distinct from general practice may be defined as a concerted, regular and determined effort to achieve perfection in the practice. The goal is not merely good health and mental balance, but acquiring the highest state of consciousness. A dynamic effort must be made to arrive at this state. While general practitioners may modify a few rules as per convenience (for example, if a separate room is not available for the practice,

218

they may make do with what is available); no slackness in the guidelines is admissible for those wanting to practice pranayama at the level of sadhana. With respect to this aim the stringent conditions for pranayama sadhana mentioned in the traditional texts assume significance.

The pranayama sadhaka must improve his involvement with life at large. He must improve every interaction, whether emotional, intellectual or physical. A state of balance at every level is emphasized time and again for the pranayama practitioner. In Maharshi Patanjali's *Yoga Sutras*, the practice of pranayama is placed after the practices of yama, niyama and asana. The five yamas are: (i) *ahimsa* (non-violence), (ii) *satya* (truthfulness), (iii) *asteya* (honesty), (iv) *brahmacharya* (moderation in sexual activity) and (v) *aparigraha* (non-possessiveness). The five niyamas are: (i) *shaucha* (cleanliness), (ii) *santosha* (contentment), (iii) *tapasya* (austerity), (iv) *swadhyaya* (self-observation) and (v) *Ishwara pranidhana* (awareness of the principle of higher consciousness). A general practitioner may take to pranayama after shatkarmas and asana, but the sadhaka must overhaul his entire attitude towards life.

Special diets are prescribed during intensive and rigorous pranayama sadhana when the pranic intake through air is amplified and less energy is required through food. Dietary considerations, however, should be obtained from the guru. The *Shiva Samhita* (3:33–37) says the sadhaka must give up foods which are acidic, astringent, pungent, salty and bitter. One is also advised to take food when the right swara flows and go to sleep when the left swara flows, because pingala is heating and digests the food quickly, whereas ida is cooling and is conducive to calm sleep. Extremes such as fasting, and taking tobacco, cannabis, narcotics and hallucinogenic drugs must be strictly avoided.

The pranayama sadhana must be commenced either in spring or autumn, when the weather is moderate. The *Gheranda Samhita* says (5:9):

वसन्ते शरदि प्रोक्तं योगारम्भं समाचरेत् ।
तथायोगी भवेत् सिद्धो रोगान्मुक्तो भवेद् ध्रुवम् ॥

The practice of yoga should be commenced by a beginner in spring or autumn. By doing so he attains success, and verily he does not become liable to disease.

High mountains and cold climates, where the pure air is thick with negative ions, are very helpful for intensive pranayama sadhana. The yoga texts also state that the pranayama practitioner should not warm himself by fire, because fire depletes negative ions.

The place of practice must be treated as sacred. In Dattatreya's *Yoga Shastra* the place of practice is described (v. 107–111):

सुशोभनं मंठ कुर्यात्सूक्ष्मद्वारं तु निर्घृणम् ।
सुष्ठु लिप्तं गोमयेन सुधया वा प्रयत्नतः ॥
मत्कुणैः मशकैः भूतैः वर्जितं च प्रयत्नतः ।
दिने-दिने सुसम्मृष्टं सम्मार्जन्या ह्यतन्द्रितः ।
वासितं च सुगंधेन धूपितं गुग्गुलादिभिः ॥

To practise pranayama, the yogi should prepare a small cloister. The door should be small and the room should be free of all germs. The floor and walls should be wiped carefully with cow-dung or lime, so that the room remains free of bugs, mosquitoes and spiders. It should be swept daily and perfumed with incense and resin.

Four sittings of pranayama practice should be undertaken daily at the following times: early morning, midday, evening and midnight. While practising one must sit facing east or north. Nadi shodhana pranayama should be practised for at least three months until the count of 20:80:40:40 is achieved, before commencing any other pranayama.

The sadhaka should avoid excessive company. Dattatreya says, "The pranayama yogi should avoid the company of others and not allow himself to be touched by others." One becomes highly sensitive in the beginning stages of pranayama sadhana and is easily disturbed by external influences. The resulting fluctuations hamper the steadiness of sadhana. Interactions also involve a pranic element. Exchanges that are not uplifting, such as criticism, gossip or catering to emotional demands, deplete one of prana as well as create or reinforce the negative samskaras that one is trying to eliminate through the sadhana. Emotional dependency expressed through an exchange translates into pranic dependency and makes it difficult to generate prana as well as remain self-reliant – the two hallmarks of a yogi.

Deep faith in the practice itself is most essential. Only through a commitment born of faith will one be able to continue the practice, irrespective of the signs of progress and the inclination to give up when the circumstances are unfavourable. The *Shiva Samhita* says (3:18):

फलिष्यतीति विश्वास: सिद्धे: प्रथमलक्षणम् ।

The first condition of success is the firm belief that it (the vidya) must succeed and be fruitful.

However, even if all the conditions are fulfilled, the sadhaka will not be able to achieve his goal without the grace of guru. The guru and the sadhaka's devotion to him are indispensable when the pranayama practice is taken to the level of sadhana. The *Shiva Samhita* says (3:11):

भवेद्वीर्यवती विद्या गुरुवक्त्रसमुद्भवा ।
अन्यथा फलहीना स्यान्निर्वीर्याप्यतिदु:खदा ॥

Only the knowledge imparted by a guru, through his lips, is powerful and useful; otherwise it becomes fruitless, weak and painful.

In pranayama sadhana for the awakening of higher consciousness, the sadhaka prepares to become a channel. Therefore, the guidance of a guru is essential, not just to correct the mechanics of the practice but to transmit intuitive knowledge. With the establishment of a link with the guru, the sadhana becomes the means to receive the direction of one's spiritual growth and the final goal is reached.

19

Nadi Shodhana Pranayama

Nadi shodhana is the first pranayama described in the classical yogic texts. Ideally, other classical pranayamas should be attempted only after practising nadi shodhana as instructed by the teacher for a specific period. The word *nadi* means 'energy channel' and *shodhana* means 'to cleanse' or 'to purify'. Therefore, nadi shodhana is a practice whereby the pranic channels are purified and regulated. This prepares one for the practice of other pranayamas, so that maximum benefits can be derived and one does not experience any pranic imbalance.

Nadi shodhana is also a complete practice in itself and the higher stages achieve the ultimate aim of pranayama: kevala kumbhaka. Nadi shodhana is practised by alternating the inhalation and exhalation between the left and right nostrils, thus influencing the ida and pingala nadis and the two brain hemispheres. This leads to control of the oscillations of the body-mind network, bringing balance and harmony throughout the system.

Nadi shodhana is truly a balancing pranayama, because whether the imbalance lies in the physical or mental body, this practice can restore equilibrium. Swami Satyananda has said, "If one wants to lead a spiritual life, this very pranayama is sufficient. It will steady the way to meditation and samadhi."

Nadi shodhana in scriptures

All the classical yogic texts describe nadi purification as a necessary step to achieve *kevala kumbhaka*, spontaneous retention of breath. Many equate pranayama with kumbhaka, while others explain the process to achieve kumbhaka as pranayama. In the first case, nadi shodhana is treated as an indispensable preliminary practice of 'pranayama' and in the second as the first pranayama, or even the only pranayama. The *Gheranda Samhita* says (5:35):

मलाकुलासु नाडीषु मारुतो नैव गच्छति ।
प्राणायाम: कथं सिध्येत्तत्त्वज्ञानं कथं भवेत् ।
तस्मादादौ नाडीशुद्धिं प्राणायामं ततोऽभ्यसेत् ॥

The vayu (prana) does not enter the nadis as long as they are full of impurities. How then can pranayama be accomplished? How can there be knowledge of the tattwas? Therefore, first the nadis should be purified, and then pranayama should be practised.

It recommends the practices of shatkarma and three specific forms of nadi shodhana, combining bija mantras and tattwa sadhana to achieve such purification. Thereafter, it says, "sitting firmly in a posture, let him begin regular pranayama" (5:36). Among the 'regular pranayamas' or kumbhakas, the first is *sahita* – alternate nostril breathing or nadi shodhana (with or without mantra and visualization), achieving higher ratios of inhalation, retention and exhalation over a period of practice.

In the *Hatha Yoga Pradipika* (2:5) it is said:

शुद्धिमेति यदा सर्वं नाडीचक्रं मलाकुलम् ।
तदैव जायते योगी प्राणसंग्रहणे क्षम: ॥

All the nadis and chakras are full of impurities. When they are purified, the yogi is able to retain prana.

This text treats nadi shodhana as a practice separate from, and a prelude to, all other pranayamas. It describes the traditional form of nadi shodhana – alternate nostril breathing with internal retention, and recommends that it be practised four times a day, gradually increasing the retention to 80 counts.

Dattatreya's *Yoga Shastra* equates pranayama with the practice of nadi shodhana and lists this pranayama alone, describing its successive higher stages. He recommends that at the beginning it be practised four times a day for 20 counts with retention to the best of one's ability. If practised in this way for three months, it will purify all the nadis (v. 131–132):

कुर्यादेवं चतुर्वारमनालस्यो दिने दिने ।
एवं मासत्रयं कुर्यान्नाडीशुद्धिस्ततो भवेत् ॥

This (nadi shodhana) should be performed four times a day every day without sloth. This will bring about nadi shuddhi in three months.

The same assertion has been made in the *Shiva Samhita* (3:25):

इत्थं मासत्रयं कुर्यादनालस्यो दिने दिने ।
ततो नाडीविशुद्धि: स्यादविलम्बेन निश्चितम् ॥

When this (nadi shodhana to 20 counts four times a day) has been practised every day for three months, without sloth, the nadis will surely be purified without delay.

The *Shiva Samhita* describes the signs of nadi purification as a harmonized body, emitting a pleasant scent and a sweet voice (23:31). Dattatreya's *Yoga Shastra* ascribes the attributes of a light, bright, lean and thin body to nadi purification (v. 135–136). However, to achieve this, the texts say that discipline and balance in food, cravings, sensory experiences, physical activity, company, thought, behaviour and speech are essential, along with the practice (SS 3:33, YSD v. 137–140). If all the rules are followed, nadi purification itself leads the practitioner to experience kevala kumbhaka for as long as desired.

Acquisition of various *siddhis* (psychic powers) may also result, but the practitioner is warned against their influence, and recommended to chant Pranava (the mantra *Om*) to get rid of the associated negative samskaras. This is only the first stage (*arambha avastha*) of kevala kumbhaka, and if the practice of nadi shodhana is continued, the second stage (*ghata avastha*) takes place (YSD v. 178–180):

प्राणापानौ मनोवायू जीवात्मपरमात्मनौ ।
अन्योन्यस्याविरोधेन एकतां घटतो यदा ।
तदा घटाद्वयावस्था प्रसिद्धा योगिनां स्मृता ॥

When the unity of prana and apana, manas and prana, and atman and paramatman is attained and their distinctness removed, this stage is called ghatadvayavastha or ghatavastha, for which a regular practice of restraining and sustaining prana is essential. This stage is known by yogis only.

At this stage, the yogi may practice the pranayama only once a day. This leads to pratyahara, described by Dattatreya as a practice where sensory withdrawal has been perfected to the extent that the yogi feels that whatever he sees, hears, smells, tastes or touches is the Supreme. The *Shiva Samhita* describes it as a stage where the yogi can hold the breath for three hours (3:57). The next stage of parichayavastha comes only when the yogi has mastered this stage (YSD v. 212–215):

तत: परिचयावस्था जायतेऽभ्याससयोगत: ।
वायु: सम्प्रेरितो यत्नादग्निना सह कुण्डलीम् ॥
बोधयित्वा सुषुम्नायां प्रविशेदविरोधत: ।
वायुना सह चित्तं तु प्रविशेच्च महापथम् ॥

The stage of parichayavastha comes thereafter if the yogi continues the yoga practice. The prana, acquainted with internal fire, awakens the kundalini and enters without obstacle into the sushumna nadi; the mind also enters into the great path with the prana.

The aim of pranayama having been achieved, thereafter the practices of pancha dharana, dhyana and finally, samadhi, are perfected and nishpatti avastha attained. Swami Sivananda states, "A yogic student will automatically experience all these avasthas one by one, as he advances in his systematic, regular practices. An impatient student cannot experience any of these avasthas through occasional practices."

Practice of nadi shodhana

Nadi shodhana is a complete practice in itself and, as stated in the scriptures, can lead to the experience of kevala kumbhaka and samadhi. However, the diligence of a sadhaka is required to arrive at this state. In texts such as *Shiva Samhita*, the various remarkable stages following the practice of nadi shodhana presume such a calibre of the aspirant. These scriptures were written by highly accomplished yogis, who actually described their advanced practices. Nevertheless, the practice of nadi shodhana will give substantial benefits to an average practitioner as well.

As a daily practice, nadi shodhana may be used to vitalize the pranic energies, release pranic blockages and achieve a balance between the sympathetic and parasympathetic nervous systems, so that life's situations can be handled better. As a therapeutic tool, it can be applied for almost all physical and mental disorders, although this must be done under expert guidance. For those who wish to use nadi shodhana as a spiritual practice, it may indeed awaken the dormant shakti and direct it through sushumna, the path of spiritual awakening, leading to deep states of meditation.

The practice is presented here in three parts, beginning, intermediate and advanced. Proper advice should be obtained before commencing any of these levels. As with all techniques, each stage should be mastered before proceeding to the next, so that the duration of inhalation, exhalation and retention can be controlled without strain and without the need to take extra breaths in between rounds. One should not be alarmed by the long ratios of the advanced level. They are difficult to master and are intended only for the serious sadhaka. The practitioner who becomes competent in all the stages of beginner and intermediate levels will gain the full benefit of the practice, physically, mentally and spiritually. Progress beyond this point is sadhana to be undertaken only under the strict guidance of a master.

General guidelines

Posture: One may assume postures such as sukhasana, ardha padmasana and vajrasana during the preliminary stages, but in the more advanced stages these postures will not lock the body and keep it steady. Therefore, it is better to choose one of the locked meditative postures such as siddhasana, siddha yoni asana, padmasana or swastikasana. Advanced stages of kumbhaka with ratio and bandhas should not be attempted unless one steady posture can be held comfortably throughout the practice. Any kind of tension will block the free flow of prana and distract the awareness. One should check the sitting position periodically to see that the back, neck and head remain straight, steady and still. There should be no shaking or nervous tremors in any part of the body.

Stages of practice: Four techniques are described here with progressive stages in each, which allow for a smooth development from beginning to advanced levels. However, this is intended to take place over a long period of time. Each stage should be practised for at least two weeks before proceeding to the next. Mastery of some stages may take months, and there should not be any hurry. More benefit can be obtained by perfecting the details of breathing than by achieving advanced stages. Control of the respiratory system requires gradual development. Time is needed for the body and mind to adjust to the effect of extended breath and retention.

Familiarity with the techniques of expanding the breath capacity (see Chapter 16: 'Preliminary Breathing Practices') will enable one to practise each new stage of nadi shodhana through both nostrils, before proceeding to alternate nostril breathing. This type of breathing is recommended at the commencement of each stage. Even in daily sadhana, practising through both nostrils to the appropriate ratio will help to create the breathing rhythm before the actual practice of nadi shodhana is commenced.

Techniques 1 and 2 prepare the lungs and the nervous system for techniques 3 and 4, which introduce *antar* and *bahir kumbhaka* (internal and external breath retention). The full benefits of this practice will be obtained by systematically perfecting each level, rather than by struggling prematurely with the advanced techniques. It is important to experience each stage fully and become established in that new pattern of breathing and its effects on the nervous system, energy levels, emotions, mental clarity and subtle aspects of the personality.

Breath: Beginners should be familiar with abdominal breathing before taking up nadi shodhana. In nadi shodhana soundless breathing is practised to ensure that the breath is not forced or restricted in any way. As one progresses with the technique, the duration of inhalation, exhalation and retention should be extended within the limits of comfort. With the increase in ratio and duration, the breathing becomes very light and subtle. In the more developed stages, this gives a feeling as if the air is just floating in and out of the nostrils. Progress through the stages is easier if one develops the ability to relax with the breath. Increased ratios and length of breath should not be at the expense of relaxation, rhythm and awareness. The flow of breath must be smooth and without jerks throughout the practice.

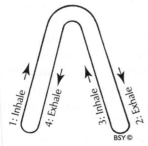
Alternate nostril breathing

Counting of rounds: One round of nadi shodhana comprises two complete breaths: breathing in through the left nostril, out through the right, in through the right nostril, and out through the left. As a standard procedure, each

229

round starts from the left nostril. The number of rounds to be practised daily depends on the individual and the time available. For general purposes, five to ten rounds (10–15 minutes daily) is sufficient. The teacher will be able to give proper advice if one wishes to extend the practice further.

Bandhas: Jalandhara, uddiyana and moola bandhas are used during the intermediate and advanced stages of nadi shodhana. These bandhas are described in Appendix D and should be practised independently before attempting to include them in the practice itself.

Precautions: Nadi shodhana should never be rushed or forced. The practitioner should proceed carefully under the guidance of a competent teacher. At the slightest sign of discomfort, the duration of inhalation/exhalation/retention should be reduced. If necessary, the practice may be discontinued for some time. For beginners the ratio of 1:2 for inhalation and exhalation without retention is favourable. Those suffering from high blood pressure, heart disease or peptic ulcer should not proceed beyond this level of practice. The ratio of inhalation and exhalation must always be 1:2 regardless of the count or duration of retention. One should never breathe through the mouth.

Awareness: During nadi shodhana the mind may tend to wander. One should be aware of this wandering tendency while continuing the practice and the count. This will automatically bring the awareness back to the practice. The awareness should be focused on the breath and the counting throughout the practice. The spiritual awareness should be on ajna chakra. Using a mantra will greatly assist in the process. When you tie an animal to a pole with a strong rope, it cannot move; in the same way, when the mantra is practised with nadi shodhana, the mind cannot move. Initially when the vital capacity is less, a short mantra like Om is easier, but when the count of inhalation has reached 24, one can use the Gayatri mantra (also see Chapter 7: 'Prana and Mantra').

Sequence: Nadi shodhana should be practised after shatkarma and asanas, and before other pranayamas. In order to remove nasal obstruction, if one of the nostrils is blocked, the practitioner should perform jala neti or breath-balancing exercises before commencing the practice. In the advanced stages, sometimes bhastrika pranayama is practised before nadi shodhana to facilitate longer retention. The best time to practise is around sunrise, although one may practise at any time during the day, except after meals.

Hand position: Nasagra/Nasikagra Mudra (nosetip position)

The following hand position is used during nadi shodhana pranayama to facilitate the smooth opening and closing of the nostrils required for alternate nostril breathing.

Technique:
Raise the right hand in front of the face. Place the tips of the index and middle fingers gently on the eyebrow centre. Both fingers should be relaxed.

Hold the thumb just above the right nostril and the ring finger just above the left.

These two fingers control the flow of breath in the nostrils by alternately pressing one nostril, blocking the flow of breath, then releasing and pressing the other.

The little finger is placed beside the ring finger.

When practising for long periods, the right elbow may be supported in the palm of the left hand, although care is needed to keep the head, neck and back straight in order to prevent chest restriction.

Practice note: While blocking a nostril, the finger is placed gently on the outside of the nostril or underneath

Variation

231

the opening of the nostril. The side of the nose should not be forced into the septum, because the pressure on the nerves inside the nostrils may compete with the effect that the flow of air is meant to have on the nerves in the opposite nostril.

Beginner's level

The following two techniques of nadi shodhana may be practised by everyone and are used to maintain the balance of body and mind in daily life as well as in therapeutic situations.

Technique 1: preparatory practice

Stage 1: Sit in any comfortable meditation posture, preferably siddhasana, siddha yoni asana or padmasana.
Keep the head and spine upright.
Relax the whole body and close the eyes.
Practise yogic breathing for some time.
Adopt nasagra mudra with the right hand and place the left hand on the knee in chin or jnana mudra.
Close the right nostril with the thumb.
Inhale and exhale through the left nostril 5 times, keeping the respiration rate normal.
Be aware of each breath.
After completing 5 breaths release the pressure of the thumb on the right nostril and press the left nostril with the ring finger, blocking the flow of air.
Inhale and exhale through the right nostril 5 times, keeping the respiration rate normal.
Lower the hand and breathe through both nostrils together 5 times, keeping the respiration rate normal.
This is one round.
Practise 5 rounds.
The breathing should be silent.
Practise this stage until it is mastered, before commencing the next stage.

Stage 2: Begin to control the duration of each breath.
Breathe deeply without strain.
Count the length of the inhalation and exhalation through
the left, right and both nostrils.
While inhaling, count mentally, "1, Om; 2, Om; 3, Om",
until the inhalation ends comfortably.
While exhaling, count, "1, Om; 2, Om; 3, Om".
Inhalation and exhalation should be equal.
Practise 5 rounds.
The breathing should be silent.

Practice note: The length of the breath will spontaneously
increase after some days of practice. When the count
reaches 10 without any strain, go on to technique 2.

Contra-indications: One should not practise while suffering
from colds, flu or fever.

Benefits: Increases awareness of and sensitivity to the breath in
the nostrils. Minor blockages are removed and the flow of
breath in both nostrils becomes more balanced, activating
both brain hemispheres. The long, slow, balanced breathing of stage 2 has profound effects, calming and balancing
the energies.

Technique 2: with alternate nostril breathing

In this technique the basic pattern of alternate nostril breathing is established.

Stage 1: Begin with equal inhalation and exhalation, using
the ratio 1:1.
Close the right nostril with the thumb and inhale through
the left nostril.
At the same time count mentally, "1, Om; 2, Om; 3, Om",
until the inhalation ends comfortably. This is the basic count.
Breathe deeply without strain.
Close the left nostril with the ring finger and release the
pressure of the thumb on the right nostril. While exhaling
through the right nostril, simultaneously count, "1, Om;
2, Om; 3, Om". The length of inhalation and exhalation
should be equal.

Next, inhale through the right nostril, keeping the same count in the same manner.

At the end of inhalation, close the right nostril and open the left nostril. Exhale through the left nostril, counting as before.

This is one round.

Practise 5–10 rounds.

Practice note: After one week, if there is no difficulty, increase the length of inhalation/exhalation by one count. Continue to increase the count in this way until the count of 10:10 is reached. Do not force the breath in any way. Be careful not to speed up the counting during exhalation to compensate for shortage of breath. Reduce the count at the slightest sign of discomfort.

Stage 2: After perfecting the above, the 1:1 ratio may be changed to 1:2.

Initially, halve the length of the inhalation. Inhale for a count of 5 and exhale for a count of 10.

Repeat on the other side.

This is one round.

Practise 5–10 rounds.

Practice note: During the ensuing practice, continue extending the breath by adding one count to the inhalation and two to the exhalation, up to the count of 10:20. The extension of count should be built up slowly.

Contra-indications: Stage 2 of technique 2 begins the process of introversion, which is not recommended for a depressed or withdrawn person. The extension of stage 2, involving longer counts, is not recommended for people with heart problems.

Benefits: Technique 2 gives more pronounced balancing of the breath and the brain hemispheres. It is calming, relieves anxiety, improves concentration and stimulates ajna chakra. The ratio 1:1 in stage 1 establishes a calming rhythm for the brain and heart, assisting people with cardiovascular and nervous disorders specifically, and stress-related conditions generally. As the count is extended, the breath slows down. The respiration becomes more efficient because the air flow is smoother and less turbulent. This ratio helps people with respiratory problems such as asthma, emphysema and bronchitis. The ratio 1:2 in stage 2 gives profound relaxation. The heartbeat and pulse rate slow down, and blood pressure drops.

Intermediate level

At this stage, internal kumbhaka is introduced. Kumbhaka is the aim of pranayama, as it activates the spiritual energy. Mastery of each stage requires conditioning the body and mind to longer periods of retention over a period of time. The brain becomes trained not to signal for inhalation or exhalation during slight rises in levels of carbon dioxide in the blood. Bandhas are also introduced, which lock the shakti or energy internally, preventing it from being dissipated in the body and mind, and directing it into the sushumna passage.

Technique 3: with antar kumbhaka (inner retention)

In this technique antar kumbhaka or internal breath retention is introduced. The inhalation and exhalation should be silent, smooth and controlled.

Stage 1: Begin breathing with equal inhalation, inner retention and exhalation.

Close the right nostril and inhale slowly through the left nostril for a count of 5.

At the end of inhalation, close both nostrils and retain the air in the lungs for a count of 5.

Open the right nostril and exhale for a count of 5.

At the end of exhalation, inhale through the right nostril for a count of 5, keeping the left nostril closed.

Again, retain the breath for a count of 5 with both nostrils closed.

Open the left nostril and exhale for a count of 5.

This is one round using the ratio 5:5:5.

Maintain constant awareness of the count and of the breath.

Practise 5–10 rounds.

Practice note: When the ratio of 5:5:5 is comfortable, the count can be lengthened. Gradually increase the count by adding 1 unit to the inhalation, 1 unit to the retention and 1 unit to the exhalation. The count of one round will then be 6:6:6. When this has been perfected and there is no discomfort, increase the count to 7:7:7. Continue in this way until the count of 10:10:10 is reached. Do not force the breath. At the slightest sign of strain reduce the count.

Stage 2: After perfecting the ratio of 1:1:1, change to the ratio 1:1:2. Initially use a shorter count. Inhale for a count of 5, perform internal kumbhaka for a count of 5 and exhale for a count of 10.

Practice note: After mastering the count of 5:5:10, gradually increase the count by adding 1 unit to the inhalation, 1 unit to the retention and 2 units to the exhalation. The count of one round will then be 6:6:12. When this has been perfected and there is no discomfort, increase the count to 7:7:14. Gradually increase the count over several months of practice until the count of 10:10:20 is reached.

Stage 3: Change to the ratio 1:2:2.

Inhale for a count of 5, hold the breath inside for a count of 10 and exhale for a count of 10. Practise until the ratio and count are comfortable and there is no tendency to speed up the count during retention or exhalation due to shortness of breath.

Practice note: When this has been perfected, the count can be gradually increased by adding 1 unit to the inhalation, 2 units to the retention and 2 units to the exhalation. The count of one round will then be 6:12:12. In this manner, gradually increase the count to 10:20:20.

Stage 4: Change to the ratio 1:3:2.

Reduce the count of inhalation to 5. Hold the breath inside for a count of 15, and exhale for a count of 10.

Practise until the ratio is comfortable and there is no tendency to speed up the count during retention or exhalation due to shortness of breath.

Practice note: When this has been perfected and there is no discomfort, the count can be gradually increased by adding 1 unit to the inhalation, 3 units to the retention and 2 units to the exhalation. The count of one round will then be 6:18:12. In this manner, gradually increase the count to 10:30:20.

Stage 5: Change to the ratio of 1:4:2.

Begin with the count of 5:20:10.

Once this count has been established, it can be gradually increased.

Practice note: Add 1 unit to the inhalation, 4 units to the retention and 2 units to the exhalation. The count of one round will then be 6:24:12. In this manner, gradually increase the count to 10:40:20.

Contra-indications: Technique 3 is not suitable for women in the later half of pregnancy. It is not recommended for persons with heart problems, high blood pressure, emphysema or any major disorders. From stage 2 onward it is not recommended for asthmatics.

Benefits: The inner retention of breath, which characterizes technique 3, activates various brain centres and harmonizes the pranas. The benefits increase with the progression of the ratios. The ratio 1:4:2 is most widely recommended in the yogic texts. It gives profound psychological and pranic effects and is used as a preparation for kundalini awakening.

Advanced practice with addition of bandhas

The three bandhas: *jalandhara* (throat lock), *moola* (perineal lock) and *uddiyana* (abdominal lock), are to be added in the following practices. Before applying the bandhas, they should be perfected as individual practices. For details of the bandhas refer to Appendix D. The ratio and count of the practice should be reduced when adding the bandhas, so that strain is avoided. Extend the count gradually as previously instructed.

With jalandhara bandha:
> Reduce the count of the practice.
> Inhale through the left nostril, practise jalandhara bandha while holding the breath inside.
> Release jalandhara and exhale through the right nostril.
> Inhale through the right nostril.
> Practise jalandhara bandha during internal retention.
> Release jalandhara and exhale through the left nostril.
> This is one round, practise 5–10 rounds.
> Once the bandha can be held without strain, gradually build up the count.

With jalandhara and moola bandhas:
> Reduce the count of the practice.
> Inhale through the left nostril.
> Close both nostrils and hold the breath inside.
> Perform jalandhara bandha and then moola bandha.
> Continue to hold the breath.
> Release moola bandha and then jalandhara bandha.
> Exhale through the right nostril.
> Inhale through the right nostril and hold the breath inside.
> Practise jalandhara bandha and moola bandha.
> Release moola bandha and then jalandhara bandha.
> Exhale through the left nostril.
> This is one round. Practise 5–10 rounds.
> When the bandhas can be held without strain, gradually build up the count.

Precaution: The practise of nadi shodhana pranayama with bandhas should be performed under the guidance of a competent teacher or guru.

Benefits: This practice purifies and balances the pranic forces.

Advanced level

This level of practice requires very good control of the breath, as external retention is introduced here. The inhalation remains the base for each ratio to build on.

The practitioner should not attempt the higher ratios by hastening the inhalation and shortening exhalation and kumbhaka accordingly. Inhalation should be a steady, soundless breath with the same count for each round. Then the timing of the practice will remain constant. One should become well-established in each stage before proceeding to the next. At this level, it takes longer to stabilize the breathing ratios. The practitioner may be able to do one round easily, while the next round will leave him breathless. Each stage may take weeks or months to perfect.

Bhastrika pranayama may be practised beforehand in order to reduce the carbon dioxide level, so that extended ratios become easier. The practitioner should first become proficient in each stage without the application of bandhas. Then the practice may be performed with the bandhas before proceeding to the next stage. The count should be increased gradually, according to one's capacity. One should experiment with the practice in order to find the ratio that suits one's own level. The final result of this level of practice is kevala kumbhaka, spontaneous cessation of the breath, which brings the mind into a state of deep meditation. With practice, faith and perseverance, this will undoubtedly occur.

Technique 4: with antar and bahir kumbhaka (internal and external retention)

In this technique bahir kumbhaka or outer breath retention is introduced. The practitioner should not try to hold the breath outside for long at first, even though it may seem easy.

Stage 1: Begin with the ratio 1:1:1:1 and a count, such as 5:5:5:5.

Inhale through the left nostril, counting to 5.

Retain the breath in antar kumbhaka, counting to 5.

Exhale through the right nostril, counting to 5.

After exhalation, close both nostrils and hold the breath outside, counting to 5.

The glottis may be slightly contracted to hold the air outside. Exhale slightly through the right nostril immediately before inhaling. This will release the lock on the lungs and the glottis and bring the respiratory system smoothly back into operation.

Inhale slowly through the right nostril, counting to 5.

Retain the breath, counting to 5.

Exhale through the left nostril, counting to 5.

Again, hold the breath outside, counting to 5 with both nostrils closed.

If necessary, exhale slightly through the right nostril before breathing in at the start of the next round.

This is one round.

Practise 5 rounds.

Practice note: When the ratio has been perfected with an easy count, gradually increase it by adding 1 unit to the inhalation, internal retention, exhalation and external retention. The count should slowly be increased from 5 to 6, 6 to 7 and so on, until the count of 10:10:10:10 is reached. Do not increase the count until the exhalation and breath retentions are comfortable.

Stage 2:The next ratio is 1:1:2:1. It should be commenced with a low count and extended gradually as previously instructed. Begin with the count of 5:5:10:5.

Practice note: Once this ratio has been established, the count can be gradually increased. Add one unit to the inhalation, one unit to the internal retention, 2 units to the exhalation and one unit to the external retention. The count for one round would thus become 6:6:12:6. Over time, the count can be slowly increased. Do not increase the count until exhalation and breath retentions are comfortable.

Stage 3: The next ratio is 1:2:2:1. Begin with the count of 5:10:10:5.

Increase the count when the exhalation and breath retentions are comfortable.

Stage 4: The next ratio is 1:2:2:2. Begin with the count of 5:10:10:10.

Build up the count gradually without strain.

Stage 5: The next ratio is 1:3:2:2.

Begin with the count of 5:15:10:10.
Increase the count gradually, without strain.
Stage 6: The final ratio is 1:4:2:2.
Begin with the count of 5:20:10:10.
Increase the count gradually, without strain.

Addition of bandhas

When technique 4 has been mastered, it may be practised in conjunction with jalandhara, moola and uddiyana bandhas. First practise jalandhara bandha with internal and external breath retention only. When this practice has been perfected, combine jalandhara and moola bandha with internal and external breath retention. After this, combine jalandhara and moola bandhas during internal retention and maha bandha during external retention.

Variation: Anuloma Viloma (mental nadi shodhana)

Anuloma viloma is a mental adaptation of nadi shodhana pranayama, and has a subtle and balancing effect. Simple nadi shodhana is practised without using nasagra mudra, but with the help of the mind and imagination. This technique subtly demonstrates the power of the mind. Even though one may be imagining the breath in the alternate nostrils at first, in time one will actually feel the breath moving in the nostrils by mental command. The advantage of this technique is that it can be practised in one's daily sadhana and at other times as well. It can be done while sitting, lying, standing or walking.

Anuloma viloma can be practised as per the beginning and intermediate levels of nadi shodhana. By the time the advanced level is reached, the breathing should be very subtle, and anuloma viloma will become superfluous. Anuloma viloma has a calming effect on the nervous system, and can be practised during stressful situations without other people's knowledge. It is an on-the-spot tranquillizer, which also promotes clarity of mind and awareness, without adverse side effects.

241

Technique

Assume any comfortable posture.

Close the eyes and relax the whole body.

Become totally aware of the breathing process.

Feel as though nothing else exists except the breath.

Mentally direct the breath in and out of the left nostril. Feel the breath flowing in and out of the left nostril only. The use of imagination may be necessary in the beginning.

Continue breathing through the left nostril mentally for one or two minutes.

Repeat the same procedure with the right nostril.

Feel that the whole flow of breath is moving in and out of the right nostril only.

Continue breathing through the right nostril mentally for one or two minutes.

Be aware of each breath throughout the practice.

Now mentally direct the breath in and out of the alternate nostrils.

Mentally inhale through the left nostril and exhale through the right.

Then, mentally inhale through the right nostril and exhale through the left.

This is one round of anuloma viloma (mental alternate nostril breathing).

Practise 27 rounds, or as required.

Variation: Prana Shuddhi

Assume any comfortable posture.

Close the eyes and relax the whole body.

Become aware of the breathing process.

Now imagine the flow of breath moving up and down the sides of the nostrils in an inverted V-shape pathway.

At the end of inhalation the two flows of breath converge at the eyebrow centre.

During exhalation the two breaths diverge from the eyebrow centre and flow down the sides of the V-shaped pathway.

242

Imagination and awareness are required to maintain the visualization.

A single inhalation and exhalation is one round.

Practise 27 rounds.

Practice note: These practices help one become centred and increase the awareness. One can count each round mentally, starting from 54 or 27 and ending at zero. The awareness should be focused on the visualization and experience of the breath flowing in the nostrils and the counting.

Physiology of nadi shodhana

Nadi shodhana pranayama affects brain hemispherity by alternately stimulating the right brain and then the left brain. The flow of breath through the nostrils stimulates the opposite side of the brain, via nerve endings just beneath the mucous layer inside the nostrils. Each side of the body is governed by nerves originating in the opposite side of the brain. The stimulation of the nostrils by the flow of breath increases nervous activity in the brain on the opposite side of each nostril.

The autonomic nervous system is also stimulated and relaxed by this practice. The sympathetic nervous system is stimulated by increasing the flow of breath in the right nostril. This increases the heart rate, produces more sweaty palms, dilates the pupils and opens up the lungs – all part of the fight or flight reaction. By increasing the flow of breath through the left nostril, the parasympathetic nervous system is stimulated. This lowers the heart rate, relaxes the body and improves digestion.

The practice of nadi shodhana also brings about ionic field homogenization. The ida nadi is a storehouse of negative ions and the pingala nadi of positive ions. During the practice of nadi shodhana, as one inhales through the left nostril the negative ion concentration in ida nadi quickly increases from its rest or basal concentration. It then reaches a maximum and begins to fall off gradually, because the concentration of ions is greater in the regions of low pranic density (e.g. there

243

is a high ionic concentration in the region of prana, udana, samana and a low concentration in apana and vyana.) The ionic concentration is thus not homogeneous yet. When the breath is held, the concentration of ions becomes equal in all parts of ida nadi. At the chakras where ida and pingala are in the closest proximity, the negative ions from ida migrate towards pingala attracted by its positive ions, and many are annihilated as they merge. This has the effect of depleting the number of ions in both ida and pingala, but more so in pingala, because of the high concentration of negative ions in ida. This also causes energy to be liberated in various forms such as heat, light and pranic energy, which has to be absorbed, transformed or removed in part.

During exhalation through the right nostril, the heat component of the energy produced by the above ionic annihilation process is liberated. Pingala nadi has a very small concentration of positive ions and is thus prepared to receive the influx of positive ions in the next part of the round. During external retention, the ionic concentrations in both ida and pingala are homogenized and a state of equilibrium is reached.

Inhalation through the right nostril increases the positive ion concentration in pingala. It rises quickly to a maximum level and then decreases slowly just as in the case of ida. During retention, the ion concentration in pingala is homogenized, and ion migration to ida (and annihilation) takes place. So, the process of nadi shodhana produces a kind of ionic seesaw.

Benefits of nadi shodhana

Nadi shodhana is a panacea for all imbalances. When the balance in the autonomic nervous system is restored, the root causes of many diseases are tackled and over a period of time removed. Regular practice of nadi shodhana also helps to maintain the pineal gland, thereby influencing the pituitary gland and the flow of hormones into the blood. Nadi shodhana activates the frontal brain and ajna chakra, thereby inducing tranquillity, clarity of thought and concentration. It also helps to remove depressive tendencies and vertigo. It purifies and regulates the entire pranic system, the nadis and chakras. As prana flows freely through every system, the vitality improves at all levels. At the spiritual level, the practice of nadi shodhana prepares one to enter higher meditative states.

20

Tranquillizing Pranayamas

The tranquillizing practices of pranayama are designed to relax the body and mind, while simultaneously increasing the pranic capacity and conscious awareness. These pranayamas stimulate the parasympathetic nervous system and draw the awareness within. Some bring about greater psychic sensitivity, while others cool the system. The tranquillizing techniques are usually practised after nadi shodhana, which balances the sympathetic and parasympathetic nervous systems by regulating the breath flow in the alternate nostrils. Therefore, the tranquillizing practices are done through both nostrils together and in some cases through the mouth. These practices should be avoided by persons who are excessively introverted, oversensitive or psychically unbalanced, as they may exacerbate these conditions.

Sheetali and Sheetkari Pranayamas

These two practices were designed to reduce body heat and are very effective during hot weather. The root word *sheet* means 'cold' while *sheetal* means 'calm, passionless and unemotional'. So, these practices cool both the body and mind. Sheetali and sheetkari are cooling practices, because the inhalation takes place through the mouth, rather than the nose. When the breath is drawn in through the mouth, evaporation of the moisture on the tongue and the inner surfaces of the mouth cool the air. This cooled air then cools the blood vessels throughout the lungs, which gradually eliminate excess body heat. The technique and effects of sheetali and sheetkari are the same, only the methods of inhalation vary.

Sheetali Pranayama
Technique 1: basic method

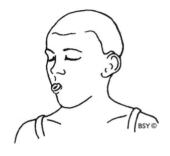

Sit in any comfortable meditation posture with the hands on the knees in chin or jnana mudra.

Close the eyes and relax the whole body.

Extend the tongue outside as far as possible without straining.

Roll the sides of the tongue up so that it forms a tube.

Inhale through the rolled tongue in one long, smooth and controlled breath.

At the end of inhalation, draw the tongue inside, close the mouth and exhale through the nose.

Practise yogic breathing throughout.

The inhaled breath should produce a sucking sound.

A feeling of icy coldness will be experienced on the tongue and the roof of the mouth.

This is one round.

Practise 11 rounds and gradually extend to 21.

Practice note: The awareness should be focused on the rolled up tongue, and the sound and cooling sensation of the inhaled breath. About one-third of the population is genetically unable to roll the sides of the tongue into a tube. For practitioners who cannot perform this action, sheetkari pranayama gives similar benefits. The duration of the inhalation should gradually be lengthened to increase the cooling effect. For general purposes 11–21 rounds are sufficient; however, in very hot weather up to 60 rounds may be performed.

247

Sequence: Practise after asanas and other yogic practices that heat the body, in order to restore temperature balance.

Technique 2: with antar kumbhaka (internal retention)

At the end of inhalation, retain the breath inside for one or two seconds.

The duration of retention may be gradually increased as the technique is mastered.

Jalandhara bandha may also be combined with this practice during internal retention.

Precautions: This practice should be avoided in a polluted atmosphere or during cold weather. Breathing through the nose filters the incoming air and adjusts it to the body temperature. However, in this practice the body's natural filtration system in the nose and the warming effect of the blood-sinusoids in the mucous membrane of the nose are bypassed. Therefore, this pranayama should be practised only in fresh, clean and warm air, so that the lungs are not contaminated or chilled. Practise inner retention for a short time only, as prolonged kumbhaka has a heating effect.

Contra-indications: People suffering from low blood pressure or respiratory disorders, such as asthma, bronchitis and excessive mucus, should not practise this pranayama. Those with heart disease should practise without breath retention. This practice cools down the activity of the lower energy centres and should be avoided by those suffering from chronic constipation. This pranayama should not be practised in winter or in cool climates.

Benefits: This practice cools the body and affects important brain centres associated with biological drives and temperature regulation. It cools and reduces mental and emotional excitation, and encourages the free flow of prana throughout the body. It induces muscular relaxation, mental tranquillity and may be used as a tranquillizer before sleep. Whenever one faces a situation where the blood pressure is rising, sheetali may be practised in order to restore equilibrium.

Sheetali gives control over hunger and thirst, and generates a feeling of satisfaction. It also reduces inflammations, fever, bile and acidity, and is useful in eliminating peptic and mouth ulcers. The sound produced during sheetali is an imitation of the respiration of a serpent. It is said that one who practises it regularly will not be affected by the bite of serpents and scorpions.

Sheetkari Pranayama
Technique 1: basic method

Sit in any comfortable meditation posture.

Close the eyes and relax the whole body.

Hold the teeth lightly together.

Separate the lips, exposing the teeth.

The tongue may be kept flat or folded against the soft palate in khechari mudra (see Appendix C).

Inhale slowly and deeply through the teeth.

At the end of the inhalation, close the mouth.

Exhale slowly through the nose in a controlled manner.

This is one round.

Practise 11 rounds, gradually increasing to 21.

Advanced practice: As for sheetali pranayama technique 2.

Awareness: On the hissing sound and the cooling sensation of the inhaled breath.

Contra-indications: As for sheetali pranayama. Practitioners with sensitive teeth, missing teeth or dentures should practise sheetali pranayama instead.

Precautions: As for sheetali pranayama.

Benefits: As for sheetali pranayama, with the additional advantage that it keeps the teeth and gums healthy.

249

Kaki Pranayama (crow's beak breath)

Kaki is so called because during inhalation the pursed lips form the shape of a crow's beak. Those practitioners who are unable to practise sheetali or sheetkari will find it easy. Kaki is really a mudra but is included here as a pranayama practice because of its close similarity to sheetali and sheetkari.

Technique 1: basic method

Sit in any comfortable meditation pose.
Close the eyes and relax the whole body.
Purse the lips, as in whistling, leaving a hollow space in the middle.
Open the eyes and focus them at the nose tip in nasikagra drishti.

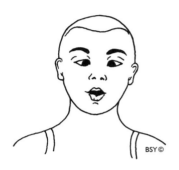

Inhale slowly and deeply, drawing the air in through the lips.
At the end of inhalation close the lips and exhale slowly through the nostrils.
Keep the eyes focused on the nose tip.
If the eyes become tired, close them during exhalation.
Practise for 3–5 minutes.

Technique 2: with jalandhara and moola bandhas

Sit in siddhasana or siddha yoni asana.
Practise the basic method of kaki pranayama.
After inhalation, retain the breath.
Maintain nasikagra drishti and perform jalandhara and moola bandhas.
Hold the retention and the bandhas for a few seconds.
Release moola bandha, then jalandhara bandha.
Slowly raise the head and exhale through the nose.
Again breathe in through the mouth.
Keep the eyes focused in nasikagra drishti throughout the practice.

If they become tired, close them during exhalation. Practise for 5–10 minutes.

Contra-indications: People suffering from heart disease should practise without retention. Those suffering from depression, low blood pressure and chronic constipation should avoid this practice.

Benefits: The practice of kaki pranayama is said to make one as healthy as a crow, which never falls ill. It is an overall tonic, cools the body and mind, dispels fatigue and restlessness, and alleviates disorders such as high blood pressure. It has the added benefits of nasikagra drishti, purifies the blood and stimulates the digestive secretions, aiding the digestive process generally.

Ujjayi Pranayama (psychic breath)

Ujjayi means 'victorious' and comes from the root *ujji*, 'to conquer' or 'acquire by conquest'. Ujjayi is one of the most important, yet one of the simplest pranayamas. It is practised by contracting the glottis and breathing through the throat. When done correctly, ujjayi breathing sounds like a cat purring or a baby snoring. When a healthy child sleeps, he always breathes by contracting the glottis, so that the sound of the breath comes from the throat. This kind of breathing is replicated in ujjayi. Of course, the breath flows through the nostrils, but the glottis is contracted so a light snoring sound is produced by the breath in the throat.

Ujjayi is a deep breathing practice which is perfected by relaxing the breath rather than forcing it. It is the one pranayama that may be practised in any position – standing, sitting or prone. Ujjayi is also known as the psychic breath, as it induces a meditative state and leads to very subtle states of mind. It is an indispensable part of many meditative techniques such as mantra japa, ajapa japa, kriya yoga and prana vidya.

Technique 1: basic method

Sit in any comfortable meditation asana.

Close the eyes and relax the whole body.

Take the awareness to the breath in the nostrils and allow the breathing to become calm and rhythmic.

After some time, transfer the awareness to the throat.

Feel or imagine that the breath is being drawn in and out through the throat and not through the nostrils, as if it is taking place through a small hole in the throat.

As the breathing becomes slower and deeper, gently contract the glottis, so that a soft snoring sound, like the breathing of a sleeping baby, is produced in the throat.

When practised correctly, there will be a spontaneous contraction of the abdomen.

Both inhalation and exhalation should be long, deep and controlled.

Relax the face as much as possible.

Do not contract the throat too strongly.

The contraction should be slight and applied continuously throughout the practice.

Practise yogic breathing, while concentrating on the sound produced by the breath in the throat.

The sound of the breath should be audible to the practitioner alone.

Practise for 3–5 minutes.

Practice note: Those suffering from a slipped disc or vertebral spondylitis may practise ujjayi in vajrasana or makarasana.

Technique 2: with khechari mudra

When ujjayi breathing has been mastered, fold the tongue back into khechari mudra (see Appendix C).

When the tongue becomes tired, release it, while continuing the ujjayi breathing. When the tongue is rested, again fold it back.

Practise for 3–5 minutes.

Practice note: *Khechari* means 'one who moves through space'. It activates the psychic, physiological and endocrine

252

processes responsible for cellular revitalization and longevity. If khechari mudra is correctly practised in conjunction with ujjayi over a long period of time, the bindu and vishuddhi chakras are stimulated, so that the special secretion formed in bindu is purified by vishuddhi, bestowing rejuvenation to the entire body. Sant Kabir says about this process: "When this nectar is tasted, all fears, diseases, guilt and ignorance are burned way. Then, one will shine from within like the full moon night." Normally when one closes the eyes, one sees darkness. But if one closes the eyes when the nectar is flowing, one will see only light. The whole brain and consciousness are illumined. This is the aim of practising ujjayi with khechari.

Technique 3: with antar kumbhaka (inner retention)
Practise ujjayi with khechari mudra.
The inhalation and exhalation should be smooth and controlled.
Inhale slowly and deeply with ujjayi.
Retain the breath inside with awareness at ajna or bindu.
The ujjayi exhalation should be as long as is comfortable.
Practice note: Avoid strain when performing kumbhaka. Initially one or two seconds is sufficient. The duration may be increased gradually as the technique is mastered. Inner retention helps to develop introversion and concentration.

Technique 4: with jalandhara and moola bandhas
Inhale with ujjayi.
Retain the breath.
Practise jalandhara bandha for a comfortable duration.
Release jalandhara and exhale with ujjayi.
Inhale with ujjayi.
Retain the breath.
Practise jalandhara and moola bandhas, holding the breath inside for a comfortable duration.
Release moola bandha, then jalandhara bandha and exhale with ujjayi.

Once the bandhas can be held without strain, gradually build up the number of rounds.

Contra-indications: Those suffering from heart disease should not combine bandhas or breath retention with ujjayi. People who are too introverted by nature should not perform ujjayi. Anyone with low blood pressure must first correct the condition before taking up the practice.

Benefits: Ujjayi is classified as a tranquillizing pranayama, but it also has a heating effect, stimulating the process of oxidation. This practice soothes the nervous system, calms the mind and increases psychic sensitivity. It has a profoundly relaxing effect at the psychic level. It helps to relieve insomnia and may be practised in shavasana just before sleep, but without khechari mudra. It slows down the heart rate and lowers high blood pressure.

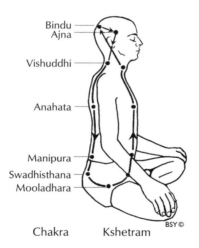

Technique 5: in the frontal psychic passage
Sit in any comfortable posture.

Practise ujjayi with khechari mudra.

Visualize a thin silver or transparent tube, connecting the navel to the throat, along the frontal part of the body.

While inhaling, imagine the breath moving along this passage from the navel to the throat.

While exhaling, imagine the breath moving down the tube from the throat to the navel.

Continue with this practice for some time.

Now, with inhalation, mentally repeat the mantra *So*, and with exhalation repeat the mantra *Ham*.

Alternatively, the guru mantra may also be synchronized with the breath.

Practise for 5–10 minutes.

Practice note: The rotation of ujjayi breath in the psychic passage creates a link between the mind and body. Therefore, the consciousness should also ascend and descend along the psychic pathway with the breath. *Soham* is the mantra of the breath. While inhaling the breath makes the sound *So*, and while exhaling it makes the sound *Ham*. One may first repeat the mantra mentally, but one will be able to hear the sound in the breath as the concentration deepens.

Technique 6: in the spinal psychic passage

Prepare for the practice in the same manner as above.

Visualize the thin silver or transparent tube in the spinal column, joining mooladhara and ajna chakras.

With each inhalation the breath and awareness ascend from mooladhara to ajna.

With each exhalation the breath and awareness descend from ajna to mooladhara.

Continue with this practice for some time.

Now, with inhalation, mentally repeat the mantra *So*, and with exhalation repeat the mantra *Ham*.

Alternatively, the guru mantra may also be synchronized with the breath.

Practise for 5–10 minutes.

Practice note: The yogic scriptures say that the mantra of the breath should be practised in the 'pathway to heaven'. This pathway is the sushumna nadi, located in the spinal cord. When this path is perfected immortal life is experienced. Its starting point is below the tail bone at mooladhara chakra, which symbolizes earth. The top of the spinal cord ends directly behind the eyebrow centre, at ajna chakra, which is called the gateway to heaven. Rotation of the ujjayi breath and the mantra in this passage is a powerful meditative technique.

Bhramari Pranayama (humming bee breath)

The word *bhramar* means 'bee'. This practice is so called because the practitioner imitates the same deep, low pitched humming sound as that of the black bee. It is used in nada yoga to awaken awareness of the inner psychic sounds.

BSY©

Technique 1: basic method

Sit in a comfortable meditation asana with the hands resting on the knees in jnana or chin mudra.

Close the eyes and relax the whole body.

The jaws should be relaxed with the lips gently closed and the teeth slightly separated. This allows the sound vibration to be heard and felt more distinctly.

Raise the arms sideways and bend the elbows, bringing the hands to the ears. Use the index fingers to close the flaps of the ears.

Bring the awareness to the centre of the head, where ajna chakra is located, and keep the body absolutely still.

Inhale through the nose.

While exhaling slowly in a controlled manner, produce a deep, steady humming sound, like that of the black bee. Be aware of the continuous humming sound within the head. The humming should be smooth and even for the duration of the exhalation. The sound should be soft and mellow, making the front of the skull reverberate.

At the end of exhalation, the hands may remain in the upraised position, or be returned to the knees and then raised again for the next round.

This is one round.

Practise 11 rounds and gradually increase to 21.

Variation: with ujjayi pranayama
Inhalation may also be performed by contracting the throat as in ujjayi pranayama.

Practice note: Gradually increase the duration of inhalation/exhalation and the number of rounds. Bhramari can be practised for up to half an hour, particularly to assist the healing process, or in cases of extreme mental tension or anxiety. Bhramari may be practised at any time to relieve mental tension. However, the best time to practise is late at night or in the early morning, as there are fewer external noises to interfere with internal perception. Practising at this time awakens psychic sensitivity.

Contra-indications: Bhramari should not be performed while lying down. People suffering from severe ear infections should not practise this pranayama.

Benefits: The vibration of the humming sound creates a soothing effect on the mind and nervous system, relieving cerebral tension, stress, anxiety and insomnia. It speeds up the healing of body tissue and post-operative patients benefit greatly from the practice. Bhramari is also helpful in pregnancy and childbirth. It eliminates throat ailments and strengthens and improves the voice. It is a powerful technique for enhancing memory and concentration. It induces a meditative state by harmonizing the mind and directing the awareness inward.

Technique 2: with antar kumbhaka (inner retention)
Inhale slowly and deeply through the nose.
Retain the breath inside with awareness at ajna or bindu.
The exhalation should be as long as is comfortable to
enhance the mind's absorption in the humming sound.
Practice note: Inner retention should be gradually increased
as it helps in developing introversion and concentration.
Avoid strain when performing kumbhaka; one or two
seconds is sufficient at first. The duration may be increased
gradually, as the technique is mastered. People with heart
disease must practise without breath retention.

Technique 3: with jalandhara and moola bandhas
Once antar kumbhaka has been mastered, jalandhara and
moola bandhas may be incorporated. For details of these
practices refer to Appendix D.
The full form of jalandhara can be practised if the hands
are returned to the knees between rounds. If the hands
remain raised the simple variation of jalandhara may be
practised.
Inhale for a long, smooth breath and retain the breath
inside.
Practise jalandhara and then moola bandha during
internal retention for a comfortable duration.
Release moola bandha and then jalandhara bandha.
Exhale with the humming sound, as in technique 1.
This is one round.
Gradually build up the number of rounds.
Ujjayi may be practised during inhalation.

Technique 4: with Pranava in the spinal passage
Bhramari may be practised with the mantra *Om* during
exhalation, instead of the humming sound. The pronunciation of the 'O' sound is very short and the 'Mmmmm'
sound is long.
Inhale with ujjayi, ascending the spinal passage from
mooladhara to ajna chakra.

While exhaling, descend in the spinal column from ajna to mooladhara chakra with the mantra *Om*.

Practise for 5–10 minutes.

Contra-indications: Those who are introverted or depressed should avoid this technique.

Technique 4: with shanmukhi mudra

All techniques of bhramari may be performed with shanmukhi mudra (see Appendix C).

In technique 1, allow the nostrils to remain open while performing shanmukhi mudra.

In technique 2, close the nostrils during internal retention with the middle fingers of each hand while performing shanmukhi mudra.

Concentrate on the subtle sound vibrations in the centre of the head and any images appearing in front of the closed eyes.

Moorchha Pranayama (swooning or fainting breath)

Moorchha means 'fainting' or 'swooning'. This pranayama is intended to arouse the feeling of unconsciousness and is best learned under expert guidance. *Moorchha* also means to expand, pervade and congeal. It expands the consciousness, awakens bindu chakra and helps in storing prana.

Technique

Sit in any comfortable meditation asana.

Keep the head and spine straight. Relax the whole body.

Observe the breath until it becomes slow and deep.

Perform khechari mudra.

Slowly inhaling through both nostrils with ujjayi pranayama, gently and smoothly bend the head slightly back.

Retain the breath inside and perform shambhavi mudra.

Straighten the arms by locking the elbows and pressing the knees with the hands.

Retain the breath and shambhavi for as long as is comfortable.

259

Exhale and relax the arms. Close the eyes and slowly bring the head back to the upright position.

Relax the whole body for a few seconds, keeping the eyes closed.

Experience lightness and tranquillity in the mind and body. This is one round.

Practise until a fainting sensation is felt.

Awareness: Physical – on the breath, head movement and eyebrow centre. Spiritual – on the void behind the eyebrow centre.

Sequence: After asanas and other pranayamas and before meditation; also beneficial before sleep.

Contra-indications: This technique should not be practised by those suffering from heart disease, high blood pressure, epilepsy, brain disorders or atherosclerosis of the carotid or basilar arteries.

Precautions: Discontinue the practice as soon as the fainting sensation is felt. The aim is to induce a swooning sensation, not complete unconsciousness.

Benefits: Moorchha pranayama is an excellent preparation for meditation as it draws the mind inwards and enables a psychic state to be experienced. It cuts out the distractions of the outside world, inhibits identification with the physical body and brings about mental tranquillity. It helps alleviate tension, anxiety, anger and neuroses, and raises the level of prana.

Practice note: The essence of moorchha pranayama is internal breath retention. Stopping the breath acts directly on the mind via the pranic body to induce a state of void. The sensation of fainting and light-headedness arises for two reasons. Firstly, pressure on the blood vessels in the neck causes fluctuations in the pressure within the cranial cavity. Secondly, the carotid sinuses, vital to maintaining autonomic control of the body's circulation, are continuously compressed, changing the tone of the autonomic nervous system and inducing a swooning sensation. The practice of antar kumbhaka further reduces the oxygen supply to the brain.

Chandra Bheda Pranayama (moon piercing breath)

Chandra means 'moon' and indicates ida nadi. *Bhedan* means 'to pierce'. This pranayama pierces ida nadi and fills it with shakti by breathing in through the left nostril only and out through the right nostril only. In this way there is a predominant stimulation of the parasympathetic nervous system and right brain hemisphere. This practice should only be done under expert guidance, as the awakened forces of manas shakti are not controlled easily. Generally, this technique is not publicized.

Technique 1: basic method

Sit in any comfortable meditation asana.

Keep the head and spine straight. Relax the whole body. Observe the breath until it becomes slow and deep.

Practise nasagra mudra.

Close the right nostril, inhaling slowly and deeply through the left.

At the end of inhalation, close both nostrils and retain the breath inside.

Bend the head forward in jalandhara bandha and hold the breath and the lock for as long as is comfortable.

Raise the head and exhale slowly through the right nostril. This is one round.

Practice 10 rounds, gradually increasing the length of inhalation and exhalation.

The breathing ratios of 1:1:1, then 1:2:2, and later 1:4:2 may be applied.

Technique 2: with moola bandha and shambhavi mudra

Moola bandha and shambhavi mudra may also be applied during internal breath retention.

Practise 10 rounds only.

Technique 3: Chandra Anga Pranayama (moon part breath)

Perform the same technique and stages as described for chandra bheda.

However, both inhalation and exhalation are performed through the left nostril only.

Contra-indications: People who are introverted by nature or have serious mental disturbances should not practise this pranayama. Those suffering from sluggish digestion or excess mucus should also not practise it.

Benefits: Creates mental introversion and calmness, and stimulates psychic capabilities. Cools the system and helps arouse all the attributes associated with ida nadi.

21

Vitalizing Pranayamas

All pranayamas are vitalizing in the sense that they enhance the pranic system. However, these techniques do so in a dynamic way, arousing body and mind, creating alertness and heat at both the physical and subtle levels. The tranquillizing techniques are cooling and soothing, while the vitalizing techniques produce the opposite effect. The vitalizing pranayamas can be used to increase the energy or to move out of introspective or dull states of mind. They may be regarded as more advanced techniques and should not be practised in hot weather or before sleep.

Whether one uses vitalizing or tranquillizing pranayamas, the awareness should remain constant, over and above the technique and its effects. From this viewpoint one can study the actions of body and mind under a whole range of conditions.

Swana Pranayama (panting breath)

In preparation for bhastrika and kapalbhati pranayama, it is useful to first practise swana pranayama. *Swana* means 'panting'. It is actually a simple form of agnisara kriya (see Appendix A). In swana pranayama, abdominal movement is combined with oral respiration. The word 'agnisara' is very meaningful in this context. *Agni* means fire, *sar* means movement. This practice is the movement of the fire element which is centralized in the visceral area from where the heat mechanism is stimulated. Agnisara kriya utilizes bahir kumbhaka at the time of moving the abdomen, whereas swana pranayama involves rapid respiration using the same abdominal movement. This is a different action from normal abdominal breathing, which uses the diaphragm. With swana pranayama, the abdominal muscles themselves are used.

BSY©

Technique 1: basic method

Sit in either bhadrasana with the hands on the knees or in simhasana with the palms of the hands on the floor, fingers pointing towards the body (see Appendix B).

Keep the head upright and breathe in slowly and deeply through the nose.

Extend the tongue out of the mouth, then forcefully breathe in and out through the mouth 10 times by pushing the abdomen in and out.

Be aware that the movement is harmonious and rhythmical. On exhalation the stomach moves inward, on inhalation it extends outward.

This breathing is exactly like an animal panting.

Begin slowly and rhythmically; gradually increase the speed and number of breaths up to 25 per round.

Breathe normally in between each round before continuing with the next.

Practise 5 rounds.

Contra-indications: This practice should be done on an empty stomach or at least four hours after eating. It should not be attempted by people suffering from stomach or intestinal ulcers, hernia, heart disease, high blood pressure, overactive thyroid gland or chronic diarrhoea.

Benefits: It improves digestion, tones the visceral organs, muscles, nerves and blood vessels. Fatty tissue on the abdomen is reduced and the lungs emptied of stale air. It helps relieve flatulence, constipation, poor digestion and loss of appetite.

Technique 2: with jalandhara and moola bandhas

Practise the basic method but after the last exhalation, close the mouth, inhale deeply through the nose, retain the breath and perform jalandhara and moola bandhas.

Hold the breath for as long as is comfortable, release moola and jalandhara bandhas and exhale through the nose.

Take a few normal breaths before continuing with the next round.

Practise 5 rounds.

Bhastrika Pranayama (bellows breath)

Bhastra are the bellows used to pump fire. The practice is so called because the diaphragm movement here imitates a pair of bellows and fans the internal fire, creating physical, pranic and psychic heat.

Posture: The rapid breathing performed in this practice requires a steady asana. Padmasana and siddhasana or siddha yoni asana are best as they lock the body into a stable position and allow freedom of abdominal movement. Other sitting postures may be used if the above are not possible.

Preparation: Both nostrils must be clear and flowing freely. Mucus blockages can be removed by neti. If the swara is greatly imbalanced, then one of the balancing methods may be used prior to the practice. Beginners should be familiar with abdominal (diaphragmatic) breathing before starting. Proficiency in antar and bahir kumbhaka, as well as jalandhara, uddiyana and moola bandhas are necessary before introducing the later stages of practice. Control of the nostrils is through nasagra mudra; the thumb controlling the right nostril, the ring finger controlling the left.

Practice techniques: Bhastrika is graded over four techniques. Techniques 1 and 2 are beginner's level as they establish the basic method of practice. Technique 3, the intermediate level, increases the number of breaths in each round, introduces internal kumbhaka, and moola and jalandhara bandhas. Technique 4, the advanced level, introduces external kumbhaka and maha bandha, and increases the number of rounds further. The practitioner should proceed slowly and be sensitive to his own capacity. Each technique should be practised until it has been consolidated before proceeding to the next.

Intensity of breathing: Bhastrika may be practised at three degrees of intensity: slow, medium and fast, depending on the capacity of the practitioner:

1. Slow or mild bhastrika is practised to approximately one breath every two seconds, with no undue force on inhalation or exhalation. It is like amplified normal breathing. Slow bhastrika should be used by beginners and those practising for therapeutic reasons, although it may also be practised at all stages up to the advanced level.
2. Medium bhastrika increases the speed of respiration to approximately one breath every second.
3. Fast bhastrika means a breathing speed of around two breaths per second. Both medium and fast breathing are suitable for intermediate and advanced practitioners.

Technique 1: preparatory practice

Sit in a comfortable meditation posture, with the hands resting on the knees in either chin or jnana mudra.

Keep the head and spine straight.

Close the eyes and relax the whole body.

Take a deep breath in and breathe out forcefully through the nose.

Immediately afterwards breathe in with the same force. Forceful inhalation results from fully expanding the abdominal muscles and forceful exhalation from firm contraction of the abdominal muscles. Do not strain.

During inhalation, the diaphragm descends and the abdomen moves outward. During exhalation, the diaphragm moves upward and the abdomen moves inward. The movements should be slightly exaggerated.

Continue in this manner, counting 10 breaths.

Take a deep breath in and breathe out slowly.

This is one round.

Breathe normally in between each round.

Practise up to 5 rounds.

Practice note: Practise slowly at first, with approximately one breath every two seconds, observing the push-pull of the diaphragm and abdominal muscles. Beginners may take several normal breaths in between rounds, so there is no strain. As one becomes accustomed to the breathing, gradually increase the speed to one breath per second, then two breaths per second, without the breath becoming shallow.

The action of the diaphragm and the abdominal muscles are exactly like bellows. The ribcage muscles play only a minimal role. The diaphragm is used to create equal force on inhalation (relaxing on exhalation) and the abdominal muscles are used to create force on exhalation (relaxing on inhalation). Both create a pull-push action. Concentration just below the sternum will help.

Only the abdomen moves in and out during the practice. There should be no other movement in the body; it should be like a statue, regardless of the velocity bhastrika attains. One may close the eyes during the practice. If the eyes are kept open, they should be fixed on a point. In either case, there should be total steadiness throughout the practice.

When attempting bhastrika for the first time, a loss in power and coordination of the diaphragm and abdominal muscles may be felt after a few rounds. This occurs due to insufficient toning and control of these muscles. Further preparation and consolidation of this technique are necessary before proceeding. Practise abdominal breathing as detailed in Chapters 15 and 16: 'Basic Breathing Methods' and 'Preliminary Breathing Practices', before continuing with bhastrika. One should be able to perform the basic method with ease before proceeding to the other techniques.

If bhastrika is practised during the hot season, do 5–10 rounds of sheetali or sheetkari pranayama afterwards to cool the body.

Awareness: Physical – on the breathing process and the physical movement of the abdomen. Spiritual – on manipura chakra.

Precautions: Bhastrika is a dynamic practice, requiring a large expenditure of physical energy, and must be practised in a relaxed manner. Avoid violent respiration, facial contortions and excessive shaking of the body. A feeling of faintness, excessive perspiration or vomiting indicates that the practice is unsuitable or is being performed incorrectly. If any of these symptoms are experienced, the advice of a competent teacher should be sought.

This practice purifies the blood. However, if the stages are rushed, all the impurities will be ejected from the body in a rush, which may exacerbate conditions caused by detoxification. A slow, conscientious approach to this practice is absolutely imperative. Bhastrika is full, rapid breathing. Hypoventilation can occur if the air is not fully expelled from the lungs on each exhalation. This is another indication that the technique is not being performed correctly.

Contra-indications: Bhastrika should not be practised by people with high blood pressure, heart disease, hernia, gastric ulcer, stroke, epilepsy, retinal problems, glaucoma or vertigo. The elderly, those suffering from lung diseases such as asthma and chronic bronchitis, those recovering from tuberculosis, or in the first trimester of pregnancy

268

are recommended to practise only under the guidance of a competent teacher.

Technique 2: with alternate nostrils

Sit in a comfortable meditation asana, preferably padmasana, siddhasana or siddha yoni asana.

Keep the head and spine straight.

Close the eyes and relax the whole body.

Raise the right hand in front of the face and perform nasagra mudra.

Close the right nostril with the thumb.

Breathe in and out forcefully through the left nostril 10 times, without straining. There should be a snuffing sound in the nose, but no sound should come from the throat or chest.

The abdomen should expand and contract rhythmically with the breath. The pumping action should be performed by the abdomen alone. The chest, shoulders and face remain relaxed.

After 10 breaths, take a deep breath in and out through the left nostril.

Close the left nostril and repeat the same process breathing through the right nostril.

Place the raised hand on the knee.

Repeat the same process breathing through both nostrils.

Ten breaths through the left nostril, the right nostril and both nostrils together makes one complete round.

Practise up to 5 rounds.

Practice note: The number of rapid breaths may be gradually increased according to capacity.

Technique 3: with antar kumbhaka (inner retention)

Close the right nostril with the thumb.

Breathe in and out forcefully through the left nostril.

The abdomen should expand and contract rhythmically with the breath.

After completing the forceful breaths, take a deep breath

in through the left nostril, expanding both the abdomen and the chest, close both nostrils and retain the breath inside for a few seconds.

Exhale through the left nostril.

Close the left nostril and repeat the same process through the right nostril.

After completing the forceful breaths, take a deep breath in through the right nostril, expanding both the abdomen and the chest, close both nostrils and retain the breath inside for a few seconds.

Exhale through the right nostril.

Lower the upraised hand to the knee.

Repeat the same process through both nostrils together.

After completing the forceful breaths through both nostrils together, inhale slowly and deeply through both nostrils.

Close both nostrils and retain the breath inside for a few seconds.

Breathe out slowly through both nostrils.

This completes one round.

Practise up to 5 rounds.

Practice note: Begin with 20 breaths. As the practice progresses, the number of breaths can be increased gradually. If the exhalation seems locked after retention, a slight inhalation before exhalation releases the locked condition of the glottis and brings the respiratory muscles back into action.

Technique 4: with bahir kumbhaka (external retention)

After inner retention has been mastered, external retention may be added.

At the end of each round, inhale deeply through both nostrils and then exhale completely.

Hold the breath outside for a few seconds.

Practise up to 5 rounds.

The duration of external retention can be gradually increased up to 30 seconds. Do not strain.

Technique 5: with bandhas

After antar and bahir kumbhaka have been mastered, the bandhas may be added.

At the end of each round, inhale deeply and hold the breath inside.

Practise jalandhara bandha and then moola bandha.

The duration of inner retention can gradually be increased up to 30 seconds.

After the inner retention, release moola bandha, jalandhara bandha, and then exhale.

Hold the breath outside and practise maha bandha.

Release maha bandha and inhale.

Practise up to 5 rounds.

Practice note: The number of breaths may be increased by 5 per month to a maximum count of 50 respirations through the left, right and both nostrils. However, it is not necessary to increase the number of breaths in each of the techniques. Increase the number of breaths per round only when it can be done without any discomfort. The practise of each technique with 20 rapid breaths will bring noticeable benefits. Those wishing to increase the number of breaths to more than 50, or the number of rounds to over 10, should do so only under the guidance of an expert teacher.

The same systematic pattern of building up the practice should be followed for external retention as was practised for internal retention. This allows the body, nervous system, mind and emotions to adjust gradually. After practising simple external retention for some time, add the bandhas until maha bandha is achieved. Continue with bhastrika until the breath stops by itself. Then discontinue the practice. In the course of practice, the frequency, depth and velocity of bhastrika become more and more intense.

Benefits: When bhastrika is practised systematically and conscientiously, the benefits are innumerable. Due to the rapid exchange of air in the lungs, there is an increase in the exchange of oxygen and carbon dioxide into and out

271

of the bloodstream. This stimulates the metabolic rate throughout the body down to the cellular level, producing heat and flushing out wastes and toxins. If one is caught in the cold without sufficient warm clothing, bhastrika can be practised to warm the body quickly.

Bhastrika is a process of hyperventilation, leading to respiratory alkalosis, which has a soothing effect on the respiratory centre. It reduces the level of carbon dioxide in the blood; hence a better kumbhaka can be performed after the practice. The rapid and rhythmic movement of the diaphragm also massages and stimulates the visceral organs, toning the digestive system and improving its blood circulation. The massage also strengthens the muscles of the intestines and other organs in the abdominal cavity, providing the organs adequate support from the front, so that they do not cause a stretch on the lumbar spine, which is often the cause of lower back pain. It is a useful practice for women during labour, if they have had proper preparation.

Bhastrika helps balance the *doshas* or humours: *kapha*, phlegm; *pitta*, bile; and *vata*, wind. It helps to alleviate inflammation in the throat, accumulation of phlegm and sinusitis, and builds up resistance to cough, cold and excess mucus. It also balances and strengthens the nervous system, inducing peace, tranquillity and one-pointedness of mind. Hysteria, psychosis and chronic depression respond well to bhastrika.

The practice of bhastrika increases vitality and lowers levels of stress and anxiety by raising the energy and harmonizing the pranas. It increases the generation of samana vayu, which replenishes the pranic store and stimulates the whole pranic system. While practising, all the pranas in the body begin to vibrate, but at the end of the practice the mind is completely stilled. In fact, the meditative state can be reached effortlessly through the practice of bhastrika. The yogic texts state that bhastrika enables prana to break through the three knots in the sushumna passage, making

272

way for the kundalini shakti to flow upwards freely. The *Hatha Yoga Pradipika* says (2:66–67):

कुंडली बोधकं क्षिप्रं पवनं सुखदं हितम् ।
ब्रह्मनाडीमुखे संस्थकफाद्यर्गलनाशनम् ॥

This (bhastrika) quickly arouses kundalini. It is pleasant and beneficial, and removes obstruction due to excess mucus accumulated at the entrance to brahma nadi.

सम्यग्गात्रसमुद्भूतग्रंथित्रयविभेदकम् ।
विशेषेणैव कर्तव्यं भस्त्राख्यं कुंभकंत्विदम् ॥

This kumbhaka called bhastrika enables the three granthis (psychic/pranic knots) to be broken. Thus, it is the duty of the yogi to practise bhastrika.

Kapalbhati Pranayama (frontal brain cleansing breath)

The Sanskrit word *kapal* means 'cranium' or 'forehead' and *bhati* means 'light' or 'splendour' and also 'perception' or 'knowledge'. Hence kapalbhati is the practice that brings a state of light or clarity to the frontal region of the brain. This pranayama invigorates the entire brain and the centres responsible for subtle perception and insight. It is also a cleansing practice and is therefore listed among the shatkarmas. Another term for this practice is kapalshodhana, the word *shodhana* meaning 'to purify'.

Although kapalbhati is similar to bhastrika, there are important differences. In bhastrika the breathing rate increases with practice; while in kapalbhati the speed becomes slower and slower. As one progresses in bhastrika, the breath gets faster and shorter; whereas in kapalbhati the breath is faster in the beginning, but with practice becomes slower and longer.

Bhastrika uses equal force in both inhalation and exhalation, expanding and contracting the thoracic area above and below its resting or basal volume. Kapalbhati, however, uses forced exhalation only, reducing the thoracic volume in

273

exhalation, while inhalation remains a restful process from extreme exhalation to the basal volume. In normal breathing inhalation is active and exhalation passive. Kapalbhati reverses this procedure, making exhalation a forced, active process, while inhalation remains the same restful process.

Types of Inhalation/Exhalation in Kapalbhati and Bhastrika

Type of breathing	Inhalation	Exhalation	Lung volumes
Normal	Active	Passive	Increased from and decreased to basal volume
Kapalbhati	Passive	Active	Decreased from and increased to basal volume
Bhastrika	Active	Active	Increased and decreased beyond basal volume

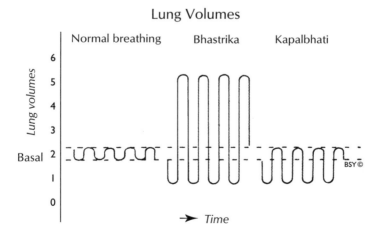

Lung Volumes

274

Kapalbhati further reverses the natural process by compressing the lungs below basal resting volume, whereas normal breathing expands and contracts the lungs, using an active process on inhalation and a passive process on exhalation. The brain centres which control normal breathing function are trained to become more versatile through the practice of these techniques.

From the point of view of the pancha pranas, the role of prana (the active inhalation) and apana (the passive exhalation) are reversed, reducing samana, which on the mental level means a reduction in the activity of vrittis, or mental oscillations. This can be experienced during kapalbhati. At the same time the powerful upward flow created by the whole breathing attitude stimulates udana in the head and neck, which is in keeping with the meaning of the term 'kapalbhati'.

There are five techniques; each should be practised progressively until it can be performed without effort, before proceeding to the next.

Technique 1: preparatory practice (shatkarma method)

Sit in a comfortable meditation asana.

The head and spine should be straight with the hands resting on the knees in either chin or jnana mudra.

Close the eyes and relax the whole body.

Exhale through both nostrils with forceful contraction of the abdominal muscles.

The following inhalation should take place passively, allowing the abdominal muscles to relax.

Inhalation should be spontaneous recoil, involving no effort.

Complete 10 rapid breaths in succession.

Inhale and exhale deeply.

Allow the breath to return to normal.

This is one round.

Practise up to 5 rounds.

Practice note: When it is performed as a shatkarma, kapalbhati clears excess mucus from the nasal passages and should be practised before pranayama. The rapid breathing should be from the abdomen; the shoulders and face remain relaxed. Beginners may take several breaths in between rounds. The number of respirations may be increased from the initial count of 10 up to 50, as the abdominal muscles become stronger. Advanced practitioners can increase up to 100 breaths per round. Kapalbhati should be performed on an empty stomach. If practised late at night, it may prevent sleep. If pain or dizziness is experienced, one should stop the practice and sit quietly for some time. The practice should be performed thereafter with more awareness and less force. If the condition continues, one should consult a competent teacher.

Contra-indications: Kapalbhati should not be practised by those suffering from heart disease, high blood pressure, vertigo, epilepsy, stroke, hernia or gastric ulcer. It is not recommended during pregnancy.

Benefits: Kapalbhati purifies the whole body by accelerating the replacement of alveolar air, stimulating the exchange of oxygen and carbon dioxide and at the same time increasing oxygen concentration in the alveoli. The total effect is one of cleansing and increasing metabolism throughout the body. The increased metabolic rate and oxygen supply to the brain have an awakening effect on the brain, and the nervous system is balanced and strengthened. The practice also tones the digestive organs and helps in respiratory disorders such as asthma, emphysema, bronchitis and tuberculosis.

Kapalbhati is particularly useful for spiritual aspirants as it arrests sensory distractions, thoughts, visions and mental chatter, calming the mind in preparation for meditation. At the same time, it energizes the mind so one is not overcome by sleep while sitting for meditation. The effects also help those engaged in mental work.

Technique 2: with alternate nostrils

Sit in a comfortable meditation asana.

Raise the right hand and perform nasagra mudra.

Close the right nostril with the thumb.

Exhale forcefully and then inhale passively through the left nostril 10 times. The pumping action should be performed by the abdomen alone; the chest, shoulders and face remain relaxed.

After the 10 breaths, take a deep breath in and out through the left nostril.

Close the left nostril and repeat the same process through the right nostril.

After the 10 breaths, take a deep breath in and out through the right nostril.

Replace the raised hand on the knee.

Repeat the same process through both nostrils.

After the 10 breaths, take a deep breath in and out through both nostrils.

Ten breaths through the left, the right and both nostrils form one complete round.

Practise up to 5 rounds.

Practice note: Beginners may take several breaths in between rounds. The number of respirations may be gradually increased up to 50, as the abdominal muscles become stronger.

Technique 3: with antar kumbhaka (inner retention)

After perfecting technique 2, antar kumbhaka may be commenced.

At the end of the round, inhale deeply and retain the breath for a comfortable length of time without straining.

Exhale slowly with control.

Practise up to 5 rounds.

Technique 4: with bahir kumbhaka (outer retention)

After perfecting antar kumbhaka, bahir kumbhaka may be added.

At the end of the round, inhale deeply.
Exhale slowly and completely.
Retain the breath outside for a comfortable length of time.
Practice up to 5 rounds.

Technique 5: with bandhas

After mastering internal and external retention the bandhas may be added.

Jalandhara and moola bandhas may be combined during internal retention and maha bandha during external retention.

At the end of each round, inhale deeply.

Hold the breath inside without straining.

Practise jalandhara bandha and moola bandha during internal retention.

Release moola bandha, jalandhara bandha, and then exhale.

Hold the breath outside and practise maha bandha.

Retain the breath and the bandha for a comfortable length of time without straining.

Release maha bandha and inhale.

Practise up to 5 rounds.

Practice note: Proceed slowly with awareness of the effects of the practice. Build up the number of breaths, number of rounds and length of retention gradually. Do not strain by practising for extended periods. If breathlessness is experienced, discontinue the practice or reduce the number of rounds to a comfortable level.

Awareness: Physical – on rhythmic, forceful exhalation. Spiritual – on the void at the eyebrow centre or on all-pervading calmness.

Sequence: Practise just before meditation techniques.

Surya Bheda Pranayama (vitality stimulating breath)

The Sanskrit word *surya* means 'sun', which refers to pingala nadi, while *bheda* means 'to pierce', 'pass through' or 'awaken'. Surya bheda pierces or purifies pingala nadi. This practice is similar to chandra bheda, but it stimulates prana shakti, the opposite energy force. In the preparatory practice, by inhaling through the right nostril, the left brain hemisphere and pingala nadi are activated. By retaining the breath after inhalation, the prana is held in pingala. By exhaling through the left nostril the energy is released along with any impurities that remain in ida. In the final practice, only the right nostril is used for both inhalation and exhalation.

Surya bheda is a powerful practice and should be learned under proper guidance, so that its effects may be checked. Internal retention and bandhas should be perfected before attempting this practice.

Technique 1: preparatory practice with alternate nostrils
Stage 1: Assume a comfortable meditation asana.

Place the hands on the knees in either chin or jnana mudra.

Close the eyes and relax the whole body.

When the body is comfortable and still, watch the breath until it spontaneously becomes slow and deep.

Adopt nasagra mudra.

Close the left nostril and inhale slowly and deeply through the right nostril.

At the end of inhalation, close both nostrils and retain the breath inside.

Lower the head in jalandhara bandha.

Hold the breath and the lock for as long as is comfortable.

Raise the head and when the head is upright, exhale slowly through the left nostril.

This is one round.

Repeat the same process: inhalation through the right nostril and exhalation through the left nostril.

Practise 10 rounds, gradually increasing the length of inhalation/retention/exhalation.

279

Stage 2: Practise the basic method as described above and include the breathing ratios of 1:1:1, then 1:2:2, and build up to 1:4:2.

Stage 3: After mastering stage 2, add moola bandha and shambhavi mudra during retention.

Precautions: Surya bheda should be practised only on an empty stomach, as it will interfere with the natural flow of energy associated with digestion. This pranayama may cause imbalance if performed for prolonged periods. It is not recommended for general practitioners and should only be utilized by those with ida nadi predominance.

Contra-indications: People suffering from heart disease, hypertension, epilepsy, hyperthyroid, peptic ulcer, acidity or anxiety should avoid this practice.

Benefits: Surya bheda activates the sympathetic nervous system and associated physical and mental states. It creates heat in the body and counteracts imbalances of the *vata* (wind) and *kapha* (phlegm) *doshas* (humours). Increased eyeball pressure, which is the cause of glaucoma, is lessened with the practice of surya bheda. It also helps the conditions of sinusitis, rheumatism, rhinitis and neuralgia.

By activating pingala nadi, it stimulates and awakens the pranic energy. This increases extroversion and dynamism, enabling physical activities to be performed more efficiently and helping to alleviate depression, anxiety and phobias. It is especially recommended for those who are dull and lethargic or who find it difficult to adjust in the external world. It makes the mind more alert and perceptive and is an excellent pre-meditation pranayama. The *Gheranda Samhita* says (5:68):

कुम्भक: सूर्यभेदस्तु जरामृत्युविनाशक: ।
बोधयेत् कुंडलीं शक्तिं देहानलं विवर्धयेत् ॥

Surya bheda prevents old age and death, increases the body heat and awakens the kundalini.

Technique 2: with right nostril

After a sustained period of practice of technique 1, this technique may be attempted. In this practice the same instructions and stages as for technique 1 are followed. The only difference is that both inhalation and exhalation are performed through the right nostril only. The purpose of the practice is to create an effect exclusively on the left hemisphere of the brain and exclude the right hemisphere for the time being. The flow of pingala is activated and the flow of ida is blocked.

Stage 1: Assume a comfortable meditation asana.

Place the hands on the knees in either chin or jnana mudra.

Close the eyes and relax the whole body.

When the body is comfortable and still, watch the breath until it spontaneously becomes slow and deep.

Adopt nasagra mudra.

Close the left nostril with the ring finger and inhale slowly and deeply through the right nostril.

Exhale slowly through the right nostril, keeping the left nostril closed with the ring finger.

This is one round.

Stage 2: Adopt nasagra mudra.

Close the left nostril with the ring finger. Inhale slowly and deeply through the right nostril.

At the end of inhalation close both nostrils. Maintain the internal retention for a comfortable length of time.

Exhale slowly through the right nostril, keeping the left nostril closed with the ring finger.

Slowly increase the duration of the inhalation, retention and exhalation without straining.

Stage 3: After mastering stage 2, add jalandhara and moola bandhas during retention.

Awareness: On the breath in the right nostril.

Duration: When first practising surya bheda pranayama, 10 rounds are sufficient. Over time, however, as the practice becomes comfortable, the duration may be increased to 10 minutes. Slowly increase the length of retention over months. A ratio of 1:1:1 may be introduced to stabilize the practice. Once this is mastered, it may be increased to 1:1:2 and then 1:2:2.

Plavini Pranayama (inundating breath)

Plavana means 'to float', and the practice of plavini enables one to float on water. This is an unusual form of pranayama, which is not commonly used. It is similar to vatsara dhauti, except that the air should be retained inside. In the *Hatha Ratnavali* it is known as bhujangini mudra.

Technique

Sit in any meditative asana and prepare for pranayama.
Inhale through the nose and gulp the air down the throat, as if swallowing food or drink.
Inhale and swallow the breath 5 times consecutively, making sure to retain the air inside.
This makes one round.
There should be no physical movement while retaining the air inside, or the air will escape.
Practise up to 3 rounds.

Sequence: Plavini should be practised after asana and pranayama. It can be followed by an inverted asana, so that the air passes through the intestines and out of the anus. Pashinee mudra is especially useful for this purpose. Plavini can also be practised when fasting.

Benefits: Plavini releases gas and acidity from the stomach. It relieves the sensations of hunger and thirst during fasting. Yogis practise it before going into samadhi for several days so that the stomach remains full during their fast.

Appendices

Supplementary Practices

Jala Neti (nasal cleansing with water)

Jala neti is a process of cleaning the nasal passages with salt water and is essential in allowing free breathing as required in many of the pranayama practices.

Equipment: A special *neti lota*, neti pot, should be used. The pot can be made of plastic, pottery, brass or any other metal which does not contaminate the water. The nozzle on the end of the spout should fit comfortably into the nostril so that the water does not leak out. Even a teapot may be used if the tip of the spout is not too large or sharp.

Salt water: The water used in the practice should be pure and at body temperature. The water should be mixed with clean salt in the proportion of one teaspoonful per half a litre of water. Make sure the salt is fully dissolved in the water. The addition of salt ensures the osmotic pressure of the water is equal to that of the body fluids, thereby minimizing any irritation to the delicate blood vessels and the mucous membrane. A painful or burning sensation is an indication of too little or too much salt in the water.

Posture: Either sit in a squatting position known as kagasana or assume a standing position, bending the shoulders and head forwards. The latter position is more suitable for practising neti over a sink or wash basin, while kagasana may be more comfortable if practising in the garden or the shower.

Technique
Stage 1: washing the nostrils
Fill the neti pot with the prepared salt water.

In the standing position, stand squarely, with legs apart so that the body weight is evenly distributed between the feet. Lean forward and tilt the head to one side.

Breathe through the mouth.

Gently insert the nozzle into the uppermost nostril.

There should be no force involved.

The nozzle should press firmly against the side of the nostril so that no water leakage occurs.

Tilt the neti pot in such a way that water runs into the nostril and not down the face.

Keep the mouth open. Raising the elbow of the hand which holds the neti pot helps to adjust the body position so that the water flows out through the lower nostril.

When half the water has passed through the nostrils, remove the nozzle from the nostril, centre the head and let the water run out of the nose.

Remove any mucus from the nose by blowing gently.

Tilt the head to the opposite side and repeat the process, placing the nozzle of the lota in the upper nostril.

After completing this process, the nostrils must be thoroughly dried.

Stage 2: drying the nostrils
1. Stand erect.

Close the right nostril with the right thumb and breathe

in and out through the left nostril 10 times in quick succession, as in kapalbhati pranayama.

Repeat through the right nostril, with the left nostril closed.

Perform once more through both nostrils.

2. Bend forward from the waist so that the trunk is horizontal. Repeat the same process as described above, but tilt the head to the right, closing the right nostril.

Repeat again, tilting the head to the left and closing the left nostril.

Finally, repeat again with the head centred, breathing through both nostrils.

Practice note: This step helps to drain trapped water from the sinus cavities.

3. Stand erect with the feet apart. Close the right nostril and exhale forcefully while bending forward rapidly from the waist. Inhale normally while returning to the upright position. Repeat 5 times.

Repeat with the right nostril open and then with both nostrils open. Do not blow the nose too hard as the remaining water may be pushed into the ears.

If necessary, perform shashankasana for several minutes to allow the drainage of any remaining water.

Duration: The practice should take about 5 minutes. Neti may be practised daily, once or twice a week, or as required. After some practice, a full neti pot may be used for each nostril.

Sequence: Jala neti is ideally practised in the morning before asana and pranayama. However, if necessary, it may be performed at any time, except after meals.

Precautions: The water should only pass through the nostrils. If any water enters the throat or mouth it causes no harm, but indicates that the position of the head needs to be adjusted.

Make sure that the nose is properly dried after the practice, otherwise the nasal passages and sinuses may become irritated and manifest the symptoms of a cold.

Only practise neti when necessary. Prolonged practise is not advisable unless instructed by a competent teacher.

Contra-indications: People who suffer from chronic bleeding in the nose should not do jala neti without the advice of a competent teacher. Those who consistently have great difficulty passing water through the nose may have a structural blockage and should seek expert advice. People prone to or having ear infections should not practise neti. During colds, flu or sinusitis, when the nose is totally blocked, neti should be avoided.

Benefits: Jala neti removes mucus and pollution from the nasal passages and sinuses, allowing air to flow without obstruction. It helps prevent and manage respiratory tract diseases. It helps to maintain good health of the ears, eyes and throat.

Jala neti relieves muscular tension of the face and helps the practitioner to maintain a fresh and youthful appearance. It has a calming and soothing influence on the brain. It alleviates anxiety, anger and depression, removes drowsiness and makes the head feel light and fresh.

Jala neti stimulates the various nerve endings in the nose, improving the sense of smell and the overall health of the individual. A balance is brought about between the right and left nostrils and the corresponding left and right brain hemispheres, inducing a state of harmony and balance throughout the body and mind. Most importantly, however, neti helps to awaken ajna chakra.

Variations: Practitioners may suck water up the nostrils directly from a glass or bowl. This is the original form of the practice called vyutkrama kapalbhati, or *usha paan,* which literally means 'morning drink'.

Other liquids may also be used instead of water for the practice of neti. These include warm milk – *dugdh neti,* warm clarified butter or ghee – *ghrita neti,* and yoghurt. If oil is used instead of ghee, it must be natural and without added chemicals. The most powerful form of neti is practised with the mid-flow of one's own urine, and is known as *amaroli neti*. This form is particularly useful for alleviating inflammation of the nasal passages. Each liquid bestows a different benefit. None of these variations should be attempted unless instructed by a competent teacher.

Sutra Neti (nasal cleansing with thread)

The practice of passing a length of thread through the nose is called sutra neti. Traditionally, a specially prepared cotton thread, *sutra*, was used for the practice. Several strands were tightly wrapped together and dipped in melted beeswax. The width was about 4 mm and the length 36 to 45 cm. Nowadays, however, the practice is more conveniently performed by using a thin, rubber catheter lubricated with melted ghee, butter, edible oil or one's own saliva, so that it slides easily through the nasal passage. The size of the catheter depends on the individual nasal passage. Beginners may prefer size 4, but progress to size 6.

Technique 1: basic method

Take any comfortable standing, sitting or squatting position.
Relax the whole body.
Tilt the head slightly back. Gently and slowly insert the narrow end of the catheter or waxed end of the thread into whichever nostril is flowing more freely.
As the thread is inserted, twist it so that it enters the nostril easily. Always keep the tip pointing downward towards the base of the nose.
Never push the catheter straight up because the nasal cavity is behind the nose, not at the top of the nose.
When the thread reaches the back of the throat, insert the index finger and thumb, or the middle and index fingers, into the mouth.

BSY©

Pull the catheter or thread gently and slowly out through the mouth, leaving a few inches of thread hanging out of the nostril.

This action may cause retching at first, but it will become easier with practice.

Hold each end of the sutra or catheter with the fingers. Very slowly and gently pull it backward and forward, no more than 15 times on the first attempt.

Remove it slowly through the nose and repeat the process with the opposite nostril.

Technique 2: advanced practice

After completing technique 1, leave the thread with one end passing through the mouth and the other through the nostril.

Gently insert the waxed end emerging from one nostril into the other nostril and pull the end through the mouth.

In the final position, both waxed ends emerge from the mouth. Loosen the hard wax at the tip of each end so that the individual strands again become separated.

Push the two ends together so that they merge with one another, and twist the thread so that the two ends become joined. If the join is too thick, some of the threads may be cut away so that the join may pass easily through the nostrils. The thread is now circular.

Slowly draw the join into the mouth, progressively sliding the thread through the nostrils.

Eventually the join should be located between the entrance to the two nostrils.

Disconnect the join.

The thread now enters one nostril and emerges from the other; it no longer passes through the mouth.

Gently pull the sutra to and fro, a few times only to begin with. If there is the slightest discomfort, stop the practice immediately.

Pull one end of the thread and slowly withdraw it from the nose.

Breathing: Breathing is performed through the mouth.

Duration: The practice takes about 10 minutes. Once every few days or once a week is sufficient.

Sequence: Sutra neti should be performed before jala neti as the latter will flush out all the impurities and particles in the nose which have been dislodged by sutra neti.

Precautions: Do not use force under any circumstances. The interior of the nose is very delicate and any undue force could cause damage. After persistent attempts, if the thread or catheter will not pass through the nose, consult a competent teacher. Make sure that the sutra is perfectly clean before inserting it into the nostril. It is best not to try sutra neti until jala neti has been perfected.

Contra-indications: Those people who suffer from chronic bleeding in the nose should not practise sutra neti. Anyone with nasal ulcers, polyps, or severe malformations of the nasal septum or turbinates should first seek the advice of a yogic or ayurvedic doctor.

Benefits: The benefits are the same as for jala neti. In addition, however, sutra neti can rectify the problem of deviated nasal septum. If one or both nostrils are not flowing freely due either to deformed bone or fleshy outgrowths, the regular friction of sutra neti causes these obstructions to disappear within a few months.

Practice note: Although the catheter is easier and quicker, it does not clean the nasal passages as effectively as the cotton thread. Technique 2 is possible with some types of catheter only.

Agnisara Kriya or Vahnisara Dhauti (activating the digestive fire or cleansing with the essence of fire)

This practice may be performed as a preparation for bhastrika and kapalbhati pranayamas. The words *agni* and *vahni* both mean fire; *sara* means essence, and *kriya* means action. The essence or nature of fire is attributed to the digestive process. If the abdominal organs are not working properly, the digestive fire smoulders and needs to be stoked

291

or fanned to increase its power. Agnisara kriya does just that, as well as purifying the digestive system and its associated organs, and allowing the optimum assimilation of nutrients from food ingested.

Technique

Sit in bhadrasana with the big toes touching, or in padmasana.

Inhale deeply.

Exhale, emptying the lungs as much as possible.

Lean forward slightly, straightening the elbows.

Push down on the knees with the hands and perform jalandhara bandha.

Contract and expand the abdominal muscles rapidly for as long as it is possible to hold the breath outside comfortably.

Do not strain.

Release jalandhara bandha.

When the head is upright, take a slow, deep breath in.

This is one round.

Relax until the breathing normalizes before commencing the next round.

Duration: Beginners may find this practice difficult and quickly become tired due to lack of voluntary control over the abdominal muscles. The muscles must be slowly and gradually developed over a period of time.

Three rounds of 10 abdominal contractions and expansions is sufficient at first. With regular practice, up to 50 abdominal movements may be performed with each round. The time of breath retention should be gradually increased over a period of time.

Sequence: Practise after asanas and before pranayama. Agnisara kriya should be practised on an empty stomach, preferably in the early morning before breakfast, and ideally after the bowels have been emptied.

Precautions: During summer months, this practice should be performed with care as it may raise the body heat and blood pressure excessively. During this period, it should always be followed by a cooling pranayama such as sheetkari or sheetali.

Contra-indications: People suffering from high blood pressure, heart disease, acute duodenal or peptic ulcers, overactive thyroid gland or chronic diarrhoea should not perform this kriya. Pregnant women should refrain from this practice.

Benefits: Agnisara kriya stimulates the appetite and improves the digestion. It massages the abdomen, strengthens the abdominal muscles and encourages optimum health of the abdominal organs. It also stimulates the five pranas, especially samana, and raises the energy levels markedly. It alleviates depression, dullness and lethargy.

Appendix B

Asanas Relevant to Pranayama

There are several positions in which to practise pranayama: sitting, standing or lying down. However, all have one component in common: a straight spine, neck and head, without which the flow of breath and prana will be hampered in many ways.

Standing posture

This posture is not very common in pranayama practice because it is less stable than the other asanas. However, it does allow for comfortable deep breathing as there is less abdominal restriction. It may be used at times when sitting or lying is impossible, although a little more concentration is required to keep the body steady.

Technique

Stand with the feet placed shoulder-width apart and parallel to each other. This gives the best standing base to maintain balance.

Adjust the pelvis, which forms a base for the rest of the body, so that the trunk is supported in an upright position, neither leaning too far forward or backward, nor to the right or left. Keep the spine straight.

Let the arms hang on either side of the body, the hands either in front of the thighs or to the sides. The shoulders should not slouch forward or be pulled backward. Adjust the position of the head so that it is balanced on the shoulders, looking directly ahead.

With eyes open, concentrate on a fixed point to help maintain balance. With eyes closed, balance needs a more subtle control. If the body is placed correctly, very little strain is necessary. No tension other than that necessary to maintain the upright position is required.

Try to imagine a plumb-line through your body, centring all the parts; the head is balanced on the trunk, the trunk is balanced on the pelvis, and the pelvis is balanced on the top of the legs. Then, when body and breath are steady, you may commence pranayama.

Shavasana (corpse pose)

The lying position or *shavasana* (corpse posture) is used in preparatory practices to teach the student how to breathe correctly in a relaxed state. It also helps in becoming more intimately aware of the respiratory processes. Shavasana enables each part of the body to be absolutely relaxed, from the muscles of the limbs to the eyelids, tongue, lungs and abdomen. Practise on a flat, even and hard surface, with a folded blanket on the floor. A small pillow or folded blanket can be placed under the head or neck if necessary.

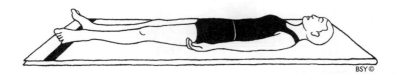

Technique

Lie on your back on the floor, ensuring that the spine, neck and head are in a straight line.

The feet should be approximately 45 cm apart, with the toes pointing outward.

Place the arms beside and about 15 cm away from the body with the palms upwards, and let the fingers curl naturally. Close the eyes.

Consciously and systematically relax every muscle by becoming aware of each part of the body in sequence, working from the feet up to the top of the head.

After some time a feeling of *pratyahara* (sense withdrawal) will be experienced, and the breath will become regular and even.

Remain aware, without strain or concentration.

At this stage the breathing practices may be commenced.

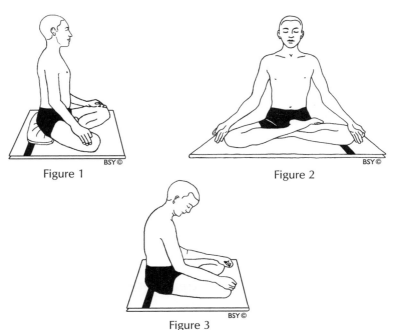

Figure 1

Figure 2

Figure 3

Sitting postures

In order to fulfil the requirements of steadiness and a straight back, neck and head, the classical meditation postures are best: padmasana, ardha padmasana, siddhasana or siddha yoni asana and vajrasana. All of these asanas allow for the free flow of breath when performed correctly. For regular practices and for advanced techniques, one of these asanas should be assumed as they have stood the test of time and scientific investigation.

Sukhasana (the easy pose) can be used if the other postures are too difficult. However, you should aim to sit in one of the other postures eventually, because in sukhasana there is a tendency for the body to slump forward and compress the abdominal region. Not only is breathing enhanced by the correct upright position, but the flow of nerve impulses, tissue fluids and prana is also improved.

The sitting postures for pranayama provide a stable base for the trunk, as well as a pelvic position which keeps the trunk upright and steady. The location of the spine in relation to the pelvis should be such that the weight of the head and trunk bears down squarely on the base provided by the legs. This is achieved by projecting the buttocks slightly backwards and the lower back slightly forwards. Check that you are sitting on the ischial tuberosities (body prominences on the lower side of the buttocks). Incorrect posture will give a tendency for the back to slump because extra strain is imposed on the lower back muscles, which tend to relax over a period of time.

The head must also be in alignment with the base, to prevent undue muscular effort in holding it upright, and to allow for a free flow of air through the trachea. The poor posture shown in Figure 3 indicates how excessive strain is placed on the spine and neck, and the lungs are compressed by the abdominal organs when the body is not held upright. Figure 2 shows the correct balanced posture with trunk, neck and head all held in alignment over the base provided by the legs. If this posture is difficult, a small pillow or folded blanket under the buttocks can give support, as shown in Figure 1. Many people will find this cushion necessary and it is quite acceptable when sitting for extended periods.

In the asana, try to elongate the spine from the base to the top, lifting it upward. Then relax your shoulders and arms, still keeping the spine straight. If the body is properly balanced, the back will be straight but relaxed. Inhaling as the spine is stretched up and exhaling as the shoulders relax down is quite a helpful and natural action.

The arms should be slightly bent so there is no tension in the muscles. They can rest on the knees or in the lap in a particular mudra. The elbows are generally bent slightly to relax the upper and lower arm muscles. It is important that the abdomen and chest should not be cramped. The lungs, diaphragm and abdomen should be able to expand and contract with ease and without undue force.

Sitting on the floor with the support of a wall is quite acceptable for beginners, but not as a continual crutch. The spinal column (particularly the sacroiliac joints) has to be strengthened, and this cannot be done if you continue using a wall for support. Sit on the floor with the back flat and supported against the wall. The back of the head should also touch the wall. The legs may be straight or folded into a cross-legged position. Sitting in a chair is also acceptable, provided the conditions of a straight and upright spine can be met. Those who are experiencing difficulty in achieving a comfortable asana and particularly sufferers of back pain are recommended to practise other yoga asanas.

The best method of learning to sit without support is simply to practise. Sit without back support wherever you are, but sit correctly with a straight and relaxed spine, maintaining stillness, if only for a minute. Increase this time daily. Soon you will be able to do away with all back support, chairs and walls, and sit freely and confidently.

Although asana is a posture, what you sit on is part of the asana. Ideally, a flat, firm surface like the floor or ground is best, with a folded woollen blanket for comfort. Traditionally, spiritual practices were done in a clean place, neither too high nor too low, covered with kusha grass, layers of cloth and a deerskin (to keep away snakes and insects).

Sukhasana (easy pose)
Sit with the legs stretched in front of the body.
Fold the right foot under the left thigh; fold the left foot under the right thigh.
Place the hands on the knees in chin or jnana mudra.
Keep the head, neck and back straight.
Practice note: Once the practitioner can perform any of the other sitting asanas comfortably, sukhasana should be disregarded, as it does not give the necessary support to the spine for correct breathing practices.

Ardha Padmasana (half-lotus pose)
Sit with the legs stretched out in front of the body.
Fold the left leg and place the left foot beside the right thigh.

299

Fold the right leg and place the right foot on top of the left thigh.

Place the hands on the knees in chin or jnana mudra.

Keep the back, neck and head straight.

Contra-indications: Those who suffer from sciatica or knee problems should not perform this asana.

Benefits: The same benefits as given for padmasana but at a reduced level.

Practice note: This pose is to be practised in preference to sukhasana. By alternately placing either foot in the elevated position, the practitioner will slowly prepare the legs for the practice of padmasana and other classical meditative poses. However, this asana should also be dropped when full padmasana, siddhasana or siddha yoni asana can be maintained comfortably.

BSY©

Padmasana (lotus pose)

Sit with the legs extended forward in front of the body.

Fold one leg and place its foot on top of the opposite thigh. The sole of the foot must be upward and the heel should touch the pelvic bone. Fold the other leg and place its foot on top of the other thigh.

Both knees should, ideally, touch the ground in the final position.

300

The head and spine should be kept steady and upright, shoulders relaxed.

Place the hands on the knees in chin or jnana mudra.

Relax the arms with the elbows slightly bent.

Contra-indications: Those who suffer from sciatica or weak or injured knees should not perform this asana. This asana should not be attempted until flexibility of the knees has been developed through practice of the pre-meditation asanas. It is not advisable during pregnancy as the circulation in the legs is reduced.

Benefits: This asana can be held for long periods of time, steadily and comfortably. There is the added advantage that the flow of blood and prana in the legs is reduced, redirecting this energy to the upper parts of the body and brain, stimulating the higher centres of consciousness.

Practice note: A small cushion or folded blanket can be put under the buttocks to help keep the knees down and the back from leaning forward or backward. This asana should not be attempted until the practitioner has developed supple legs by doing the pre-meditative exercises.

Siddhasana (accomplished pose for men)

Sit with the legs extended forward in front of the body.

Bend the right leg and place the sole of its foot flat against the left thigh with the heel pressing the perineum, the area between the genitals and the anus.

Bend the left leg and place its foot on top of the right calf muscle.

Press the pelvic bone with the left heel directly above the genitals.

Push the toes and the outer edge of this foot into the space between the right calf and thigh muscles; it may be necessary to adjust the right leg for this. Grasp the right toes, either from above or below the left calf, and pull them upward into the space between the left thigh and calf. The legs should now be locked with the knees on the ground and the left heel directly above the right heel.

301

Make the spine steady, straight and erect as though it were
planted in the ground.
Place the hands on the knees in chin or jnana mudra.
Relax the arms with the elbows slightly bent.

Contra-indications: Siddhasana should not be practised by
those with sciatica or sacral infections.

Benefits: This is not only a pose of physical steadiness but
for mental steadiness also. It has a calming effect on the
entire nervous system. The spine can maintain its straight-
ness which is necessary for productive pranayama over
longer periods.

More blood and prana is directed upwards and the pressure
on the perineal body activates a partial moola bandha and
vajroli mudra, which redirects sexual nervous impulses
back up the spinal cord to the brain. It is considered by
some to be the best posture for dhyana and pranayama.

Practice note: Siddhasana can be practised with either leg
uppermost.

This technique can also be used for long periods of time,
especially with a cushion placed beneath the buttocks, for
the same reason as for padmasana.

302

Siddha Yoni Asana (accomplished pose for women)

Sit with the legs extended in front of the body.

Bend the right leg and place the sole of the foot flat against the inner left thigh.

Place the heel firmly against or just inside the labia majora of the vagina.

Adjust the body position so that it is comfortable, while simultaneously feeling the pressure of the right heel.

Bend the left leg and place the left heel directly on top of the right heel so it presses the clitoris; then wedge the left toes down into the space between the right calf and thigh.

Pull the right toes up into the space between the calf and thigh and the left toes down into the space on the right side. Make the spine fully erect and straight as though it were planted solidly in the earth.

Place the hands on the knees in chin, jnana or chinmaya mudra. This can be practised with either leg uppermost.

Contra-indications: As for siddhasana.

Benefits: The benefits are the same as for siddhasana. It has a direct effect on the nerve plexus concerned with the female reproductive system, and gives some control over the neuro-psychic impulses, necessary for productive pranayama and dhyana. It is one of the best poses for women to adopt for most pranayama practices. This asana gives complete steadiness, calmness and serenity.

Swastikasana (auspicious pose)
Sit with the legs straight in front of the body.
Bend the left knee and place the sole of the left foot against the inside of the right thigh so there is no contact between the heel and the perineum.
Bend the right knee and place the right foot in the space between the left thigh and calf muscle so that there is no contact between the heel and the pubis.
Grasp the toes of the left foot and pull them up into the space between the right calf and thigh.
Adjust the position so that it is comfortable. The knees should be firmly on the floor.
Straighten the spine. Place the hands on the knees in chin, jnana or chinmaya mudra.
Variation: Sit with the legs straight in front of the body.
Bend the left leg and place the sole against the inside of the right thigh.
Similarly, bend the right leg and place the heel of the right foot on the floor in front of the left foot with the sole resting against the left shin. The heels will now be one in front of the other.

The hands may be placed on the knees in jnana, chin or chinmaya mudra, or they may be placed in the lap.

Close the eyes and relax the whole body.

Contra-indications: Swastikasana should not be performed by people with sciatica or sacral infections.

Benefits: Swastikasana is a healthy position to sit in, especially for those suffering from varicose veins, tired and aching muscles or fluid retention in the legs.

Practice note: This is the easiest classical meditation asana and is a simplified version of siddhasana.

Vajrasana (thunderbolt pose)

Kneel on the floor. Bring the big toes together so they cross, and separate the heels. The knees should be together, the heels are apart.

Lower the buttocks on to the insides of the feet, with the heels touching the sides of the hips.

Place the hands on the knees, palms down.

The back and the head should be straight, but not tense.

Close the eyes, relax the arms and the whole body.

Benefits: Vajrasana alters the flow of blood, prana and nervous impulses in the pelvic and visceral regions. People with sciatica or sacral disabilities should use this asana for pranayama. This position provides ideal conditions for abdominal breathing.

Practice note: Beginners may find that their ankles ache after a short time in vajrasana. To remedy this, release the posture, stretch the legs forward and shake the feet until the stiffness disappears. Then resume the posture.

Simhasana (lion pose)

Sit in vajrasana with the knees apart. Place the hands between the knees with the fingers pointing towards the body. Lean forward, resting the body on the straight arms.

Tilt the head backward, open the mouth and extend the tongue as much as possible.

Practice note: This posture is used for swana pranayama.

Bhadrasana (gracious pose)

Sit in vajrasana.

Separate the knees as far as possible, while keeping the toes in contact with the ground.

Separate the feet just enough to allow the buttocks to rest flat on the floor between the feet.

Try to separate the knees further, but without strain.

Place the hands on the knees, palms down.

When the body is comfortable, practise nasikagra drishti (concentration on the nose tip).

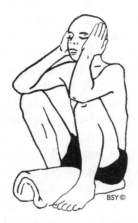

Nadanusandhana Asana (discovering the psychic sound pose)
Squat on a rolled up blanket or cushion, keeping this beneath the buttocks and between the legs. The cushion should be high enough so that the back is not cramped. The head and spine must be straight.
Rest the elbows on the knees and place the fingers on the top of the head and the thumbs in the ears.
Alternately, the index fingers can be used to seal the ears.

307

Appendix C

Mudras Relevant to Pranayama

The Sanskrit word *mudra* is translated as 'attitude' or 'gesture'. Attitude is something which reflects mind in body, and body in mind. With a little observation, we can learn a lot about someone's mental state by the way they walk, sit, act, and so on. A person who is frightened will walk quite differently from someone who is angry. This 'body language' is a constant communication between the annamaya kosha (physical body) and the other koshas, via the network of nadis in the pranayama kosha. Even simple hand or facial gestures will have a corresponding 'gesture' in the subtle body.

Tantra has developed this knowledge into a system of mudras which are specific attitudes of the body relating to specific attitudes of mind. The mudra may be a whole body position or a simple finger position, but the effect is transmitted through all levels of the pancha kosha, and the appropriate 'signal' transferred from gross to subtle.

This flow of information through the pranamaya kosha is a two-way process. People experiencing altered states of consciousness have been known to perform mudras spontaneously, representing a transmission from subtle to gross. Conversely, we can reverse the signal and send a message to the mind by adopting a physical attitude or mudra. The effects are very subtle. It would require great sensitivity for someone to be able to perceive a change of consciousness simply by joining the thumb and index finger together, but with practise the mind becomes conditioned to this signal, and when this hand position is adopted, the signal for meditation is transmitted.

Within the pranamaya kosha, these mudras represent a linking of various circuits within the network of nadis, creating a flow of prana which has gross and subtle implications. Mudras induce a change in the pranic circulatory system; they activate the nadis, ensuring a smooth flow of prana and eliminating wastage of prana. Therefore, they are able to guide prana towards a specific organ, as intended by a specific mudra. The hand mudras in particular gradually re-channel the energy back into the system, others influence specific nadis and organs, and so on. As a number of mudras are used in yogic practices, those relevant to pranayama are described here.

Nasikagra or Nasagra Mudra (nose tip position)

This is one of the most common hand mudras in pranayama practice. It is used to control the flow of the breath in each of the nostrils. Variations of the technique exist, but the one given below is easy for beginners, practical and efficient; it combines utility with subtle pranic manipulation.

The right hand is used because it is more associated with 'giving' on a pranic level; whereas the left is more associated with 'receiving'. However, if the right hand cannot be used for some reason, the left can be substituted.

Technique

Assume a comfortable meditation asana.

Take the awareness to the hands.

Hold the right hand in front of the face.

Place the tips of the index and middle fingers gently at the eyebrow centre. Both fingers should be relaxed.

The thumb is placed beside the right nostril, and the ring finger beside the left nostril.

The right nostril can be closed or opened by pressing or releasing the right side of the nostril with the thumb, as

Variation

required. The ring finger controls the flow of air in the left nostril in the same way. The little finger is not used and is comfortably folded.

Each side of the nostrils should be pressed with light pressure only, so the septum does not bend to one side or the other; be firm but gentle.

The arm should be in front and near the centre of the chest, but not touching or crowding the chest so as to obstruct the expansion of the lungs.

The elbow should point downward, because if it is out at the sides, it can cause the arm to ache after some time.

Keep the arms and shoulders relaxed; the less tension, the more rounds you will be able to complete without physical discomfort and interruption of the pranayama practice.

Practice note: The two concave depressions on each side of the nostrils are the most efficient positions to place the thumb and ring finger for the control of the two nostrils, as less pressure is needed to close the nostril. The fingers do not have to make such a large movement when changing from one nostril to the other. This lessens disruptions, however minimal, to both the body and the pranayama practice itself.

Variation: Another variation of nasikagra mudra is where the index and middle fingers are bent or folded into the palm of the hand. However, this eliminates the added benefit

310

of the index and middle fingers pressing the eyebrow centre, gently stimulating bhrumadhya, the *kshetram* or trigger point of ajna chakra. Choose the position which suits you best.

Jnana Mudra (psychic gesture of knowledge)
Assume a comfortable meditation posture.

Fold the index fingers of both hands so that they touch the inside root of their respective thumbs. The other three fingers should be straight but relaxed.

Place the hand on the knees with the palms facing downward.

Relax the hands and arms.

Practice note: This mudra is used for meditation and pranayama practices.

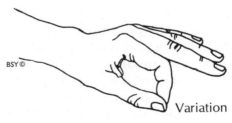

Variation

Variation: The tip of the thumb touches the tip of index finger to form a circle.

Chin Mudra (psychic gesture of consciousness)
This mudra is performed in the same way as jnana mudra except that the palms of both hands face upwards, with the backs of the hands resting on the knees.

311

Benefits: Jnana mudra and chin mudra are simple but important psycho-neural finger locks which make meditation asanas more powerful. The palms and fingers of the hands have many nerve root endings which constantly emit energy. When the index finger touches the thumb, a circuit is produced which allows the energy that would normally dissipate into the environment to travel back through the body and up to the brain.

When the fingers and hands are placed on the knees, the knees are sensitized, creating another pranic circuit that maintains and redirects prana within the body. In addition, placing the hands on the knees stimulates a nadi which runs from the knees, up the inside of the thighs and into the perineum. This nadi is known as *gupta* or the hidden nadi. Sensitizing this channel helps to stimulate the energies at mooladhara chakra.

When the palms face upward in chin mudra, the chest area is opened up. The practitioner may experience this as a sense of lightness and receptivity, which is absent in the practice of jnana mudra.

An understanding of the relationship between prana and the ki energy of oriental acupuncture brings another interesting aspect to some of these mudras. There are meridians of ki energy (related to prana in the nadis), which have their terminal points (*sei* or well points) in the fingertips. The sei point of the lung meridian is located on the thumbs; the large intestine meridian at the tip of the index finger; the heart constrictor vessel at the tip of the middle finger; the triple heater meridian on the ring finger and small intestines and heart sei points on the little finger.

Energy is normally being discharged from the fingertips, and it has been suggested that the energy flowing along the lung meridians to the thumb while performing jnana or chin mudra is transferred to the large intestine meridian. The body's vital energy is therefore conserved.

Chin mudra is said to have an influence on abdominal breathing, and here we can see a pranic connection between the lungs and abdomen through their respective meridians.

Note: The word jnana *means 'wisdom' or 'knowledge', and thus jnana mudra is the gesture of intuitive knowledge. Chin, on the other hand, is derived from the word* chit *or* chitta, *which means 'consciousness'. Chin mudra, therefore, is the psychic gesture of consciousness.*

Symbolically, the middle, ring and small fingers represent the three qualities of nature. The middle finger symbolizes sattwa *(purity, wisdom, true understanding), the ring finger* rajas *(action, passion, movement) and the little finger* tamas *(inertia, lethargy, darkness). These three states or gunas have to be transcended (from tamas to rajas to sattwa) in order to pass from darkness into light and from ignorance to knowledge. The bent index finger represents the individual manifestation of consciousness (jivatma). The thumb signifies the all-pervading consciousness or reality (paramatma). The index finger and the thumb touching each other shows that, though they seem separate, the individual being is in fact one with the Supreme.*

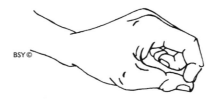

Chinmaya Mudra (gesture of manifested consciousness)
Assume a meditation asana.
Relax into the posture.
Hold the fingers in the same way as for jnana mudra.
Fold the three straightened fingers so that the tips touch
or point towards the palm.
The index finger can either touch the root or the tip of
the thumb.
Place the hands on the knees with the palms facing either
up or down.
Benefits: This mudra influences prana and stimulates move-
ment in the thoracic area. The acupuncture meridian
points concerned here affect respiration.

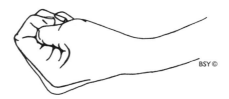

Aadi Mudra (primal or first attitude)
Assume a meditation asana.
Relax into the posture.
Fold the thumb into the palms of the hands; then slowly
curl each finger over the thumb to make a fist.
Place the hand on the knees with the palms either up or
down.
Benefits: This mudra influences upper chest breathing.

Brahma Mudra (attitude of all-pervading consciousness)

Assume a meditation asana.

Relax into the posture.

Turn the thumbs inward across the palms and fold the fingers over the thumbs.

Then place the back of the hands on the thighs and bring the knuckles of the hands together.

The thumb side of the hand is away from the body; the fingernails are visible; the little finger side of the hand is close to the body.

Place both hands close against the body at the level of the pelvic bone.

Benefits: This mudra helps to stimulate full yogic breathing, i.e. using the abdomen, chest and clavicles for each respiration. The knuckles, being pressed together, connect all the hand meridians. The tips of the fingers form another circuit as they touch the palm.

Comparative practice

Practise these four mudras (chin, chinmaya, aadi and brahma respectively) and see if you can discern any difference in the intensity of your breathing and type of breath used. While practising any pranayama which does not utilize nasikagra mudra, perform chin mudra and become aware of its effect on the lungs. Does it influence abdominal or diaphragmatic breathing? Practise this for 10 minutes and then change to chinmaya mudra. Is there any alternation of your breathing pattern? Do you feel any influence on the thoracic region and the intercostal muscles? Then perform aadi mudra and watch if there is any effect on the upper chest region and clavicles. Lastly, change to brahma mudra and feel if there is any effect on your complete breath. In this way, experiment, but remember that sensitivity will grow only with regular practice.

Bhairava and Bhairavi Mudra (fierce or terrifying attitude)
Assume a meditation asana.
Relax into the posture.
One hand is placed on top of the other, both with their palms facing upward. Both hands rest in the lap.
When the right hand is placed on top of the left, it is called bhairava mudra.
When the left hand is placed on top of the right, it is bhairavi mudra.
Practice note: These mudras may be adopted during any pranayama or meditation practice, where nasikagra mudra is not being used.

Note: *Bhairava is a terrifying form of Shiva. Bhairavi is his consort or Shakti, that is, the power that manifests this particular aspect of existence.*

Prana Vayu Mudras (vital air gestures) and the elements
It is interesting to note how many ways the five common elements of earth, water, fire, air, ether and space are not only macrocosmically but also microcosmically represented. These *pancha bhutas* (five elements) govern or dominate specific parts of the body and are also symbolized in each finger. This has significance when performing hand mudras, as different elements are symbolically joining together. The thumb represents fire; the index finger, air; the middle finger, ether; the ring finger, earth; and the little finger, water, although there is some variation in the classical texts.

316

The prana vayu mudras represent a subtle relationship between our existence in gross matter and our relationship to the more universal elements and forces, which interpenetrate all levels of creation. It reminds us to stop separating ourselves from the outside world, to stay still for a moment and feel the oneness vibrating and permeating all and everything.

Prana Mudra: The tip of the thumb (fire), middle finger (space) and ring finger (earth) are placed together. The mantra used with this mudra is *Om Pranaya Swaha*. Prana vayu centres in the chest area.

Apana Mudra: The tip of the thumb, index and middle fingers are placed together. The mantra is *Om Apanaya Swaha*. Apana vayu centres in the pelvic area.

Samana Mudra: The tip of the thumb, little finger and ring finger are placed together. The mantra used is *Om Samanaya Swaha*. Samana vayu centres in the abdomen.

Udana Mudra: The tip of the thumb, index and little fingers are placed together. The mantra is *Om Udanaya Swaha*. Udana vayu centres in the arms, legs, neck and head.

Vyana Mudra: The tip of the thumb, index, middle, ring and little fingers are placed together. Its mantra is *Om Vyanaya Swaha*. Vyana vayu permeates the whole body.

Technique

Sit comfortably in a meditation asana with the spine straight but relaxed.

Perform prana mudra, keeping your awareness on your natural breath and the region of the body where the prana vayu manifests. Continue for a few minutes, then begin to chant its mantra mentally.

Do the same with each of the prana vayu mudras in turn, spending up to 10 minutes on each one. Slowly, your awareness of these subtle energies will begin to stir.

Practice note: These mudras may be used with any pranayama or pre-pranayama practice, when alternate nostril breathing with nasikagra mudra is not used.

317

Note: *The five different kinds of prana vayu are represented and invoked by hand mudras. When performing these mudras, it does not mean that you will automatically feel that particular vayu surging through its normally specified location in the body, but on a subtle or pranic level this particular energy will be stimulated. While dealing with prana and its subtleties, one should have knowledge of these mudras, until finally a deeper awareness dawns of the vital energies, and of those same energies pervading the cosmos.*

Shanmukhi Mudra (closing the seven gates)

Sit in any comfortable meditative asana, preferably padmasana or siddha/siddha yoni asana.

Hold the head and spine straight.

Close the eyes and place the hands on the knees.

Relax the whole body.

Raise the arms in front of the face with the elbows pointing sideways.

Close the ears with the thumbs, the eyes with the index fingers, the nostrils with the middle fingers, and the mouth by placing the ring fingers above and little fingers below the lips.

Release the pressure of the middle fingers and open the nostrils. Inhale slowly and deeply, using full yogic breathing. At the end of inhalation, close the nostrils with the middle fingers.

318

Retain the breath inside for as long as is comfortable.
After some time, release the pressure of the middle fingers and slowly exhale.
This is one round.
Inhale again immediately to start another round.
To end the practice, lower the hands to the knees, keeping the eyes closed, and slowly externalize the mind, becoming aware of external sounds and the physical body.

Contra-indications: Those suffering from depression should not perform this mudra.

Benefits: Physically, the energy and heat from the hands and fingers stimulate and relax the nerves and muscles of the face. Mentally, it introverts the awareness. Spiritually, it induces the state of *pratyahara* or sense withdrawal.

Practice note: This mudra is used in conjunction with various pranayama and meditation techniques, kriya yoga and nada yoga.

Khechari or Nabho Mudra (tongue lock)

Sit in any comfortable meditative asana, preferably padmasana or siddha/siddha yoni asana, with the head and spine straight and the hands in chin or jnana mudra.
Close the mouth. Roll the tongue back so that the lower surface touches the upper palate.
Fold the tongue upward and backward, so that the lower surface lies in contact with the upper palate.
Stretch the tip of the tongue backward as far as is comfortable.
Do not strain.
Perform ujjayi pranayama.
Breathe slowly and deeply.
Hold the tongue lock for as long as possible without straining.
At first there may be some discomfort and ujjayi pranayama may irritate the throat, but with practice it will become more comfortable.

When the tongue becomes tired, release and relax it, then repeat the practice.

With practice, the tongue will automatically ascend into the soft palate to stimulate many vital nerve centres in the brain.

Precaution: Discontinue this mudra if a bitter secretion is tasted. Such a secretion is a sign of toxins in the system.

Benefits: Khechari mudra stimulates a number of pressure points located in the back of the mouth and the nasal cavity. These points influence the whole body. A number of glands are also massaged, stimulating the secretion of certain hormones and of saliva. This practice reduces the sensations of hunger and thirst, and induces a state of inner calm and stillness. It preserves the vitality of the body and is especially beneficial for inner healing. Ultimately, this mudra has the potential to stimulate prana and awaken kundalini shakti.

Shambhavi Mudra or Bhrumadhya Drishti (eyebrow centre gazing)

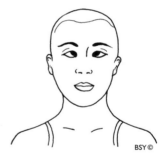

Sit in any comfortable meditation pose.

Keep the head and spine upright and straight.

Place the hands on the knees in either chin or jnana mudra.

Close the eyes and relax the whole body.

Relax all the muscles of the face, including the forehead, the eyes and behind the eyes.

Slowly open the eyes and look forward at a fixed point, keeping the head and the whole body absolutely still.

Next, look upward and inward, focusing the eyes at the eyebrow centre.

When performed correctly, the curve of the eyebrows will form a V-shaped image with the apex at the eyebrow centre. If the V-formation cannot be seen, the eyes are not converging as they should.

Hold the gaze for only a few seconds at first. Release at the slightest sensation of strain.

Close the eyes and relax them.

Try to suspend the thought process and meditate on the stillness in chidakasha, the dark space in front of the closed eyes.

Precaution: The eyes are very sensitive and consequently the final position should not be held for too long. If the nerves are weak, any strain can cause retinal detachment. Release the position when strain is experienced.

Contra-indications: People suffering from glaucoma should not practise this mudra. Those with diabetic retinopathy or who have just had cataract surgery, lens implant or other eye operations should not perform shambhavi without expert guidance.

Benefits: Shambhavi strengthens the eye muscles and releases accumulated tension in this area. It calms the mind, thus removing emotional stress and anger. Concentration, mental stability and the state of thoughtlessness are developed.

Agochari Mudra or Nasikagra Drishti (nose-tip gazing)

Sit in any meditation pose with head and spine straight.

Rest the hands on the knees in chin or jnana mudra.

Close the eyes and relax the whole body.

Open the eyes and focus them on the tip of the nose.

When the eyes are correctly focused a refraction of light, forming a V is seen just above the nosetip.

Concentrate on the apex of the V.

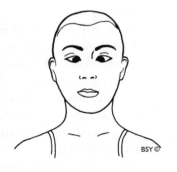

321

Become completely absorbed in the practice to the exclusion of all other thoughts.

After a few seconds close the eyes and relax them before repeating the practice. Continue for up to 5 minutes.

Contra-indications: As for shambhavi mudra. Those suffering from depression should avoid this introverting practice.

Benefits: This practice calms anger and disturbed states of mind. The powers of concentration are developed. If performed with awareness for a long period, it helps to awaken mooladhara chakra and induce meditative states.

Practice note: Nasikagra drishti should be practised with normal breathing in the beginning until the eyes have adjusted to the downward gaze. Later the practice can be combined with antar kumbhaka (inner retention) but not with bahir kumbhaka (external retention).

Unmani Mudra (attitude of mindlessness)

The word *unmani* literally means 'no mind' or 'not thinking'. The state of unmani arises during meditation. Unmani implies that state which is beyond thought, a state where all attachment to the world of objects is dispelled. In this state, the awareness functions without the hindrance of conflicting thoughts and analysis. This state is helpful in certain pranayama, meditation and kriya practices.

Technique

Sit in any comfortable meditation asana.

The eyes are wide open but relaxed.

Inhale slowly and deeply. Hold the breath inside. Focus the awareness at bindu in the back of the head for a few seconds. Exhale slowly, allowing the awareness to descend with the breath from bindu through the chakras in the spine: ajna, vishuddhi, anahata, manipura, swadhisthana, mooladhara.

The eyes should slowly close as the awareness descends. By the time the awareness reaches mooladhara, the eyes should be fully closed.

Even when the eyes are open, the awareness is looking within.

Do not try too hard, but allow the process to occur spontaneously.

Inhale deeply and begin the next round.

Continue for 5 to 10 minutes.

Contra-indications: As for shambhavi mudra.

Benefits: Unmani mudra induces a meditative state. It also calms general stress and agitation.

Akashi Mudra (awareness of inner space)

Sit in any comfortable meditative posture.

Fold the tongue back against the upper palate in khechari mudra.

Practise ujjayi pranayama and shambhavi mudra.

Simultaneously, bend the head back to about 45 degrees. Straighten the arms and lock the elbows, pressing the knees with the hands.

Breathe slowly and deeply in ujjayi.

Continue for as long as you feel comfortable.

End the practice by bending the elbows and releasing khechari and shambhavi mudras.

Raise the head to the upright position.

Resume normal breathing. Be aware of the inner space.

Practise 1 to 3 rounds. Gradually increase to 5 rounds.

Precaution: As soon as faintness is felt, stop the practice. This technique must be practised slowly under the guidance of a competent teacher.

Contra-indications: People suffering from high blood pressure, vertigo, brain disorders or epilepsy should not practise this mudra.

Benefits: This practice combines the benefits of kumbhaka, ujjayi, shambhavi and khechari. It induces calmness and tranquillity, and develops control over the senses. When perfected, it arrests the thought processes and induces higher states of consciousness.

Practice note: It is recommended that the practitioner be completely familiar with the practices of ujjayi, khechari and shambhavi before commencing akashi mudra. At first ujjayi pranayama may irritate the throat in this inclined position, but with practice it will become more comfortable. Maintain the final position for as long as possible, increasing the length of time in the mudra very slowly.

Bandhas Relevant
to Pranayama

The word *bandha* means to 'hold', 'tighten' or 'lock'. These definitions describe the physical action involved in the bandha practices and their effect on the pranic body. Whereas mudras redirect prana by linking up certain circuits in the pranamaya kosha, bandhas redirect and store it by blocking the flow in certain areas of the body, thus forcing it to flow or accumulate in other areas. During the practices, certain parts of the body are contracted. This action also massages, stimulates and influences the muscles, organs, glands and nerves associated with that specific area.

There are three bandhas: jalandhara, uddiyana and moola, and a fourth, maha bandha, is the combination of all three. These bandhas contract the regions of the throat, abdomen and pelvic floor respectively. When one practises internal retention in pranayama, one should assume two bandhas – jalandhara and moola. When one practises external retention, one should assume three bandhas – jalandhara, moola and uddiyana.

One gains the maximum benefit from pranayama when retention is practised with the bandhas. There are many reasons for this. Pranayama stimulates the flow of prana, and when the pranas are stimulated one must have a means of forcing this pranic energy up towards the higher centres. Therefore, one needs to create a negative pressure, similar to what is used in pumping water, which will push the pranic energy up through the spinal cord. The bandhas create such a pressure. They control the flow of prana and direct it to the required areas. When one performs moola bandha and jalandhara bandha, one is forcing apana to flow upwards and unite with prana. When prana and apana unite it generates vitality and helps to awaken the kundalini.

The bandhas also assist in releasing the three *granthis*, the main blockages or attachments that confront the sadhaka:

Brahma granthi, which controls mooladhara and swadhisthana chakras and creates fear and insecurity, attachments to material objects, sensual pleasures and selfishness.

Vishnu granthi, which controls manipura and anahata chakras and creates bondage to other people, emotional relationships and attachment to emotional situations.

Rudra granthi, which controls vishuddhi and ajna chakras and represents the obstacles created by the power of the intellect, along with attachment to siddhis and other higher psychic experiences.

As long as the knots exist, the negative power of the chakras manifest, but when they are released, the positive power of the chakras manifest. The build-up of prana during the practice of bandhas releases these knots of bondage, so that the sadhaka is free to attain what lies beyond all attachment.

A bandha is also a means to expand the pranic or ionoplasmic field which is concentrated around the chakras. This can be understood if we consider ida and pingala as rotating coils in three dimensions. When we perform jalandhara bandha, by lowering the head so that the chin presses the hollow at the base of the neck, raising the shoulders and holding the breath, the field around vishuddhi chakra is expanded. This has the effect of increasing the strength of the pranic field in this area. The amplitude of the wave form and its range of activity are increased. The ionoplasmic field now extends in a greater density from anahata to ajna.

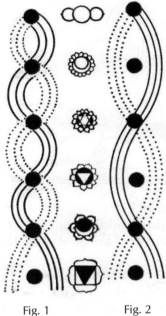

Fig. 1: Modified wave forms when moola bandha is practised by itself.

Fig. 2: Wave forms when the three bandhas are performed together.

Fig. 1   Fig. 2

Likewise, the influence of uddiyana bandha – performed by breathing out, holding the breath externally and sucking in the abdominal area – expands the field around manipura chakra. When practised by itself, this bandha extends the ionoplasmic field in greater density from swadhisthana to anahata and when combined with jalandhara bandha, the field is expanded from swadhisthana to ajna.

The third bandha, moola bandha, is practised by contracting the area of the perineum. When practised by itself the field around mooladhara is expanded and practised in conjunction with uddiyana and jalandhara bandhas, the ionoplasmic field from mooladhara to ajna is expanded.

When jalandhara, uddiyana and moola bandhas are practised simultaneously in maha bandha, one of the most important techniques in many advanced yogic sadhanas, it increases the ionoplasmic and pranic energies throughout the body and develops and activates many dormant brain cells.

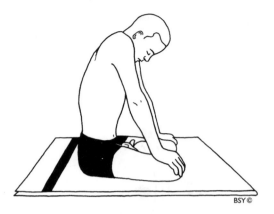

BSY©

Jalandhara Bandha (throat lock)

Sit in padmasana or siddha/siddha yoni asana with the head and spine straight. The knees should be in firm contact with the floor.

Place the palms of the hands on the knees.

Close the eyes and relax into the position.

Inhale slowly and deeply and hold the breath inside.

While retaining the breath, bend the head forward and press the chin tightly against the chest.

Straighten the arms and lock them firmly into position, pressing the knees down with the hands.

Simultaneously, hunch the shoulders upward and forward.

Remain in this locked position for as long as the breath can be comfortably held. Do not strain.

Relax the shoulders, bend the elbows and slowly release the lock. Raise the head and then exhale.

Repeat when the breath has returned to normal.

Practice note: Inhalation and exhalation must only be performed when the chin lock and arm lock have been released and the head is fully upright. Jalandhara bandha may also be practised with external breath retention.

Variation: A simpler and subtle form of jalandhara bandha is where the head is simply bent forward so that the chin presses the neck. The shoulders and the arms do not move. This variation is often used during pranayama to

328

minimize external movement and avoid disruption of the pranayama mudra such as nasagra.

Precaution: Although the neck lock reduces blood pressure, long retention of the breath strains the heart. Refrain from the practice if any vertigo or dizziness arises.

Contra-indications: People suffering from cervical spondylosis, high intracranial pressure, vertigo, high blood pressure or heart disease should not practise jalandhara bandha.

Benefits: The full form of jalandhara bandha compresses the carotid sinuses, which are located on the carotid arteries, the main arteries in the neck. The simple variation exerts a subtler pressure. These sinuses help to regulate the circulatory and respiratory systems. Normally, a decrease in oxygen and increase in carbon dioxide in the body leads to an increased heart rate and heavier breathing. This process is initiated by the carotid sinuses. By exerting pressure on these sinuses, this tendency is prevented, allowing for decreased heart rate and increased breath retention. This practice produces mental relaxation, relieving stress, anxiety and anger. It develops meditative introversion and one-pointedness. The stimulus on the throat helps to balance thyroid function and regulate the metabolism.

Uddiyana Bandha (abdominal lock)

Sit in a meditation pose which enables the knees to touch the ground.

Place the palms of the hands flat on the knees.

Close the eyes and relax the whole body.

Inhale deeply through the nostrils, then exhale fully, accentuating the contraction of the abdominal muscles and emptying the lungs as much as possible.

Hold the breath out and perform jalandhara bandha.

Contract the abdominal muscles inward and upward, making the abdomen concave.

Hold this locked body position for as long as the breath can be comfortably retained outside. Then release uddiyana followed by jalandhara and raise the head fully before inhaling.

329

Allow the breath to return to normal before commencing the next round.

Contra-indications: People suffering from heart problems, stomach or intestinal ulcer, ulcers, hernia, colitis, diaphragmatic hernia, major abdominal problems, high blood pressure, glaucoma and raised intracranial pressure should not perform this practice. It should also be avoided by pregnant women, though after childbirth it is useful for re-toning the abdominal and uterine muscles.

Benefits: All the abdominal organs are toned, massaged and strengthened. It stimulates the function of the pancreas and liver and strengthens the internal organs. The digestive fire is stimulated and the adrenal glands are balanced, removing lethargy and soothing anxiety and tension. It also improves blood circulation throughout the torso.

Uddiyana bandha stimulates the solar plexus, which has many subtle influences on the distribution of energy throughout the body. It creates a suction pressure which reverses the energy flow of apana and prana, uniting them with samana and stimulating manipura chakra.

Practice note: Uddiyana should be practised on an empty stomach and with empty bowels. It is practised with external breath retention only.

Moola Bandha (perineal contraction)

Sit in siddhasana or siddha yoni asana so that pressure is applied to the perineal/vaginal region.

The area to be contracted is the physical location of mooladhara chakra.

For men this is located in the perineum, between the anus and the sexual organ.

For women, the trigger-point is located behind the cervix where the uterus and vagina meet.

Close the eyes and relax the whole body.

Inhale deeply, retain the breath inside and contract the perineal/vaginal muscles as tightly as possible, without strain.

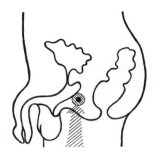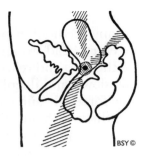

Maintain awareness in this region, perform 5 contractions, then exhale.

At first practise short contractions and as control improves increase the duration of the contraction.

Contra-indications: As for jalandhara bandha. This practice should only be performed under experienced guidance, as it raises the energies very fast and can precipitate symptoms of hyperactivity if wrongly prescribed. Do not practise during menstruation.

Benefits: Moola bandha bestows many physical, mental and spiritual benefits. It stimulates the pelvic nerves and tones the uro-genital and excretory systems. It is a means to attain sexual control and alleviate many sexual disorders.

Practice note: Moola bandha is the contraction of certain muscles only in the pelvic floor. Initially, the anal and urinary sphincters will also contract, but as greater awareness and control is developed this should be minimized and eventually cease so that moola bandha can be isolated and performed without contraction of these areas. Moola bandha can also be performed during external retention.

Maha Bandha (the great lock)

Maha bandha is a powerful combination of all three bandhas, jalandhara, uddiyana and moola, performed during external breath retention. This practice concentrates the pranas internally and increases the level of energy during periods of inner awareness.

Technique

Sit in any meditation pose with the knees on the floor; spine erect, head straight.

Close the eyes and relax the whole body.

Inhale slowly and deeply through the nose.

Exhale forcefully and completely.

Retain the breath outside.

Successively perform jalandhara, uddiyana and moola bandhas, in this order.

Hold the bandhas and the breath for as long as is comfortable without straining.

While holding maha bandha, rotate the awareness for a few seconds from mooladhara to manipura to vishuddhi a number of times.

Start from mooladhara each time.

After a comfortable period, release moola, uddiyana, then jalandhara bandha in this order.

Inhale slowly only when the head is upright.

This is one round.

Allow the breath to return to normal before commencing the next round.

Practise up to 5 rounds.

Contra-indications: As for the three bandhas.

Benefits: Maha bandha gives enhanced benefits of all three bandhas. It affects the hormonal secretions of the pineal gland and regulates the entire endocrine system. The degenerative and ageing processes are checked and every cell of the body is rejuvenated. It introverts the mind prior to meditation. When perfected, it can fully awaken prana in the main chakras. It leads to the merger of prana, apana and samana in manipura chakra, which is the culmination of all pranayamas.

Practice note: The three bandhas should be mastered separately before attempting maha bandha.

'Hatha Yoga Pradipika' Pranayama Sutras

The *Hatha Yoga Pradipika* by Swatmarama is a tantric text which deals systematically with the science of evolution. Along with the *Goraksha Samhita*, *Gheranda Samhita* and *Hatharatnavali*, it is one of the most reliable texts on hatha yoga. Below are selected sutras from Chapter 2 which have provided source material for some of the content of this book. The sutras are arranged in verse order.

Thus being established in asana, and having control (of the body), taking balanced diet, pranayama should be practised according to the instructions of the guru. (2:1)

When prana moves, chitta (the mental force) moves. When prana is without movement, chitta is without movement. By this (steadiness of prana) the yogi attains steadiness and should therefore restrain the vayu (air).   (2:2)

As long as the vayu (air and prana) remain in the body, that is called life. Death is when it leaves the body. Therefore, retain the vayu.   (2:3)

The vital air does not pass in the middle channel because the nadis are full of impurities, so how can the state of unmani arise, and how can perfection or siddhi come about?   (2:4)

When all the nadis and chakras which are full of impurities are purified, then the yogi is able to retain prana.　(2:5)

Therefore, pranayama should be done daily with a sattwic state of mind, so that the impurities are driven out of sushumna nadi and purification occurs.　(2:6)

Sitting in baddha padmasana, the yogi should inhale through the left nostril and hold the breath to capacity, and then exhale through the right nostril.　(2:7)

Then, inhaling through the right nostril, gradually fill the abdomen, perform kumbhaka as before, then exhale completely through the left nostril.　(2:8)

Inhale with the same nostril through which exhalation was done, hold the breath to utmost capacity and exhale through the other nostril slowly and not forcibly.　(2:9)

When prana is inhaled through the left nostril, then it must be exhaled through the other. When it is inhaled through the right, hold it inside and then exhale through the other nostril. One who practises in this way, through the right and left nostrils alternately, purifies all his nadis within three months.　(2:10)

Retention should be performed four times a day: early morning, midday, evening and midnight, so that retention is gradually held up to eighty (counts) in one sitting. (2:11)

At first there is perspiration, in the middle stage trembling, in the highest stage complete steadiness, and therefore the breath should be withheld.　(2:12)

Rub the body with the perspiration from the labour (of pranayama). The body derives firmness and steadiness from this.　(2:13)

In the beginning stages of practice, food consisting of milk and ghee is recommended. Upon being established in the practice, such restrictions are not necessary. (2:14)

Just as lions, elephants and tigers are gradually controlled, so the prana is controlled through practice. Otherwise, the practitioner is destroyed. (2:15)

By proper practise of pranayama, all diseases are eradicated. Through improper practise, all diseases can arise. (2:16)

Hiccup, asthma, cough, headache, ear and eye pain, and various other diseases are due to disturbances of the vital air. (2:17)

The vayu should be skilfully inhaled, exhaled and retained so that perfection or siddhi is attained. (2:18)

When the nadis are purified, there are external symptoms. Success is definite when the body becomes thin and glows. (2:19)

When one is able to hold the vayu according to one's will, the digestive power increases. With the nadis being purified, the inner sound or nada thus awakens and one is free from disease. (2:20)

When fat or mucus is excessive, the shatkarmas or six cleansing techniques should be practised before (pranayama). Others in whom the doshas, i.e. phlegm, wind and bile, are balanced, should not do them. (2:21)

Perform exhalation and inhalation rapidly like the bellows (of a blacksmith). This is called kapalbhati and it destroys all mucus disorders. (2:35)

According to some teachers, pranayama alone removes impurities, and therefore they hold pranayama in esteem, and not the other techniques. (2:37)

Even Brahma and other gods in heaven devote themselves to practising pranayama because it ends the fear of death. Thus it (pranayama) must be practised. (2:39)

As long as the breath is restrained in the body, the mind is devoid of thought and the gaze is centred between the eyebrows, why should there be fear of death?   (2:40)

By systematically restraining the prana (breath), the nadis and chakras are purified. Thus the prana bursts open the doorway to sushumna and easily enters it.   (2:41)

The breath (prana), moving in the middle passage, makes the mind still. This steadiness of mind is itself called the state of manomani (devoid of thought).   (2:42)

By practising the various kumbhakas, wondrous perfections are obtained. Those who are the knowers, practise the various kumbhakas to accomplish them.   (2:43)

The eight kumbhakas are surya bheda, ujjayi, sheetkari, sheetali, bhastrika, bhramari, moorchha and plavini. (2:44)

At the end of inhalation, jalandhara bandha is done. At the end of kumbhaka and beginning of exhalation, uddiyana bandha is done.   (2:45)

Contracting the perineum and the throat, and drawing the abdomen upwards, prana flows into brahma nadi.
    (2:46)

Raising apana upward, and bringing prana down from the throat, the yogi becomes free from old age and appears as if sixteen years of age.   (2:47)

Sitting comfortably, the yogi should become fixed in his posture and slowly breathe the air in through the right nostril.   (2:48)

Retention should then be held until the breath diffuses to the roots of the hair and the tips of the nails. Then slowly exhale through the left nostril.   (2:49)

Surya bheda is excellent for purifying the cranium, destroying imbalances of the wind dosha, and eliminates worms. It should be done again and again.   (2:50)

Closing the mouth, inhale with control and concentration through ida and pingala so that the breath is felt from the throat to the heart and produces a sonorous sound.
(2:51)

Do kumbhaka as before and exhale through ida. This removes phlegm from the throat and stimulates the (digestive) fire.
(2:52)

This pranayama, called ujjayi, may be performed while moving, standing, sitting or walking. It removes oedema and disorders of the nadis and dhatu.
(2:53)

By drawing the breath through the mouth, make a hissing sound, without gaping the mouth, and exhale through the nose. By practising this, one becomes a second Kamadeva (god of love).
(2:54)

He is adored by the circle of yoginis and becomes the controller of creation and dissolution, being without hunger, thirst, sleep and laziness.
(2:55)

And the sattwa in the body becomes free from all disturbances. Truly, by the fore-mentioned method, one becomes lord of yogis on this earth.
(2:56)

The wise inhale air through the tongue and practise kumbhaka as (described) before. Then, slowly exhale the air through the nostrils.
(2:57)

This kumbhaka called sheetali, cures an enlarged stomach or spleen and other related diseases, fever, excess bile, hunger and thirst, and counteracts poisons.
(2:58)

Placing both soles of the feet on the top of the thighs is padmasana which destroys all sins (bad karma).
(2:59)

Sitting properly in padmasana, and keeping the neck and abdomen in alignment, exhale prana through the nose.
(2:60)

And again, the air should be quickly inhaled up to the heart lotus. Accordingly, the resounding is felt from the heart and throat up to the cranium. (2:61)

In that way, it (the breath) is inhaled and exhaled repeatedly with the same motion as a pair of bellows being pumped. (2:62)

Thus, in this way, one keeps the breath moving with mindfulness (awareness) and body steadiness. When the body is tired, then inhale through the right nostril. (2:63)

Accordingly, when the abdomen becomes full of air, then quickly hold the nostrils (and breath) firmly, without using the index and middle fingers (i.e. using the thumb and ring finger as in nasikagra mudra). (2:64)

Having performed (pranayama and) retention systematically, exhale through the left nostril. Thereby, imbalances of wind, bile and mucus are annihilated and the digestive fire increased. (2:65)

This (bhastrika) quickly arouses kundalini. It is pleasant and beneficial, and removes obstruction due to excess mucus accumulated at the entrance to brahma nadi.
(2:66)

This kumbhaka called bhastrika enables the three granthis (psychic pranic knots) to be broken. Thus it is the duty of the yogi to practise bhastrika. (2:67)

Breathe in quickly, making a reverberating sound like the black male bee, and exhale slowly while softly making the sound of the female black bee. By this yogic practice, one becomes lord of yogis and one's mind is absorbed in bliss. (2:68)

At the end of inhalation, gradually become fixed in jalandhara bandha, then exhale slowly. This is called the fainting or swooning pranayama as it makes the mind inactive and (thus) confers pleasure. (2:69)

The inner part of the abdomen being completely filled with air, one can float like a lotus leaf on water. (2:70)

Pranayama is said to be of three types: exhalation (rechaka), inhalation (pooraka) and retention (kumbhaka). Kumbhaka is again of two types: connected (sahita) and unconnected (kevala). (2:71)

Kevala kumbhaka is perfected, sahita kumbhaka has to be practised. When (you are) freed of inhalation and exhalation, then the breath and prana is retained easily.
(2:72)

Perfection of isolated retention is freedom from inhalation and exhalation. The pranayama spoken of is verily kevala kumbhaka. (2:73)

Nothing in the three planes of existence is unobtainable by him who has mastery of kevala kumbhaka, and can retain the breath as desired. (2:74)

There is no doubt, the state of raja yoga is also attained (through kevala kumbhaka). By retention, kundalini is aroused, sushumna becomes unobstructed, and perfection of hatha yoga takes place. (2:75)

By stopping the prana through retention, the mind becomes free from all modifications. By thus practising (this yoga), one achieves the stage of raja yoga (supreme union). (2:76)

Glossary

Aadi – primary

Abhinivesha – fear of death; one of the five kleshas described by Patanjali in the *Yoga Sutras*

Adhama – inferior

Agni – fire; god of fire and purification

Ahimsa – absence of violence from within; one of the yamas, according to Patanjali's *Yoga Sutras*

Ajapa japa – continuous, spontaneous repetition of mantra; meditation practice in which mantra is coordinated with the breath

Ajna chakra – psychic/pranic centre or vortex situated at the medulla oblongata on the top of the spinal column, corresponding to the pineal gland; seat of intuition; psychic centre where guru's commands are received

Akasha – ether, space

Akshara – letter, form; sounds which do not die; imperishable

Alambusha – one of the seven lesser nadis, flowing from the anus to the mouth

Amrita – nectar which bestows immortality

Anahad nada – unstruck sound reverberating throughout the universe; transcendental, cosmic sound experienced in the highest state of meditation

Anahata chakra – psychic/pranic centre or vortex situated in the region of the cardiac plexus

Anandamaya kosha – sheath or body of bliss

Angula – a specific measurement, the width of one finger

Annamaya kosha – sheath or body of matter; the physical body

Antar – internal

340

Antaranga – internal stage

Anuloma – in a natural direction

Apana vayu – one of the pancha pranas, moving downwards from the navel to the perineum in the lower abdominal region, responsible for elimination and reproduction

Aparigraha – non-possessiveness; one of the yamas, according to Patanjali's *Yoga Sutras*

Apas – water

Arambha – beginning

Ardha – half

Ardhanarishwara – tantric symbol of the half-male/half-female form denoting the two principles of Shiva and Shakti

Asana – a steady and comfortable meditative pose; third step of Patanjali's ashtanga yoga

Asteya – honesty; one of the yamas, according to Patanjali's *Yoga Sutras*

Atma shakti – inherent power in an individual being

Atmamaya kosha – sheath of the spirit

Atman – the Self beyond mind and body; superconsciousness, spirit, soul

Atmapuri – city of the soul

Avastha – state of consciousness or condition of the mind; position

Ayama – expansion; dimension

Ayurveda – the vedic system of medical diagnosis and treatment

Baddha padmasana – locked lotus pose

Bahir – external

Bahiranga – external stage

Bandha – binding; psycho-muscular energy block

Basti – yogic enema, one of the shatkarmas

Bhairava – name of Lord Shiva in his fierce aspect; state of consciousness which precedes the ultimate experience of universal consciousness or Shiva

Bhairavi – female counterpart or shakti of Bhairava.

Bhrumadhya – trigger point for ajna chakra located at the eyebrow centre

Bhu – earth

Bhu samadhi – yogic state achieved through prolonged kumbhaka where all vital functions appear to have ceased and the yogi stays buried in earth

Bhujanga – serpent

Bhuvah – astral plane of existence

Bija – seed

Bija mantra – seed sound; a basic mantra or vibration

Bindu – point; seed

Bindu chakra – psychic/pranic centre situated at the top of the back of the head; centre or source of individual creation from where psychic vibrations first emanate

Bindu visarga – flow of fluid (bindu) secreted at the bindu chakra

Brahma – the first god in the cosmic trinity, the Creator; potentiality of mooladhara chakra

Brahma granthi – lit. 'Brahma's knot'; psychic knot in mooladhara and swadhishthana chakras, symbolizing material and sensual attachment

Brahma nadi – the most subtle pranic flow within sushumna nadi

Brahmacharya – self-restraint, celibacy; to abide constantly in Brahman; one of the yamas, according to Patanjali's *Yoga Sutras*

Brahmamuhurta – the time between 4 am and 6 am best suited to spiritual sadhana

Brahman – ever-expanding, limitless consciousness; monistic concept of absolute reality

Brahmin – of the priestly caste; a person whose life is dedicated to the study of the Vedas and dispensation of the knowledge of Brahman

Buddhi – higher intelligence, discrimination; intuitive aspect of mind

Chaitanya – consciousness

Chakra – a psychic/pranic centre in the subtle body; circle, wheel or vortex; congregation point of the nadis

Chakra sharira – body of the chakras

Chandra – moon; representing mental energy

Chandra nadi – ida nadi

Chidakasha – inner space visualized in meditation behind the closed eyes

Chinmaya – supreme intelligence

Chitra/chitrini nadi – the second of three energy currents (nadis) lying within sushumna nadi

Chitta – individual consciousness, including the subconscious and unconscious layers of mind; storehouse of memories or samskaras

Chitta shakti – mental force

342

Devadatta – one of the sub-pranas, responsible for causing yawning

Devata – illumined form, divinity; the revealed symbol of a mantra

Dhananjaya – one of the sub-pranas, responsible for decomposition of the body after death

Dharana – concentration or complete attention; sixth limb of Patanjali's ashtanga yoga

Dhwani – sound

Dhyana – meditation; seventh limb of Patanjali's ashtanga yoga

Divya chakshu – divine eye

Dosha – three humours of the body described in ayurveda: mucus (*kapha*), bile (*pitta*) and wind (*vata*)

Drishti – faculty of seeing

Gandhari – one of the seven lesser nadis, flowing from the left eye to the left big toe

Ganga – the river Ganges, the most sacred river in India; another term for ida nadi

Gayatri – famous and sacred vedic mantra suitable for everyone; vedic goddess, female counterpart of the Sun

Ghata – vessel

Granthi – psychic knot; three granthis along sushumna nadi hinder the upward passage of kundalini

Gunas – the three qualities of nature: rajas, tamas, sattwa

Guru – one who dispels the darkness of ignorance; teacher, preceptor

Ham – bija mantra of vishuddhi chakra

Hasta – hand, one of the five organs of action (*karmendriya*)

Hastijihva – one of the seven lesser nadis, flowing from the right eye to the left big toe

Hatha yoga – system of yoga for attaining physical and mental purity, and balancing the pranas in the body

Hreem – seed sound which is the tantric equivalent of Om

Ida – major nadi beginning on the left side of mooladhara and twisting up the spine through the chakras to ajna, through which manas shakti or lunar energy flows; governing the left side of the body and right side of the brain; associated with internalized awareness

Ishta devata – one's personal deity

Ishwara pranidhana – complete dedication to higher consciousness; one of the niyamas, according to Patanjali's *Yoga Sutras*

Jagrat – the stage of waking; conscious mind

Japa – continuous repetition of mantra

Jada samadhi – state of samadhi in which there is no awareness or illumination

Janah loka – plane of realized beings; one of the seven higher planes of consciousness

Jara – old age; one of three ailments suffered due to amrita consumption

Jatharagni – digestive fire

Jihva – tongue, one of the five *jnanendriyas* (organs of knowledge); one of the 19 lesser nadis

Jiva – individual soul

Jnana – true knowledge; wisdom

Jnana chakshu – eye of wisdom

Jnanendriyas – the five organs of sense perception and knowledge: ears, eyes, tongue, nose and skin

Kalaa – the limiting aspect of Shakti; the manifest universe of time and space

Kalpa taru – wish-fulfilling tree

Kanphata – one whose ears are pierced

Kapha – one of the doshas; mucus, phlegm

Karma – action in the manifest and unmanifest dimension; law of cause and effect

Karmendriyas – five organs of action: hands, feet, vocal cords, excretory and reproductive organs

Kaya sthairyam – practice of absolute steadiness and awareness of the physical body often performed as a preparation for pranayama or meditative states

Kevala – sole; pure; spontaneous

Kevala kumbhaka – spontaneous breath retention

Kilaka – pin

Klesha – pain, affliction, suffering; five causes of suffering described in Patanjali's *Yoga Sutras*, viz. ignorance (*avidya*), ego or sense of doership (*asmita*), attraction (*raga*), aversion (*dwesha*) and fear of death (*abhinivesha*)

Krikara – one of the sub-pranas, which induces hunger and thirst

Kriya – action; motion; action leading to perfection of knowledge

Kriya yoga – practices of kundalini yoga designed to speed up the evolution of humanity

Kshetram – field; sphere of action; trigger point for the activation of a chakra

Kuhu – one of the seven minor nadis, flowing from the throat to the genitals

Kumbhaka – breath retention

Kundalini shakti – also referred to as 'kundalini'; potential energy lying dormant in mooladhara chakra, often referred to as the 'serpent power'

Kundalini yoga – path of yoga which awakens the dormant spiritual force

Kunjal kriya – cleansing the stomach by voluntary vomiting using warm saline water; a form of dhauti (a shatkarma)

Koorma – one of the sub-pranas, responsible for opening and closing the eyes, blinking, and controlling the movement of the eyelids; one of the minor nadis

Lam – bija mantra of mooladhara chakra

Laya – dissolution; merging

Lila – divine play, pastime; cosmic play of consciousness and energy; activity of prakriti and its three gunas

Loka – plane of existence

Madhyama – middle; intermediate

Maha – great

Mahah loka – one of the seven higher dimensions of consciousness; plane of saints and siddhas

Mahamaya – lit. 'great illusion'; a term used to denote the feminine creative force of the universe

Mahamrityunjaya mantra – lit. 'great death conquering mantra'; a sacred and popular Shiva mantra used to generate wellbeing at all levels

Mahaprana – cosmic, universal prana

Maharshi – lit. 'great seer'; a great sage or saint

Mahashakti – lit. 'great shakti'; a term used for the primordial feminine force

Manas – finite, rational mind, concerned with senses, thought and counter-thought

Manas shakti – mental or lunar energy

Mandala – area; pictorial representation; orb; diagram within a circumference symbolizing the deeper aspects of the human psyche and capable of invoking cosmic power

Manipura chakra – psychic/pranic centre situated behind the navel in the spinal column, corresponding to the solar plexus

Manomaya kosha – sheath or body of mental experience

Mantra – subtle sound or combinations of sound vibrations revealed to sages in deep meditation, used for liberating consciousness from the limitations of mundane awareness

Mantra siddhi – the accomplishment, knowledge or power achieved through mantra sadhana

Matra – syllable of a mantra; unit of time, rhythm or beat

Maya – cause of the phenomenal world; illusion

Moola prakriti – the transcendental basis of physical nature; original source of all evolution

Mooladhara chakra – lowest psychic/pranic centre in the human body; base storehouse of prana shakti

Mrityu – death; one of three ailments suffered due to amrita consumption

Mudra – lit. 'gesture'; physical, mental and psychic attitude which expresses and channels cosmic energy

Nada – subtle sound vibration heard in the meditative state

Nada Brahma – attunement with the primordial sound vibration

Nada yoga – the yoga of subtle sound

Nadi – flow; subtle channel of energy in the pranic body

Naga – one of the sub-pranas, responsible for belching and hiccuping

Nasikagra – tip of the nose

Nauli kriya – practice of rotating the abdominal muscles; one of the shatkarmas

Nishpatti – completion

Niyama – rule; the second limb of Patanjali's ashtanga yoga comprising five rules or observances of behaviour, viz. *shaucha* (purity), *santosha* (contentment), *tapas* (austerity or penance), *swadhyaya* (self-study), and *Ishwara pranidhana* (dedication to the highest principle)

Ojas – vitality; subliminal sexual energy; kundalini shakti

Om – or 'Aum', bija mantra of ajna chakra; the universal cosmic mantra representing the four states of consciousness

Omkara – the sound of Om

Pancha bhutas – the five gross elements, viz. ether (*akasha*), air (*vayu*), fire (*agni*), water (*apas*) and earth (*prithvi*)

Pancha koshas – the five sheaths, bodies or realms of experience and existence

Pancha prana – five major divisions of pranic energy located in the physical body, viz. apana, prana, samana, udana, vyana

Pancha vayus – five minor pranas, viz. krikara, devadatta, dhananjaya, naga and koorma, responsible for such actions as sneezing, yawning, decomposition, belching and blinking respectively

Para Brahman – absolute, supreme reality

Paramatman – cosmic soul or consciousness; supreme Spirit

Parichaya – familiarity

Pashinee mudra – lit. 'folded psychic attitude'; a mudra performed in an inverted posture to induce pratyahara and bring about balance and tranquillity

Patanjali – author of the *Yoga Sutras* and propounder of ashtanga yoga; contemporary of Lord Buddha

Payaswini – one of the seven minor nadis, dominant in the right ear

Pingala nadi – major nadi beginning on the right side of mooladhara and twisting up the spine through the chakras to ajna, conducting the dynamic prana shakti; governs the right side of the body and left side of the brain; associated with externalized awareness; also called surya nadi

Pitta – one of the three doshas; bile

Pooraka – inhalation

Prana – vital energy force, essence of life permeating the whole of creation, both the macrocosmos and the microcosmos; one of the pancha pranas, also called sthoola prana

Prana nigraha – control of prana

Prana shakti – the force of prana; vital or solar energy

Prana vidya – knowledge of prana and the ability, through this knowledge, to guide it

Pranamaya kosha – sheath or body of pranic energy

Pranava – another term for the sacred syllable *Om*, the primal sound vibration

Pranayama – a series of techniques for controlling and expanding the dimension of prana; fourth limb of Patanjali's ashtanga yoga

Prani – a living being

Pranotthana – awakening of the pranas in the different nadis and chakras

Pratyahara – sense withdrawal; fifth limb of Patanjali's ashtanga yoga

Prayag – name of a celebrated place of pilgrimage at the confluence of the Ganga, Yamuna and Saraswati rivers near the town of Allahabad; confluence of ida, pingala and sushumna

Prithvi – earth

Pusha – one of the seven minor nadis, flowing from the left big toe to the right ear

Raja yoga – the royal yoga; yoga of awakening the psychic awareness and faculties through meditation

Rajas – second of the three gunas or qualities of nature; dynamism, activity, passion, oscillation

Rajasic – pertaining to rajas

Rajo guna – quality of rajas

Ram – bija mantra of manipura chakra

Rechaka – exhalation

Rig Veda – oldest of the four Vedas (vedic texts) and the most ancient sacred book of the Hindus

Rishi – inspired poet, ascetic, realized sage; one who contemplates on the self

Rudra – the third god in the cosmic trinity, the Destroyer; the destructive aspect of Shiva personifying the forces of disintegration of the cosmos

Rudra granthi – lit. 'knot of Rudra'; psychic knot in the vishuddhi and ajna chakras symbolizing attachment to siddhis or higher mental attributes

Sadhaka – one who practises sadhana; spiritual aspirant

Sadhana – spiritual practice or discipline performed regularly for the attainment of inner experience and self-realization

Sagarbha – impregnated; pranayama practised with mantra (pranayama impregnated with the power of mantra)

Sahasrara – abode of superconsciousness; highest psychic/pranic centre which symbolizes the threshold between the psychic and spiritual realms, located at the crown of the head, associated with the pituitary gland

Sahita – combined with something

Sahita kumbhaka – pranayama in which inhalation, retention and exhalation can be practised with or without bija mantra, according to the *Gheranda Samhita*

Samadhi – culmination of meditation; state of unity with the object of meditation and the universal consciousness; final stage of Patanjali's ashtanga yoga

Samana – sideways moving prana situated between the navel and the diaphragm, which is the pranic force of manipura

Samskara – mental impression stored in the subtle body as an archetype

Santosha – contentment, one of the niyamas

Saraswati – goddess of knowledge, speech and learning; name of a sacred submerged river; another term for sushumna nadi; a minor nadi situated on the tongue

Satchitananda – the supreme reality as self-existent existence-consciousness-bliss

Sattwa – third of the three gunas or qualities of nature; steadiness, purity, harmony

Sattwic – pertaining to sattwa

Satya – truthfulness; one of the yamas, according to Patanjali's *Yoga Sutras*

Satya loka – one of the seven higher dimensions of consciousness; also called Brahma loka

Satyam – the unchanging principle

Saumya – relating or sacred to the moon; having the properties of soma; one of the minor nadis

Shabda – sound; object of the sense of hearing; property of space (*akasha*)

Shakti – primal energy; manifest consciousness; subtle creative and vital energy; counterpart of Shiva

Shankhini – one of the seven lesser nadis, flowing from the throat to the anus

Shanti – peace

Shatkarma – group of six purifying practices of classical hatha yoga, viz. dhauti, basti, neti, nauli, trataka and kapalbhati

Shaucha – cleanliness; one of the niyamas, according to Patanjali's *Yoga Sutras*

Shikha – tuft of hair kept by Hindu Brahmins on the top of the back of the head

Shivalingam – black oval-shaped stone worshipped as symbol of Shiva; symbol of consciousness

Shodhana – purification

Shoonya – void; state of absolute nothingness in which no object is experienced

Shuddhi – purification

Shura – one of the minor nadis

Siddha – perfected being; accomplished soul particularly characterized by eight supernatural faculties called siddhis

Siddhi – perfection; paranormal or supernormal accomplishment; control of mind and prana

Soham – lit. 'I am That'; mantra used in ajapa japa; the unconscious repetitive sound produced by the breath, the inhalation sounding 'so' and the exhalation 'ham'

Soma – name of a plant that was the most important ingredient in ancient sacrificial offerings; its juice; the moon; nectar of the gods

Spandan – vibration

Srishti – creation; manifest universe

Sthoola prana – one of the pancha pranas moving upwards between the diaphragm and the larynx; controls the heart and the lungs; also called prana

Sukha – pleasure, comfort

Surya – the sun

Surya nadi – pingala nadi

Surya namaskara – lit. 'salute to the sun'; a series of twelve asanas for revitalizing prana

Sushumna nadi – main nadi in the centre of the spinal cord through which kundalini shakti passes

Swadhisthana chakra – lit. 'one's own abode'; psychic/pranic centre situated at the base of the spinal column, associated with the sacral plexus

Swadhyaya – self-observation; one of the niyamas, according to Patanjali's *Yoga Sutras*

Swah loka – one of the seven higher dimensions of consciousness

Swara – sound or tone; flow of the breath in the nostrils

Swara yoga – science of the breathing cycle

Tamas – first of the three gunas or qualities of nature; inertia, ignorance, dullness

Tamasic – pertaining to tamas

Tamo guna – the quality of tamas

Tantra – ancient universal science, philosophy and culture which deals with the transcendence of human nature from the present mundane level of evolution and understanding to the highest attainment of transcendental awareness, knowledge and experience; process of expansion of mind and liberation of energy

Tantric – pertaining to tantra

Tapah loka – one of the seven higher dimensions of consciousness

Tapasya – practice of austerity; one of the niyamas, according to Patanjali's *Yoga Sutras*

Tattwa – essential element, essence

Tha, ksha – the second syllable of the word 'hatha', the first syllable 'ha' stands for the sun, the second syllable 'tha' stands for the moon, and the union of these two forces is hatha yoga

Trataka – to gaze steadily; a concentration practice and a shatkarma

Turiya – superconsciousness; fourth dimension of consciousness transcending the waking, dreaming and deep sleep states

Udana – one of the pancha pranas, located in the extremities of the arms, legs and head

Upa pranas or pancha vayu – minor pranas

Upanayana samskara – a vedic ritual of investiture with a sacred thread to initiate participants into sacred learning

Upanishads – 'to sit close by and listen'; ancient vedic texts, conveyed by sages, rishis or seers containing their experiences and teachings on the ultimate reality

Uttama – highest, best; principal

Vajra nadi – one of the three major energy channels within sushumna nadi

Vajroli mudra – gesture involving contraction of the urinary passage to stimulate swadhisthana chakra and promote brahmacharya

Vam – bija mantra of swadhisthana chakra

Varna – colour of a mantra; colour; caste (especially applied to the four principal castes); species; groups of letters in the Sanskrit alphabet

Varuni – one of the seven minor nadis, flowing in the lower pelvic area

Vasana – seed or inherent desire; subtle desire of the unconsciousness

Vata – one of the three doshas; wind and gas

Vatsara dhauti – a technique of dhauti, one of the six cleansing practices of hatha yoga (shatkarma), in which air is swallowed into the stomach and belched out

Vayu tattwa – air element

Vedas – most ancient scriptural texts of Sanatana dharma, composed before 5,000 BC, revealed to the sages and expressing knowledge of the whole universe; the four Vedas are: Rig, Yajur, Sama and Atharva

Veena – Indian lute

Vijnanamaya kosha – astral or psychic (higher mental) sheath or body

Vilambha – one of the minor nadis

351

Viloma – inverted, opposite; produced in the reverse order

Vishnu – the second god of the cosmic trinity, the Preserver; the god who redeems and sustains

Vishnu granthi – lit. 'Vishnu's knot'; psychic knot in manipura and anahata chakras symbolizing the bondage of personal and emotional attachment

Vishuddhi chakra – psychic/pranic centre located at the level of the throat pit or the thyroid gland; associated with the cervical plexus

Vishwodari – one of the seven minor nadis, flowing in the area of the navel

Vritti – mental fluctuation, wave or pattern, modification arising in consciousness

Vyadhi – disease; one of three ailments suffered due to amrita consumption

Vyana – one of the pancha pranas, pervading the whole body; reserve pranic energy

Yajna – worship through sacrifice or sacrificial rite for internal and external purification; offering oblations to the fire; any work beneficial for one and all

Yam – bija mantra of anahata chakra

Yama – first limb of Patanjali's ashtanga yoga, five self-restraints or rules of conduct pertaining to ethical perfection: *ahimsa* (non-violence), *satya* (truth), *asteya* (non-stealing), *brahmacharya* (continence) and *aparigraha* (non-covetousness)

Yamuna – one of the most sacred rivers of India; another term for ida nadi

Yantra – geometric symbol designed for concentration or meditation in order to unleash the hidden potential within the consciousness; visual form of mantra used for concentration and meditation

Yashaswini – one of the seven minor nadis, flowing from the right big toe to the left ear

Yoga danda – a stick placed under the armpit to influence breath flow

Yogagni – fire of yoga

Yogi – an adept in yoga; one connected or endowed with yoga

Yoni – womb

Index of Practices

General Index

357